Academic Evaluation

Academic Evaluation

Review Genres in University Settings

Edited by

Ken Hyland
Institute of Education, University of London, UK

and

Giuliana Diani
University of Modena and Reggio Emilia, Italy

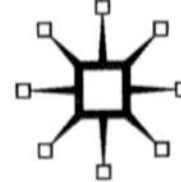

First published 2009 by
PALGRAVE MACMILLAN

Palgrave Macmillan in the UK is an imprint of Macmillan Publishers Limited,
registered in England, company number 785998, of Houndmills, Basingstoke,
Hampshire RG21 6XS.

Palgrave Macmillan in the US is a division of St Martin's Press LLC,
175 Fifth Avenue, New York, NY 10010.

Palgrave Macmillan is the global academic imprint of the above companies
and has companies and representatives throughout the world.

Palgrave® and Macmillan® are registered trademarks in the United States,
the United Kingdom, Europe and other countries.

ISBN-13: 978–0–230–22433–9 hardback

This book is printed on paper suitable for recycling and made from fully
managed and sustained forest sources. Logging, pulping and manufacturing
processes are expected to conform to the environmental regulations of the
country of origin.

A catalogue record for this book is available from the British Library.

A catalog record for this book is available from the Library of Congress.

10   9   8   7   6   5   4   3   2   1
18   17   16   15   14   13   12   11   10   09

Printed and bound in Great Britain by
CPI Antony Rowe, Chippenham and Eastbourne

Contents

Acknowledgements   vii

Introduction: Academic Evaluation and Review Genres   1
Ken Hyland and Giuliana Diani

Part I An Overview of Review Genres

1 Negotiating Research Values across Review Genres: A Case
   Study in Applied Linguistics   17
   Davide Simone Giannoni

2 Reviewing Science in an Information-Overloaded World   34
   Judy Noguchi

3 Literature Reviews in Applied PhD Theses: Evidence and
   Problems   50
   Paul Thompson

4 Back Cover Blurbs: Puff Pieces and Windows on Cultural
   Values   68
   Helen Basturkmen

Part II Disciplinary Variation

5 Reporting and Evaluation in English Book Review Articles:
   A Cross-Disciplinary Study   87
   Giuliana Diani

6 Discipline and Gender: Constructing Rhetorical Identity
   in Book Reviews   105
   Polly Tse and Ken Hyland

7 Phraseology and Epistemology in Academic Book Reviews:
   A Corpus-Driven Analysis of Two Humanities Disciplines   122
   Nicholas Groom

Part III   Cross-Linguistic Variation

8   (Non-)Critical Voices in the Reviewing of History
Discourse: A Cross-Cultural Study of Evaluation   143
Rosa Lorés Sanz

9   Academic Book Reviews in English and Spanish: Critical
Comments and Rhetorical Structure   161
Ana I. Moreno and Lorena Suárez

10   Historians at Work: Reporting Frameworks in English and
Italian Book Review Articles   179
Marina Bondi

Part IV   Diachronic Variation

11   On the Dynamic Nature of Genre: A Diachronic Study of
Blurbs   199
Maria-Lluïsa Gea-Valor and Marta Inigo Ros

12   The Lexis and Grammar of Explicit Evaluation in
Academic Book Reviews, 1913 and 1993   217
Philip Shaw

Notes on Contributors   236

Name Index   239

Subject Index   243

Acknowledgements

Ken Hyland

This book is the outcome of a collaborative project by a group of authors whose interest in academic review genres has greatly stimulated and expanded my own curiosity about evaluation in written texts. My thanks go to them. I also want to thank Polly Tse, John Swales and Vijay Bhatia, colleagues and friends whose knowledge and enthusiasm for understanding discourse is a constant inspiration. Finally, as always, my thanks go to Fiona Hyland, for her stimulating thoughts on writing and for her constant support and encouragement.

Giuliana Diani

I am particularly indebted to Professor Marina Bondi for awakening my interest in the topic of evaluative language use in academic discourse and whose encouragement convinced me to write the book. I would like to offer my warm thanks to Professor Ken Hyland for accepting the idea to get involved in the project. There would have been no book without his support.

Introduction: Academic Evaluation and Review Genres

Ken Hyland and Giuliana Diani

The expression of personal opinions and assessments is a ubiquitous feature of human interaction and, despite its apparently impersonal facade, central to academic writing. It could be argued, in fact, that among all the activities of the academy, what academics mainly do is evaluate. Their research and publishing is a continual round of comparing methods, assessing sources, weighing up outcomes, contrasting claims and considering data. They are constantly making judgements about whether samples are representative, findings are accurate and interpretations valid. The texts they produce while conducting these activities reflect this concern with evaluation and its expression pervades research articles, lectures, conference presentations, textbooks and student assignments.

Perhaps most explicitly, however, evaluation is central to a constellation of related activities, which we label *review genres*. These are texts and part texts that are written with the explicit purpose of evaluating the research, the texts and the contributions of fellow academics and include book reviews, book review articles, review articles, book blurbs and literature reviews. Academic review genres collectively represent 'the public evaluations of research' (Lindholm-Romantschuk, 1998) and play a significant role in scholarship, supporting both the manufacture of knowledge and the social cohesiveness of disciplinary communities (Hyland, 2000). Together they comprise a crucial, and highly visible, role in academic disciplines as they assess the value of research and provide a platform for members in a community to engage with each other's ideas and analyses in conventional fora.

Review genres are, in fact, crucial sites of engagement where writers argue their viewpoints, signal their allegiances and display their credibility. These genres are often more interactively complex than their more celebrated research genre cousins as they do not simply respond to a general body of more-or-less impersonal literature, but critically engage with particular texts, and therefore their authors. It is, then, somewhat surprising that their contribution has not received more attention in the applied linguistics literature. It is even more surprising when we consider that evaluation is a term that has begun to capture the imagination of theorists and analysts from a range of different perspectives across the humanities and social sciences. In this introduction we consider the nature of review genres and offer an overview of the role of evaluation in academic texts.

What are review genres?

Reviewing the work of others has been part of that academic landscape for almost 2000 years (Orteza y Miranda, 1996), but its evolution into modern review genres really began in the mid seventeenth century, when the output of books, and thus new knowledge, increased enormously. Initially, dedicated book reviews summarized and chronicled uncritically the explosion of learning in the sciences for the reading public and journals such as the *Analytical Review* and the *Monthly Epitome* emerged which were devoted entirely to this purpose (Roper, 1978). A more selective and critical approach to reporting published scholarship only came into being with the introduction of *The Edinburgh* in 1802. The style of reviews also underwent a rhetorical shift with the publication of this journal. The common practice of transcribing long passages from the reviewed text without comment was now replaced with the reviewer's own opinion, often conveyed at length and with little connection to the original (Roper, 1978, p. 45). Today, book reviews, book review articles and state-of-the-art articles all play an important role in the life of disciplinary communities.

Many international journals devote a section to *book reviews* and they play an important role in supporting both the manufacture of knowledge and the social cohesiveness of disciplinary communities. Evaluation of recent publications not only provides the research community with valuable information about titles that might otherwise pass unnoticed, but also provides an alternative forum in which academics can set out their views without engaging in the long cycle of inquiry, review and revision involved in a full-length paper. Very much a public discourse, reviews contribute to the dissemination and evaluation of research and offer a means by which junior academics can gain institutional credit and a publication profile and established writers a rhetorical platform. Here they can signal their allegiance to a particular orientation or group and proclaim a position.

While the book review focuses on a single title or cluster of related books, a second review genre spreads its net more widely. *The review article,* sometimes called the 'review essay', 'general article', 'report article' or 'state-of-the-art paper' (Noguchi, 2006) is essentially a literature survey on a specific issue or area of research. Typically solicited from experts in the field and appearing in annual volumes (such as *The Annual Review of Applied Linguistics* and *The Annual Review of Information Science and Technology*), it focuses on the most recent studies and presents a re-examination of the issue in the light of the reviewer's reading of the new publications in the field. As a result, it has some influence in helping to shape knowledge and keeping community members up to date with advancing research. In practice, as Swales (2004) points out, this influence is uncertain despite the effort invested in writing them; their post hoc quality means they count for little in prestige or credit for the writer and they seem to be referred to by students more than academics.

A third review genre perhaps has a less certain identity. The *book review article* (Diani, 2007) often appears in the book review section of academic journals yet differs from both book reviews and review articles. Something of a hybrid genre, this type of review offers a critical analysis of the ideas an author discusses in his or her book (not necessarily a new one) as a springboard for a wider evaluation of them, comprising a discussion of the issues they raise and an appraisal of what this means for the community. As with all review genres, the judgement of 'good' and 'bad' is a central feature, but this is presented as debate to construct a dialogue with the reviewed book author and other voices in the community. This debate allows the reviewer to create a 'research space' for his or her own views, exploiting the reviewed authors' reported opinions to construct a 'niche' for his or her claims on the topic (Swales, 1990). Not surprisingly, the genre is rare in the hard sciences but found in the more discursive disciplines of the humanities and social sciences, such as history, philosophy, applied linguistics, economics and sociology.

A fourth review genre, and one 'less public' than the others (Thompson, this volume), is the *review of literature* in a PhD thesis. This is a part genre where doctoral students weave an argument for their research by evaluating the previous research in an area of study. Linking local research to the concerns of the discipline is a key feature of academic argument and so literature reviews are carefully assembled to justify the value of the current research and show why it is distinct from what has gone before (Kwan, 2006). Critically engaging with prior literature allows writers to construct a story for their study, persuading the reader that some organizing principle links their work into a coherent chain of disciplinary activity through comparison, analysis and evaluation of previous research.

A final review genre is the back-cover *book blurb*. Like the book review, the blurb provides a description of the content of the book for potential readers and highlights some of its positive features for its authors' and publishers' benefit (Gesuato, 2007). This, however, is a paratextual element of a book and more of a publishing than an academic phenomenon. While perhaps similar in function to the book review, blurbs are a review genre characterized by a strong promotional orientation and strict space constraints so that evaluations are almost always positive and their purpose promotional. In this sense, however, they are entirely responsive to the growth of commercial interests marketing norms in academic publishing (Gea-Valor and Inigo Ros, this volume).

Despite differences in form and pragmatic force of the genres we have introduced here, what they all have in common is a clear awareness on the part of both reviewers and readers of the importance of evaluation. Evaluation is central to the academic entries of creating knowledge and evaluating texts, research and colleagues, and is at the heart of review genres, as we discuss further in the next section.

What is evaluation?

Evaluation is an elusive and complex concept but, judging by the growing number of books, articles and theses on the topic, including special issues of the *Journal of English for Academic Purposes* and *Textus*, it is one that has found its time. This research has been conducted under various headings, including 'affect' (Ochs, 1989), 'evidentiality' (Chafe and Nichols, 1986), 'point of view' (Simpson, 1993), 'hedging' (Hyland, 1998), 'stance' (Biber and Finegan, 1989; Conrad and Biber, 2000; Hyland, 2005a); 'metadiscourse' (Hyland and Tse, 2004; Hyland, 2005b) and 'appraisal' (Martin, 2000; Martin and White, 2005). The term 'evaluation' itself originates in the work of Hunston (1994; Hunston and Thompson, 2000). Despite differences among these terms, they all take up Stubbs' (1996, p. 197) point that 'whenever speakers (or writers) say anything, they encode their attitude towards it'. They all, in other words, address the idea of how we take a position on something and seek to position others to do the same.

Essentially *evaluation* is concerned with interpersonal uses of language and how the subjective presence of the writer or speaker intrudes into communication to convey an attitude to both those they address and the material they discuss. Thompson and Hunston (2000, p. 5) define evaluation as a 'broad cover term for the expression of the speaker or writer's attitude or stance towards, viewpoint on, or feelings about the entities or propositions that he or she is talking about'. In academic discourse it performs three central functions: first it expresses the speaker's opinion and thus reflects the value-system of that person and their community; it helps to construct a dialogue and relations of solidarity between the writer and reader; and finally it helps structure a text in expected ways.

In general terms, evaluation operates on two levels: statements which display assessments of value, roughly corresponding to opinions along a good–bad axis and those concerning the likely accuracy of claims, relating to judgements of probability. Conrad and Biber (2000) refer to these as 'attitudinal stance' and 'epistemic stance' respectively. The first group has typically been studied in terms of 'affect' and whether the speaker feels positive or negative towards something. This is an attitudinal dimension of evaluation that conveys value judgements of approval. Thompson and Hunston (2000, p. 3) observe that this relates largely to things and so evaluates nominal groups such as *a surprising result, a terrible afternoon*. The second group corresponds to 'evidentiality' and the degree of certainty or reliability that someone is prepared to publicly invest in a statement. It has been discussed in terms of hedging and modalization and relates to propositions; it therefore evaluates clauses such as *unlikely to arrive early, according to the newspaper*.

Both kinds of evaluation can be expressed lexically, for example by an evaluative term such as *interesting, perhaps* or *unclear*, or grammatically, by embedding the evaluation in the grammar of the clause like *there is little evidence to suggest that*. In addition, alongside the expression of our evaluations, we often indicate the extent we commit ourselves to them, 'turning up or lowering the volume' as Martin puts it (Martin, 2000). Writers can grade the strength of their feelings in a variety of ways, most commonly by choice of intensified lexis (*astonishing, loathe*, etc.), by repetition, by the addition of superlative morphology (*grandest, best*) or by the use of qualifying adverbs such as *extremely, quite* and *unbelievably*. Martin and White (2005), in fact, recognize two axes of such scalability. Evaluation can be graded according to the intensity or amount of the opinion along clines of positivity, extent, proximity and so on (*slightly-extremely, near-far*, etc.). Alternatively things can be graded according to prototypicality and precision, or how far they approximate to some ideal (*true, real* and the suffix *-ish*).

More tricky, however, is the fact that many words carry connotative evaluative meanings, or what Martin (2000) refers to as the differences between 'inscribed' and 'evoked' appraisal, or that what is explicitly expressed and that which projects an evaluation based on what is conventionally valued. While words like *brilliant, depressing* and *idiotic* clearly have evaluation as their chief function, others convey evaluation more stealthily. Some words take on particular meanings as a result of their tendency to repeatedly occur in certain environments, for instance, in a process referred to as 'semantic prosody'. The words *cause* and *commit* have negative connotations, for example, because corpus studies have revealed their association with harmful or unwanted consequences such as *chaos, uproar, explosions* and *death* (cause) and *murder, suicide* and *perjury* (commit). Other words, of course, can take on evaluative meanings in particular contexts or with particular users, for example, we have heard apparently neutral terms such as *nostalgic, estate agent* and *bedroom slippers* used disparagingly in conversation.

In academic contexts writers are often simultaneously trying to maintain rapport with readers, argue a position and signal their allegiance to a particular orientation or group so that in some circumstances terms like *empiricism, post modern* and *Darwinian* can all take on negative meanings. Dressen's (2003) ethnographic account is one of the few studies which has looked at implicit evaluation and she shows how subtle uses of language by geologists rely on readers' inside knowledge to convey evaluations which value fieldwork over laboratory work. Such rhetorical winks to colleagues can put evaluation beyond the interpretive reach of outsiders and render analysis problematic. Such opaque evaluations are not uncommon in review genres where it is commonplace to mitigate criticism through the connotative spin placed on particular terms or references to community understandings, as in these examples from published book reviews:

> (1) The writing is excellent if, like me, the reader appreciates the style of the Wall Street Journal. (Marketing)

> He begins with an introductory chapter of which an Oxford ordinary language philosopher would have been proud. (Philosophy)

> In this sense the work remains firmly in the criminological tradition, alongside the Home Office sponsored research. (Sociology)

Membership of a discipline involves aligning oneself with its institutional values and expected responses. The injection of evaluative meanings into apparently neutral comments diffuses criticism with audience solidarity, helping to foreground a sense of collusion which simultaneously makes the criticism less explicit and identifies the writer as a member of a community who understands these kinds of things.

The fact is that evaluation is always related to a judgemental yard-stick; a conception of relative truth, beauty, reason, usefulness or whatever against which something is judged. In this sense, when an academic evaluates some claim or proposition, he or she is really contrasting this with what is considered to be a norm within the community. These norms are constructed from the community's bodies of knowledge and epistemic understandings, what counts as appropriate methodologies, relevant literature, robust theories and effective prac-tices. This backdrop of disciplinary schema, values and ways of seeing the world allows writers to position themselves and their work in rela-tion to other members of their groups, negotiating and confirming their membership of particular communities (e.g. Bourdieu, 1977; Geertz, 1983).

Evaluation in review genres

Research into the workings of evaluation has been especially produc-tive in academic research writing (e.g. Hunston, 1994; Bondi, 1999; Hyland, 2000). While often considered an objective and faceless kind of discourse based on empirical evidence or flawless logic, academic writ-ing is actually extremely interactive and rhetorical. Research shows, for example, that academic writers use language to acknowledge, construct and negotiate social relations in a variety of ways including the use of tentativeness and possibility (Hyland, 1998), self mention (Hyland, 2001a), directives (Swales *et al.*, 1998; Hyland, 2002) and reporting verbs (Thompson and Ye, 1991; Hyland, 2000). In fact, the ability of writers to credibly represent themselves and their work by claiming solidarity with readers, evaluating their material and acknowledging alternative views, is a defining feature of academic writing.

It is true, however, that a great deal of research writing is charac-terized by the absence of inscribed evaluation. The attitudes we find there largely express writers' judgements of probability and estimations of value such as surprise, interest, importance, etc., rather than affect (Hyland, 2000). Academic texts are, however, clearly structured to evoke affinity and engagement, which means that evaluative features play an important part in creating a writer–reader dialogue to situate researchers, their research and their readers (Hyland, 2001b; Swales, 2004). One domain of academic discourse where explicit evaluation is particularly prominent is in review genres.

Here we see the workings of the community in perhaps its most nakedly normative role, where it publicly sets out to establish standards, assess merit and, indirectly, to evaluate reputations. These texts are highly interactively loaded as judgements carry significant social consequences. Not only can criticism become a potential challenge to a specific author, but the act of evaluating itself also exposes the writer as someone prepared to speak on behalf of a community. Negotiating social interactions in review genres can therefore mean charting a perilous course between critique and collegiality, minimizing personal threat while simultaneously demonstrating both disciplinary membership and an expert understanding of the issues.

While they share a similar intertextual purpose of evaluating research or its presentation, there are obviously considerable differences in the length, rationale and rhetorical conventions of review genres. Blurbs, for example, may consist of only a few lines and signify just 'patterns of puffery' (Cronin and La Barre, 2005), while literature reviews in doctoral dissertations can run to several chapters and involve complex arguments to justify current research (e.g. Kwan, 2006). Similarly, while many review genres 'provide a space where academics can participate in the ongoing conversation in their disciplines' (Salager-Meyer and Alcaraz Ariza, 2004, p. 151), the length of book review articles allow more opportunities for writers to develop an argument and engage with readers than the shorter book review. It is this engagement, however, which makes these genres rhetorically so complex. It is because a good review needs not only to offer a critical and insightful perspective, drawing on considerable knowledge of the field, but also respond to the complex demands of a delicate interactional situation, displaying an awareness of the appropriate expression of what is positive and negative: essentially, of praise and criticism.

Praise and criticism in reviews

In Brown and Levinson's (1987) classic politeness model, praise and criticism are fraught with potential face threats. Not only can criticisms undermine a hearer's 'positive face', the desire to be approved of, but compliments also carry risks, for not everyone is entitled to compliment and conveying praise implies an authority to appraise and make public one's judgements. While we might want to recognize wider, community-oriented considerations where ambition, theoretical positioning, allegiances and so on play a major role, it is also the case that the academic world is a small one and it may be prudent not to antagonize those within it. Vicious criticism can seriously undermine an author's credibility and lavish praise can be unwelcome as superficial and undiscriminating. Praise and criticism are therefore carefully managed strategies in review genres, entailing careful framings that respond to their interpersonal effects while simultaneously addressing the demands of the genre.

Praise is relatively common in review genres, particularly blurbs and book reviews, for example, and is generally used as an opening move to offer global praise for the volume, relying heavily on a restricted range of adjectives, most commonly *interesting, comprehensive, significant* and *excellent*, as we see in these examples:

> (2) This is an inspirational book, which makes a major contribution to linguistic theory. (Book blurb)

> Kim's presentation of the contemporary philosophies of mind is excellent. (Book review)

> This book is an excellent example of bringing together the study of international relations and comparative politics, setting very interesting questions and hypotheses about the interaction between domestic and international politics. (Review article)

Alternatively, credit is often attributed directly to the author rather than the volume itself:

> (3) written by a world renowned expert in the field. (Book blurb)

> Roger Brubaker has acquired a reputation in recent years as one of the most original scholars analysing the emergence of the 'New Europe'. (Book review)

> Certainly it would be hard to find two men more qualified to speak about space and time. (State-of-the-art paper)

Endorsement of a work by shifting praise from the volume to its producers helps to demonstrate the solidarity of reviewers with their communities by acknowledging the reputations of colleagues and their previous contributions to a shared endeavour. It is interesting, however, that author praise also occurs in otherwise negative reviews, perhaps to reassure readers that the book author was otherwise perfectly qualified to write the volume.

While praise is often fulsome, and naked condemnation fairly common, the full force of criticisms in review genres is typically mitigated. In a study of 160 academic book reviews, for example, Hyland (2000) found that authors took considerable care to soften criticism in a number of ways. Most often this involved pairing a criticism with praise to slightly soften the evaluation:

> (4) There are some very good essays in this collection, but considered as a whole the book does have significant shortcomings.

> Undoubtedly this book will be a valuable reference work, but it has also missed an opportunity.

> I found the book quite strong on low-level policing issues, but less convincing on the nature of drug trafficking, markets or police counter-measures.

Occasionally such pairings can be a shade Byzantine, with similes or metaphors used to make the criticism more abstract, as shown here:

> (5) Reading this book was like cutting into a loaf cake and discovering that delightful bits of chocolate had been baked into the dough. At the same time, it was disconcerting to find that each slice seemed to come from a different recipe.

Hedges are another key way of toning down criticisms and reflecting a positive relationship with both reader and the author. While hedges have both an epistemic and affective function in knowledge-making genres (Hyland, 1998), their principal purpose in review genres is to mitigate the interpersonal damage of critical comments. Modal verbs and particularly *would, might, may* and *could* and the verb *seem*, are common:

> (6) I agree that these are important groups, but a broad overview of peatland biodiversity would have been useful.

> This breadth of coverage might be off-putting to those with less linguistic background or with less knowledge of the languages discussed.

> The level of detail in the book is also rather variable, and the order in which material is presented does not always seem sensible.

Another way to mitigate negative commentary is to draw attention to the source of evaluation. Clearly, one might express an evaluation by attributing it to someone else, and we often find writers avoiding direct responsibility for a judgement by crediting it to an abstract reader or general audience. This functions to make criticism more diffuse by obscuring the link between the reviewer and the FTA while at the same time allowing the writer to insinuate membership of a community dedicated to particular standards of scholarship and a shared pursuit of knowledge:

(7) Not everyone will accept the aims of teacher education as formulated by Perraton.

Readers might quibble with the order of these two chapters.

Many readers will probably find unpalatable Bickerton's style of argumentation which rests all too often on sweeping dismissals of the views of others, or an incomplete consideration of relevant literature, plus a great deal of fanciful neuropsychology and magic.

More usually, however, review writers foreground their commentary as a personal response. This allows them to adopt a less threatening authorial voice, repositioning themselves and their authority by reacting as an ordinary reader rather than as an 'expert'. Specifying oneself as the source of a view can qualify its force by implicitly acknowledging that others may hold alternative positions. While reviews necessarily carry the biases and predispositions of their writers, the personal expression of criticism reminds the reader of this and acts to mitigate negative comment by placing it in this context:

(8) This section suffers, in my opinion, from the circularity of including...

I found this quite daunting and, if I am right about the intended audience, unnecessary.

The reviewer believes that it is not an unfair assessment to say that the work suffers broadly from two faults...

Personal attribution, then, conveys the limitation of the criticism, representing it as the writer's individual opinion rather than an objective characteristic of the volume.

So, explicit evaluation, and even outright criticism, is an integral feature of review genres, helping to substantiate their claim to be regarded as a scholarly form of writing by academics. This, then, is a knowledge-examining domain where writers cannot avoid evaluating the work of others, but they can, and typically do, address interpersonal issues with some sensitivity so that reviews are rarely as destructive as they might be and are often mitigated in various ways.

Conclusions

In this introductory chapter we have tried to set the scene for what follows in this book and to convey something of the ways social interactions contribute to the construction of a relatively neglected clutch of genres. We have argued that review genres are not only concerned with intertextual judgements of importance, value, usefulness and truth, but that these evaluations involve writers in the complex construction and negotiation of interpersonal relationships. The kinds of regularities we have outlined above help shape the social purposes of individuals to the formal constraints of the genre and the preferred practices of their disciplines. So, while each review offers a potentially threatening challenge to the author of the text reviewed, it works because of a collaborative orientation by all parties to certain disciplinary observed evaluative standards and norms of engagement.

Reviewers and their reviews are shaped by the expectations and practices of their disciplines, which means that part of a reviewer's competence lies in the appropriate expression of evaluation: What issues are deserving of comment? What standards are issues judged against? What expressions are seen as fair, warranted and collegial? In addressing these questions reviewers not only draw on readers' familiarity with the research networks and disciplinary knowledge of the field, but also on an interpretive framework, which includes an understanding of appropriate social interactions. However, the dimensions of praise and criticism sketched above do not, by any means, exhaust the possibilities of evaluation in these genres nor the variations that can occur within and between them. As the following chapters describe, interactional resources are deployed differently to manage evaluation across genres, languages, disciplines and times. Together, these chapters show how review genres display a keen orientation to the reviewed writer, a community literature, a set of values and the understandings of a disciplinary community.

References

Biber, D. and Finegan, E. (1989) 'Styles of Stance in English: Lexical and Grammatical Marking of Evidentiality and Affect', *Text*, IX, 1, 93–124.

Bondi, M. (1999) *English across Genres: Language Variation in the Discourse of Economics* (Modena: Il Fiorino).

Bourdieu, P. (1977) *Outline of a Theory of Practice* (Cambridge: Cambridge University Press).

Brown, P. and Levinson, S. (1987) *Politeness: Some Universals in Language Usage* (Cambridge: Cambridge University Press).

Chafe, W. and Nichols, J. (eds) (1986) *Evidentiality: The Linguistic Coding of Epistemology*, vol. XX (New Jersey: Ablex).

Conrad, S. and Biber, D. (2000) 'Adverbial Marking of Stance in Speech and Writing', in S. Hunston and G. Thompson (eds) *Evaluation in Text: Authorial Stance and the Construction of Discourse* (Oxford: Oxford University Press), 56–73.

Cronin, B. and La Barre, K. (2005) 'Patterns of Puffery', *Journal of Librarianship and Information Science*, XXXVII, 1, 17–24.

Diani, G. (2007) 'The Representation of Evaluative and Argumentative Procedures: Examples from the Academic Book Review Article', *Textus*, XX, 1, 37–56.

Dressen, D. F. (2003) 'Geologists' Implicit Persuasive Strategies and the Construction of Evaluative Evidence', *Journal of English for Academic Purposes*, II, 4, 273–90.

Geertz, C. (1983) *Local Knowledge: Further Essays in Interpretive Anthropology* (New York: Basic Books).

Gesuato, S. (2007) 'Evaluation in Back-Cover Blurbs', *Textus*, XX, 1, 83–102.

Hunston, S. (1994) 'Evaluation and Organization in a Sample of Written Academic Discourse', in M. Coulthard (ed.) *Advances in Written Text Analysis* (London: Routledge), 191–218.

Hunston, S. and Thompson, G. (eds) (2000) *Evaluation in Text. Authorial Stance and the Construction of Discourse* (Oxford: Oxford University Press).

Hyland, K. (1998) *Hedging in Scientific Research Articles* (Amsterdam: John Benjamins).

Hyland, K. (2000) *Disciplinary Discourses: Social Interactions in Academic Writing* (London: Longman).

Hyland, K. (2001a) 'Humble Servants of the Discipline? Self-Mention in Research Articles', *English for Specific Purposes*, XX, 3, 207–26.

Hyland, K. (2001b) 'Bringing in the Reader: Addressee Features in Academic Articles', *Written Communication*, XVIII, 4, 549–74.

Hyland, K. (2002) 'Directives: Power and Engagement in Academic Writing', *Applied Linguistics*, XXIII, 2, 215–39.

Hyland, K. (2005a) 'Stance and Engagement: A Model of Interaction in Academic Discourse', *Discourse Studies*, VII, 2, 173–91.

Hyland, K. (2005b) *Metadiscourse. Exploring Interaction in Writing* (London: Continuum).

Hyland, K. and Bondi, M. (eds) (2006) *Academic Discourse across Disciplines* (Bern: Peter Lang).

Hyland, K. and Tse, P. (2004) 'Metadiscourse in Academic Writing: A Reappraisal', *Applied Linguistics*, XXV, 2, 156–77.

Kwan, B. (2006) 'The Schematic Structure of Literature Reviews in Doctoral Theses of Applied Linguistics', *English for Specific Purposes*, XXV, 1, 30–55.

Lindholm-Romantschuk, Y. (1998) *Scholarly Book Reviewing in the Social Sciences and Humanities* (London: Greenwood Press).

Martin, J. (2000) 'Beyond Exchange: APPRAISAL Systems in English', in S. Hunston and G. Thompson (eds) *Evaluation in Text: Authorial Stance and the Construction of Discourse* (Oxford: Oxford University Press), 142–75.

Martin, J. and White, P. (2005) *The Language of Evaluation: Appraisal in English* (London: Palgrave).

Noguchi, J. (2006) *The Science Review Article: An Opportune Genre in the Construction of Science* (Bern: Peter Lang).

Ochs, E. (ed.) (1989) 'The Pragmatics of Affect', *Text*, IX, 1 (Special Issue).

Orteza y Miranda, E. (1996) 'On Book Reviewing', *Journal of Educational Thought*, XXX, 2, 191–202.

Roper, D. (1978) *Reviewing before the Edinburgh: 1788–1802* (London: Methuen).

Salager-Meyer, F. and Alcaraz Ariza, M. A. (2004) 'Negative Appraisals in Academic Book Reviews. A Cross-Linguistic Approach', in C. N. Candlin and M. Gotti (eds) *Intercultural Aspects of Specialized Communication* (Bern: Peter Lang), 149–72.

Simpson, P. (1993) *Language, Ideology and Point of View* (London: Routledge).

Stubbs, M. (1996) *Text and Corpus Analysis* (Oxford: Blackwell).

Swales, J. (1990) *Genre Analysis: English in Academic and Research Settings* (Cambridge: Cambridge University Press).

Swales, J. (2004) *Research Genres: Explorations and Applications* (Cambridge: Cambridge University Press).

Swales, J., Ahmad, U. K., Chang, Y.-Y., Chavez, D., Dressen, D. F. and Seymour, R. (1998) 'Consider This: The Role of Imperatives in Scholarly Writing', *Applied Linguistics*, XIX, 1, 97–121.

Thompson, G. and Ye, Y. (1991) 'Evaluation of the Reporting Verbs Used in Academic Papers', *Applied Linguistics*, XII, 4, 365–82.

Thompson, G. and Hunston, S. (2000) 'Evaluation: An Introduction' in S. Hunston and G. Thompson (eds) *Evaluation in Text: Authorial Stance and the Construction of Discourse* (Oxford: Oxford University Press), 3–27.

Part I
An Overview of Review Genres

1
Negotiating Research Values across Review Genres: A Case Study in Applied Linguistics

Davide Simone Giannoni

Introduction

Over the last two decades an increasing number of scholars have extended the investigation of academic discourse to those genres associated with the validation – rather than the production – of disciplinary knowledge, most notably review articles (Myers, 1991; Noguchi, 2006), book reviews (Motta Roth, 1996a; Shaw, 2004), back-cover blurbs (Basturkmen, 1999; Gea-Valor, 2005) and journal editorials (Salager-Meyer, 2002; Giannoni, 2008). All such texts share a concern for the axiology of research – that is, for what is right or wrong, certain or uncertain, desirable or undesirable in their field. For this reason, the analysis of evaluative acts is especially prominent in the literature dealing with review genres (cf. Salager-Meyer, 2001; Römer, 2008). Their wording shows an overall tendency to praise general features and criticize more specific points, with critical expressions mitigated by polar comments, hedging, indirectness, other attribution, metadiscoursal bracketing and the assumption of personal responsibility. In some instances, even negative evaluations may be foregrounded, using first-person markers, emotive language, criticism enhancers and irony.

Despite their considerable similarities, most research has focused on the description of individual genres, occasionally comparing realizations across different academic disciplines (Motta-Roth, 1996b; Diani, 2006) or languages (Giannoni, 2006; Moreno and Suárez, 2008). It might be interesting, therefore, to take an approach that considers such texts as a single 'genre family' (cf. Fishelov, 1993) whose purpose is to certify and validate new knowledge claims made in the primary literature.

The case study presented here looks at how explicit judgements of academic value are realized in a range of review texts instrumental to the reception and appraisal of four recent monographs in applied linguistics, using a multigeneric textual sample to analyse the distribution and polarity of evaluative acts targeting such publications. Apart from its familiarity, the choice of discipline was inspired by Hyland's (2000) finding that book reviews in applied linguistics are particularly rich in overt evaluation, if compared to other academic fields.

Materials and methods

Choice of texts

The material used in this investigation centres around four monographs shortlisted for the 2005 Book Prize awarded by the British Association for Applied Linguistics (BAAL) to an 'outstanding book in the field'. As explained in the organization's website, a total of 26 titles, all published in 2004, were nominated for the award by several – mostly British – international publishers. Under the regulations, a panel of expert reviewers specializing in the subject area of each title selects the four books that most deserve to be shortlisted for the prize; which is later awarded by a panel of judges taking into account such criteria as 'the production quality of the book, and the style of presentation and language' (BAAL, 2005, section 3). The following four titles were shortlisted in 2005:

1. V. Edwards. *Multilingualism in the English-Speaking World. Pedigree of Nations* (Oxford: Blackwell)
2. K. Bolton. *Chinese Englishes: A Sociolinguistic History* (Cambridge: Cambridge University Press)
3. R. Carter. *Language and Creativity: The Art of Common Talk* (London: Routledge)
4. P. Seedhouse. *The Interactional Architecture of the Language Classroom: A Conversation Analysis Perspective* (London: Blackwell)

Importantly, the BAAL website includes the two *expert reviews* (ERs) written for each shortlisted book. After collecting such texts, the tables of contents of various applied linguistics journals were searched and two *book reviews* (BRs) extracted for each of the four titles. Next, the *blurbs* (Bs) printed on the back cover or inside flaps of the books, where available, were included in the sample and finally online catalogues were inspected to retrieve the *publisher's descriptions* (PDs) of the same books. Of these four genres the book review and the book blurb have been extensively investigated, whereas expert reviews and publisher's descriptions remain relatively unresearched (for a description of book publishers' homepages, however, see Gea-Valor, 2006).

In terms of communicative purpose, such texts vary along a continuum extending from the most promotional (arguably blurbs) to the most critical (expert reviews). At the same time, they reflect different levels of interpersonal distance, depending on how far the reviewer identifies with the reviewee: maximum proximity is reached in book blurbs (which are often written by the book's author), while maximum distance occurs in expert reviews (texts of a semi-institutional nature written on behalf of a learned society). These two dimensions of pragma-rhetorical variation across review genres may be illustrated as follows:

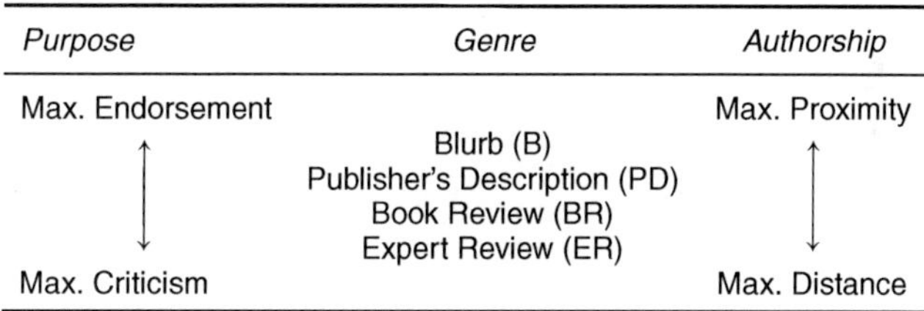

Figure 1.1   Review genres compared

The promotional use of blurbs is well documented (Bhatia, 2004; Gesuato, 2004) since the genre's main purpose is not to inform readers but to market the publication and make it 'attractive to buy' (Cacchiani 2007, p. 5). In book reviews, the purpose switches from endorsement to criticism, as the reviewer is a (supposedly neutral) third party acting as gatekeeper on behalf of the academic community. At the end of the continuum, expert reviews are those most likely to express unmitigated criticism due to the authority of the experts involved and to the necessarily competitive environment of a book prize. Being shortlisted for the prize, however, is itself a promotional incentive and BAAL informs its members that publishers 'may use the phrase "Short-listed for the BAAL Book Prize + DATE" in their publicity' (2005, section 3).

In quantitative terms, the textual sample assembled included around 20,000 tokens, with an average length of 1684 words in BRs, followed by 620 in ERs, 300 in Bs and 146 in PDs. Because of this difference, the evidence gathered from each text will be normalized per 10,000 words so as to make it comparable across genres.

Analytical framework

Among all the possible instantiations of evaluation, our concern here is with expressions that explicitly signal the 'qualities ascribed to the entities, situations or propositions that are evaluated' (Bednarek, 2008, p. 14). The explicitness is given – as argued by Shaw (2004) – by the fact that evaluation is communicated, chiefly, by lexical rather than contextual resources. The analysis will single out critical acts targeting value-laden aspects of the reviewed book and/or its author, in line with the communicative purpose of the genres in question. The range of evaluators will be explored adopting a classification based on two alternative options observed in academic reviews: (i) the claim that a certain value-laden trait is present in the reviewed work (*additive evaluation*); or (ii) the claim that it is not present (*detractive evaluation*). In turn each of these two types can be positive, negative or comparative in polarity. A total of six possible options are therefore envisaged:

Table 1.1   Classification of evaluative acts

Type and polarity	*Realizations*
Additive Evaluation	
– Positive	X is good/has goodness
– Negative	X is bad/has badness
– Comparative	X is better or worse than Y/is the best or worst
Detractive Evaluation	
– Positive	X is not bad/lacks badness/does not lack goodness
– Negative	X is not good/lacks goodness/does not lack badness
– Comparative	X is not better or worse than Y/is not the best or worst

The use of negation has complex pragmatic implications, often related to the need for mitigation when a face-threatening act is expressed: in other words, 'negation operates as a hedge, allowing features of the negated item to be retained so that the end product of the negated constituent is a toned down version of the affirmative rather than a total eradication of that affirmative' (Giora *et al.*, 2005, p. 83). From this perspective, 'not good' is equivalent to 'less than good' rather than 'bad'.

The different realizations of additive and detractive evaluation are in turn classified according to their polarity, which generally implies a good/bad axis (cf. Thompson and Hunston, 2000). Alongside this inevitable distinction, a third category has been added for those acts that perform evaluation comparatively. Although interpretable also in terms of what is good or bad, comparative evaluators deserve separate consideration because they signal goodness and badness not as values *per se* but as variables within a relationship that target both the reviewed book (which is always mentioned) and its counterparts in the literature (referred to globally or in varying degrees of detail).

By inspecting such texts manually it should be possible to distinguish both quantitatively and qualitatively between these different options in a way that is normally impossible with large corpora, where – as pointed out by Hunston (2004) and Römer (2008) – the polysemy and collocational complexity of evaluative items plays havoc with wordlists, concordances and other kinds of data generated by electronic text-processing tools.

Results

The distribution of evaluators (that is of individual lexical items signalling an explicit value) in the sample was investigated following the framework outlined above and yielded the results summarized in Table 1.2. Before turning to each category and its linguistic realizations, however, the overall significance of these results should be considered. Most noticeable is the concentration of evaluative acts, which peaks at each extreme of the continuum in Figure 1.1, with the highest number in Bs (45.2 occurrences per 10,000 words) and ERs (39.8 occurrences).

Positive additive evaluators were by far the favourite option, followed at a distance by negative additive and negative detractive realizations.

Table 1.2   Distribution of evaluators by genre (normalized per 10,000 words)

	Expert reviews	*Book reviews*	*Publisher's description*	*Blurbs*	*Mean*
Additive Evaluation	[86%] 34.1	[92%] 27.0	[100%] 11.8	[100%] 45.2	[94%] 29.5
– Positive	27.7	11.1	9.5	37.0	
– Negative	4.2	14.8	–	–	
– Comparative	2.2	1.1	2.3	8.2	
Detractive Evaluation	[14%] 5.7	[8%] 2.5	–	–	[6%] 2.1
– Positive	0.6	0.9	–	–	
– Negative	5.1	1.6	–	–	
– Comparative	–	–	–	–	
Total	39.84	29.5	11.8	45.2	31.6

This indicates that, within the review genres considered, a desirable trait is signalled nearly always as a quality possessed by the evaluated object (1), while an undesirable trait is signalled either as the presence of a negative quality (2) or less often (3) as the absence of a positive one (emphasis added):

(1) His review *clearly* demonstrates that this literature is both heterogeneous and multidisciplinary. (B.BR1)

(2) The notion of a cline, repeated whenever there are distinctions to be made, may lead to *wooliness*. (C.ER2)

(3) With regard to the status of the Irish language, the constitutional position is *not stated accurately* on p. 15. (A.ER1)

Positivity prevails in Bs (82 per cent) and PDs (80 per cent) but is also high in ERs (71 per cent). Negativity, on the other hand, is absent in Bs and PDs, rises to 23 per cent in ERs and becomes dominant in BRs (56 per cent). The considerable difference between the latter two genres may be due to the fact that ERs, despite their intensely evaluative stance, single out books chosen for their qualities rather than their defects. BRs, on the other hand, may target a book that the reviewer does not approve of and is reluctant to endorse – hence the prevalence of negativity. Comparative evaluators were altogether far less prominent, accounting for some 20 per cent of acts in Bs and PDs but only around 5 per cent in ERs and BRs. As indicated in Table 1.2, they were all of the additive type.

Additive evaluation

Evaluators of this type accounted for the vast majority of acts in all texts, where they generally encode positive comments, while the less direct option of detractive evaluation is reserved almost entirely for criticism. This does not mean that additive evaluators always communicate praise: in fact negative realizations constituted 12 per cent of all occurrences in ERs and 55 per cent in BRs. Despite the finding that additive evaluation is more frequent in ERs (34.1 vs. 27.0 occurrences), the greater balance between positive and negative acts in BRs arguably reflects the fact that ERs (especially those in our sample, limited to shortlisted books) target only a selection of high-quality publications.

Positive

This is the most common form of evaluation used in the whole sample, with the exception only of BRs. It includes a considerable range of linguistic realizations devoted almost entirely to desirable aspects of the book and its claims, but also occasionally including the author's merits. Though never prevalent – in line with Swales and Burke's (2003) findings – polarized forms such as *excellent, ground-breaking, glorious* were not uncommon. There were also various emotively-charged realizations (e.g. 'the book has won me over'; 'simply a pleasure to read'; 'I am particularly pleased') that apparently contravene the impersonal stance normally assumed in academic writing. The following sentences are typical of how positive additive evaluation is expressed in the texts considered:

(4) This close analysis has *considerable appeal,* not only because of the *empirical support* it provides, but also because it *stimulates* in the reader something of Carter's own *genuine fascination* with 'ordinary' speech. (C.BR2)

(5) Offers *important new insights* for the study of World Englishes, giving illustrations that are *interestingly distinct* from the better-known regional Englishes, e.g. in South Asia or the Caribbean. (B.PD)

Here and elsewhere there is extensive use of conceptual metaphor: a finding that confirms the close link (cf. Giannoni, forthcoming) between evaluation and metaphor in written academic discourse. At the same time, there were many cases of 'evaluative interplay', to use Bednarek's (2008) term – that is of lexical items whose evaluative force is disambiguated by their immediate collocational environment. In the first sentence below, for example, the polarity of the qualifier *novel* (which does not necessarily imply appreciation) is resolved by the use of a positive premodifier (*refreshingly*); in the second sentence, both *many* and *new* are potentially factual qualifiers that acquire a positive orientation through their juxtaposition:

(6) The present offering, however, tackles such issues from a *refreshingly novel perspective.* (C.ER1)

(7) Along the way, it offers *many new insights* into key topics in discourse studies, such as repetition in conversation, metaphor, and reported speech. (C.ER2)

Sometimes the polarity of an evaluative act is signalled metadiscursively rather than lexically. The sentence below, for example, uses the disambiguator 'has the advantage of' to foreground the positivity of a claim that could otherwise be interpreted as negative:

> (8) This is in line with the rather broad perspective Carter takes, and *has the advantage of allowing his scope to range widely* over various linguistic phenomena, while at the same time raising, and leaving open, a number of theoretical questions. (C.BR2)

In a few cases (often but not exclusively in Bs and PDs) the author's academic credentials are introduced in a way that are not only informative but also positively evaluative. His or her position, affiliation and publications are mentioned as an indication of the author's status, experience and achievements; most appropriately, such details may include reference to book prizes and other awards.

Negative

Describing the weaknesses of a book appears to be the most distinctive feature of BRs, though it also occurs in ERs. The amount of criticism levelled at reviewees may be related, as observed by Salager-Meyer and Alcaraz Ariza (2004), to the prestige of the journal: those at the top end of the spectrum tend to attract more senior reviewers and are less willing to endorse new books or authors unreservedly. Negative additive evaluators generally stigmatize flaws that undermine the scientific value of the reviewed book (in terms of depth, strength, focus, consistency and balance) or its textual quality (clarity, conciseness, organization of contents and reader-friendliness), as illustrated by the following excerpts:

> (9) Although the discussion on communicative teaching approach is significant, it is rather *confusing* to see the author discuss it immediately after the discussion of DA approach, which in my opinion may suggest that it is treated as an L2 classroom research methodology. This is quite a *disputable* viewpoint because after all it is a teaching approach rather than a research approach as DA, ethnography, or CA. (D.BR1)

> (10) The studies of specific kinds of creativity, in patterns of talk and in figures of speech, seem rather *narrow and particular* between the broad expanses of the opening and closing chapters. (C.ER2)

As reported in other studies on the language of BRs (see Hyland 1998), a large part of negative speech acts are mitigated: the examples above employ approximators of degree ('rather', 'quite a') and a 'polar comment' or praise–criticism pair sequence ('Although the discussion…is significant, it is rather confusing'). Their force is thus counterbalanced by collocations that hedge both the claim's coverage and its intensity.

Not all the occurrences were as straightforward as those shown so far. Elsewhere negativity was signalled by metatextual items pointing to contradictions or inconsistencies in the reviewed text. The excerpt below, for example, juxtaposes two statements whose negative polarity is made evident by the adverbial sequence 'Instead…really'. Thus the flaw (namely, inconsistency) is signalled without ever mentioning it:

> (11) *Chinese Englishes* implies that the text incorporates a substantial amount of comparative linguistic data from various Englishes used in the region under discussion. *Instead,* the book *really* focuses on the history of Chinese-English contact. (B.ER2)

A different phenomenon is observed in (12), where the evaluator *circumspect* is employed in a way that could convey positivity and/or negativity, according to whether it implies caution or insecurity on the reviewee's part. Without excluding the former meaning, the negative claim made in the subsequent sentence ('That being said…not the most fortunate one') clearly disambiguates the polarity of the evaluator.

> (12) Carter is himself *circumspect* and points out that, in relying on qualitative research methods, 'much has to be taken on trust' (p. 150), and 'the analyst cannot provide evidence which goes beyond the extracts cited' (p. 151). That being said, the particular choice of examples in Chapter 5 is probably not the most fortunate one. (C.BR2)

Comparative

This category of evaluators, though less frequent, appeared across all the genres considered, with the greatest frequency in Bs (8.2 every 10,000 words) and the highest proportion in PDs (20 per cent of evaluators). Although the opposite option – namely *X is worse than Y* – is potentially available to reviewers, all the comparative evaluators in the texts signal aspects of the reviewed book that make it 'better' than its predecessors. This finding suggests it is less face-threatening, when making a comparison, to criticize the literature than the reviewee; its reason may lie in an epistemology that views scientific progress as an incremental process whereby new publications generally correct and integrate established knowledge (cf. Kuhn, 1970).

Contrary to expectations, comparative qualifiers occurred only in a minority of such acts (13). This is the case because most realizations merely state that a given quantitative or qualitative aspect observed in the book is instead lacking in the literature: example (14) has two positive additive evaluators ('detailed', 'insightful') stressing the book's merits, followed by two comparative evaluators that claim its superiority ('a unique contribution') to publications that have *largely ignored* the historical dimension of research:

(13) The fact that his analysis is based on a significantly *larger database* than most other research of this type, allows him to make such a case for the robustness of his description of the interactional architecture of the language classroom across cultures and the teaching of different L2s in different institutions. (D.ER1)

(14) Bolton's *Chinese Englishes* presents us with a detailed and insightful account of English in Hong Kong and southern China from linguistic, sociolinguistic, and historical perspectives. In this respect, *it is a unique contribution* to the literature on World Englishes, *which has so far largely ignored* the historical dimensions of varieties of English around the world. (B.BR1)

In one remarkable instance, example (15), the reviewer shares the book's comparative claim that other approaches 'have neglected language', but is then careful to add – almost as a rebuttal – that 'my own work' (references provided) is excluded:

(15) Chap. 2 turns to linguistic approaches, noting that the psychological and sociocultural approaches to creativity *have neglected language* (with the exception of my own work: see Sawyer 2001 2003b). (C.BR1)

Detractive evaluation

As predicted, there were also evaluative acts signalling what traits (whether positive or negative in polarity) the reviewed book does *not* possess. Detractive evaluation can thus be regarded as a form of negation, whose realizations tend to be more reader-responsible in that part of the information is missing and has to be inferred from the context (e.g. *not new* → old; *lacks order* → is confused). In this respect detractive evaluators resemble other indirect speech acts, such as metaphor and metonymy: a finding compatible with Giora *et al.*'s (2004) claim that negation belongs to the realm of figurative language. Their presence is limited to ERs and BRs, where they account respectively for 14 and 8 per cent of all evaluators.

Positive

Positive acts were relatively scant, given that detractive evaluation is exploited above all to hedge criticism (see negative acts below) rather than praise. As shown in the following examples, negation can be embedded in the syntax (is not) or in the lexis (never, unlikely) of an evaluative act. The second sentence (17) uses the incongruous colloca-tion 'the data' or 'the reader' to introduce a tangible element of irony – a device exploited more explicitly in example (18) to commend the book's readability.

> (16) The important message is that multilingualism in the English-speaking world *is not a mechanical or additive reality* of English plus something else, but a new reality that has to be reckoned with. (A.BR1)

> (17) But there is also a kind of pleasure in the commentaries which follow each extract, which always suggests a light touch, pointing out a few notable features relevant to the argument, while *never trying* to exhaust either the data or the reader. (C.ER2)

> (18) Each of the chapters is, however, relatively self-contained and readers who prefer their histories to begin at the beginning are *unlikely to suffer* unduly by reading chapter 3 before chapter 2. (B.BR1)

Positive detractive evaluation is used therefore to stress a book's achieve-ments by countering the negative expectations that may be implicit in a certain trait. While the object of evaluation is normally the book and its content, the absence of negative traits is at times described as a deliberate act on the reviewee's part. In the example below, the additive qualifier 'cautious', placed before the detractive evaluator, underscores this kind of positive agency:

> (19) The author is cautious *not to omit* discussion of the role of lan-guage in diplomacy and defence in order to highlight the functional

importance of other languages in a serious attempt to overcome these difficulties and threats. (A.BR1)

Negative

Negative acts of this type were the second most frequent occurrence in ERs (13 per cent), where interestingly they encode criticism more often than additive evaluators (5.1 vs. 4.2 occurrences per 10,000 words). The opposite was observed in BRs, where the latter are far more common (14.8 vs. 1.6 occurrences). Negative detractive evaluation constitutes a conventionally indirect framework for face-threatening claims target-ing qualities of the reviewed book that are considered to be missing or incomplete in terms of coverage (20), scientific value (21) or some textual quality (22):

(20) Chapter 4 is the shortest chapter, and I think *it could have been longer*. It returns to some of the themes raised in Chapter 1, but I think *many could have been further developed*. (B.ER1)

(21) By touching on the notion that language debates are a veneer for deeper power struggles, *Edwards merely scratches at the surface* of the vastly complex relationship between English (and its monolingual speakers) and other languages worldwide. (A.BR2)

(22) *It is a pity that Blackwell couldn't have been a little more lavish* in the presentation of the book, as it has a rather basic and 'low budget' feel (the *lack of back-cover blurb* gives a feeling that *something is missing*). (D.ER1)

The first two examples above are representative of the personal tone of these criticisms, where both the reviewer ('I think…I think'), the revie-wee ('Edwards merely') and even her publisher ('Blackwell couldn't') emerge as participants in the knowledge production and validation pro-cess. The most scathing remark, however, occurs when the validity of a claim made in the book is (more or less bluntly) rejected, either by claiming it is incorrect or through a counterclaim:

(23) For example, *the use of bath to refer to any kind of all-over wash (p 213, 215) is not a modification that took place in Asia* – its restriction in some varieties of British English to refer to a bath in a tub is where the change took place. (B.ER1)

Negative detractive evaluators are occasionally mitigated by items that condense the negativity into privative affixes and – being completely lexicalized – are far less conspicuous than negated or negative forms, as in *unclear* for 'confused' or *lifeless* for 'dead'. The following (with *underdeveloped* for 'incomplete') is one of the two instances of this type observed in our sample.

(24) The two core studies lead to many insights with lots of data. And the extensions at the end, *though underdeveloped*, led to many connections and references I will have to follow up. (C.ER2)

Discussion

The contribution of review genres to academic communication should not be underestimated. They consolidate and synthesize the primary literature, which means that 'Scholars are dependent on other scholars in order to have their knowledge claims…certified or rejected. Otherwise they would not have any criteria other than their own subjective experience' (Andersen, 2002, p. 476). The results of this study point to similarities and divergences across such genres, based on a sample of texts targeting books shortlisted by BAAL – Britain's most representative learned society in the field of applied linguistics – for its annual book prize. Among the six evaluative options posited before the analysis, all but one (comparative detractive evaluation) were confirmed by the data, which revealed the highest concentration of explicit evaluative acts in book blurbs and expert reviews, respectively. These two genres occupy opposite ends of an ideal continuum expressing on the one hand variation in authorship (in terms of interpersonal distance between the reviewer and reviewee) and, on the other hand, variation in communicative purpose (endorsement vs. criticism). In other words, evaluative intensity seems to depend on the pragma-rhetorical functions of a review genre rather than the personal proclivities of its author. An in-depth analysis of such data shows that detractive evaluators are preferred to additive evaluators only for negative judgements in expert reviews, where they offer a conventionally indirect way of expressing face-threatening claims.

As for the polarity of such acts, positivity is prevalent in most texts, where it is encoded almost exclusively by additive evaluation. Negativity is entirely absent in publisher's descriptions and blurbs but prevalent in book reviews – a result that points to the genre's highly authoritative role in high-impact journals and confirms Lather's argument that

'A review is gatekeeping, policing, and productive rather than merely mirroring. In short a review constitutes the field it reviews' (1999, p. 3). Negative evaluation is realized above all by additive realizations in book reviews and detractive realizations in expert reviews. This suggests that positivity is the unmarked choice for reviewers, who feel a need to employ indirect realizations (detractive evaluation) almost only for negative comments. All comparative evaluators are employed to argue that the book concerned is an improvement on other contributions (but never worse or not as good) – the implication being that it is more acceptable to criticize flaws in the literature than in the book under review.

Taken together these findings indicate that, within the bounds of a single academic domain, positive and negative judgements are deployed differently across genres whose common aim is to assess a new publication in the field. Applied linguistics was chosen because of the evidence (cf. Hunston, 1993) that linguists engage in academic controversies more extensively than other scholars – a phenomenon interpreted in research articles as 'an attempt to compensate for the indefiniteness in the basic theoretical apparatus of the discipline' (Motta-Roth, 1996b, p. 22). It is worth adding, however, that the impact of negative evaluations is always linked to the relative frequency of their positive counterparts; in our case, the finding that criticism is far more common in book reviews than expert reviews is even more significant because of the smaller amount of praise found in the former. Despite suggestions that in general communication direct and indirect negative comments convey the same amount of negativity (cf. Colston, 1999), the distribution of evaluators here seems to substantiate the mitigating function of detractive realizations, whose indirectness is reserved almost entirely for negative evaluative acts. At the same time, the wording of negative comments (whether additive or detractive) relies extensively on contextual information, making them more diluted and embedded in the surrounding discourse than their positive counterparts.

Despite their apparent similarity, blurbs and publisher's descriptions were therefore distinguishable in terms of evaluative intensity, with the former containing almost four times more evaluators than the latter. This suggests a clear division of roles between the two genres: blurbs (whether written entirely or in part by the book's author) tend to concentrate on the monograph's merits and its contribution to the literature – which makes them the most value-laden genre in the group – while publisher's descriptions are mainly descriptive accounts of the book's contents, with the occasional addition of an upbeat review passage.

The evaluative acts embedded in review genres encode not only information about the reviewed book but also elements of the complex relationship between the reviewer, the reviewee and their readership. This is linked to the fact that 'expressing evaluation in a text involves both a statement of personal judgement and an appeal to shared norms and values. In that it creates a shared point of view of speaker/writer and hearer/reader, its meaning is essentially interpersonal' (Hunston, 1994, p. 191). Balancing these two sides of the praise/criticism dyad is essential to success in academic communication, whether in the primary, secondary or tertiary literature. It is hoped that a closer understanding of the evaluative repertoire used by reviewers (and book authors/publishers) to signal what is good or bad in a given context may help uncover elements of the value system that underpins disciplinary discourse, while providing EAP learners and practitioners with textual evidence of marked and unmarked realizations in the target genre.

References

Andersen, J. (2002) 'The Role of Subject Literature in Scholarly Communication. An Interpretation Based on Social Epistemology', *Journal of Documentation*, LVIII, 4, 463–81.

BAAL (2005) 'British Association for Applied Linguistics 2005 Book Prize', http://www.baal.org.uk/bkprize_about.htm, date accessed 14 February 2008.

Basturkmen, H. (1999) 'A Content Analysis of ELT Textbook Blurbs: Reflections of Theory-in-Use', *Regional English Language Council Journal*, XXX, 1, 18–38.

Bednarek, M. (2008) ' "An Increasingly Familiar Tragedy". Evaluative Collocation and Conflation', *Functions of Language*, XV, 1, 7–34.

Bhatia, V. K. (2004) *Worlds of Written Discourse* (London: Continuum).

Cacchiani, S. (2007) 'From Narratives to Intensification and Hyperbole: Promotional Uses of Book Blurbs' in M. Davies, P. Rayson, S. Hunston and P. Danielsson (eds) *Proceedings of the Corpus Linguistics Conference, University of Birmingham, 27–30 July 2007*, http://www.corpus. bham.ac.uk/corplingproceedings07/paper/79_Paper.pdf, date accessed 14 May 2008.

Colston, H. L. (1999) ' "Not Good" Is "Bad," but "Not Bad" Is not "Good": An Analysis of Three Accounts of Negation Asymmetry', *Discourse Processes*, XXVIII, 3, 237–56.

Diani, G. (2006) 'Reviewer Stance in Academic Review Articles: A Cross-Disciplinary Comparison' in G. Del Lungo Camiciotti, M. Dossena and B. Crawford Camiciottoli (eds) *Variation in Business and Economics Discourse. Diachronic and Genre Perspectives* (Rome: Officina Edizioni), 139–51.

Fishelov, D. (1993) *Metaphors of Genre. The Role of Analogies in Genre Theory* (University Park: Pennsylvania State University Press).

Gea-Valor, M. L. (2005) 'Advertising Books: A Linguistic Analysis of Blurbs', *Ibérica*, X, 41–62.

Gea-Valor, M. L. (2006) 'Is an Image Worth a Thousand Words? Net Representations of the Book Industry', *Revista de Lingüística y Lenguas Aplicadas*, I, 37–48.

Gesuato, S. (2004) 'Read Me First: Promotional Strategies in Back-Cover Blurbs', paper presented at the 2nd Inter-Varietal Applied Corpus Studies Conference, Belfast, 25–26 June 2004, http://www.units.it/~didactas/pub/unipd/presIVACS 2004.doc, date accessed 14 February 2008.

Giannoni, D. S. (2006) 'Expressing Praise and Criticism in Economic Discourse: A Comparative Analysis of English and Italian Book Reviews' in G. Del Lungo Camiciotti, M. Dossena and B. Crawford Camiciottoli (eds) *Variation in Business and Economics Discourse. Diachronic and Genre Perspectives* (Rome: Officina Edizioni), 126–38.

Giannoni, D. S. (2008) 'Popularizing Features in English Journal Editorials', *English for Specific Purposes*, XXVII, 2 (Special Issue in Honor of John Swales), 212–32.

Giannoni, D. S. (forthcoming) 'Metaphoric Values and Disciplinary Identity in English Research Articles' in J. Archibald and G. Garzone (eds) *Discourse, Identity and the Professions* (Bern: Peter Lang).

Giora, R., Balaban, N., Fein, O. and Alkabets, I. (2004) 'Negation as Positivity in Disguise' in H. L. Colston and A. Katz (eds) *Figurative Language Comprehension: Social and Cultural Influences* (Mahwah, NJ: Lawrence Erlbaum), 233–58.

Giora, R., Fein O., Ganzi, J., Levi, N. A. and Sabah, H. (2005) 'On Negation as Mitigation: The Case of Negative Irony', *Discourse Processes*, XXXIX, 1, 81–100.

S. Hunston (1993) 'Professional Conflict: Disagreement in Academic Discourse' in M. Baker, G. Francis and E. Tognini-Bonelli (eds) *Text and Technology: In Honour of John Sinclair* (Amsterdam: John Benjamins), 115–34.

Hunston, S. (1994) 'Evaluation and Organization in a Sample of Written Academic Discourse' in M. Coulthard (ed.) *Advances in Written Text Analysis* (London: Routledge), 191–218.

Hunston, S. (2004) 'Counting the Uncountable: Problems of Identifying Evaluation in a Text and in a Corpus' in A. Partington, J. Morley and L. Haarman (eds) *Corpora and Discourse* (Bern: Peter Lang), 157–88.

Hyland, K. (1998) *Hedging in Scientific Research Articles* (Amsterdam: John Benjamins).

Hyland, K. (2000) *Disciplinary Discourses: Social Interactions in Academic Writing* (London: Longman).

Kuhn, T. S. (1970) *The Structure of Scientific Revolutions*, 2nd edn (Chicago: University of Chicago Press).

Lather, P. (1999) 'To Be of Use: The Work of Reviewing', *Review of Educational Research*, LXIX, 1, 2–7.

Moreno, A. I. and Suárez, L. (2008) 'A Study of Critical Attitude across English and Spanish Academic Book Reviews', *Journal of English for Academic Purposes*, VII, 1, 15–26.

Motta-Roth, D. (1996a) 'Same Genre, Different Discipline: A Genre-Based Study of Book Reviews in Academe', *The ESPecialist*, XVII, 2, 99–131.

Motta-Roth, D. (1996b) 'Investigating Connections between Text and Discourse Communities: A Cross-Disciplinary Study of Evaluative Discourse Practices in Academic Book Reviews', paper presented at the Annual Meeting of the American Association for Applied Linguistics, 23–26 March 1996, http://www.eric.ed.gov/ERICDocs/data/ericdocs2sql/content_storage_01/0000019b/80/39/cf/88.pdf, date accessed 14 February 2008.

Myers, G. (1991) 'Stories and Styles in Two Molecular Biology Review Articles' in C. Bazerman and J. Paradis (eds) *Textual Dynamics of the Professions. Historical and Contemporary Studies of Writing in Professional Communities* (Madison: The University of Wisconsin Press), 45–75.

Noguchi, J. (2006) *The Science Review Article. An Opportune Genre in the Construction of Science* (Bern: Peter Lang).

Römer, U. (2008) 'Identification Impossible? A Corpus Approach to Realisations of Evaluative Meaning in Academic Writing', *Functions of Language*, XV, 1, 115–30.

Salager-Meyer, F. (2001) ' "This Book Portrays the Worst Form of Mental Terrorism": Critical Speech Acts in Medical English Book Reviews (1940-2000)' in A. Kertész (ed.) *Approaches to the Pragmatics of Scientific Discourse* (Frankfurt am Main: Peter Lang), 47–72.

Salager-Meyer, F. (2002) 'Market-Place, Self-Confidence and Criticism in Medical Editorials', *Revista Canaria de Estudios Ingleses*, XLIV, 65–78.

Salager-Meyer, F. and Alcaraz Ariza, M. A. (2004) 'Negative Appraisals in Academic Book Reviews. A Cross-Linguistic Approach' in C. N. Candlin and M. Gotti (eds) *Intercultural Aspects of Specialized Communication* (Bern: Peter Lang), 149–72.

Shaw, P. (2004) 'How Do We Recognise Implicit Evaluation in Academic Book Reviews?' in G. Del Lungo Camiciotti and E. Tognini Bonelli (eds) *Academic Discourse – New Insights into Evaluation* (Bern: Peter Lang), 121–40.

Swales, J. M. and Burke, A. (2003) ' "It's Really Fascinating Work": Differences in Evaluative Adjectives across Academic Registers' in P. Leistyna and C. F. Meyer (eds) *Corpus Analysis. Language Structure and Language Use* (Amsterdam: Rodopi), 1–18.

Thompson, G. and Hunston, S. (2000) 'Evaluation: An Introduction' in S. Hunston and G. Thompson (eds) *Evaluation in Text. Authorial Stance and the Construction of Discourse* (Oxford: Oxford University Press), 1–27.

2
Reviewing Science in an Information-Overloaded World

Judy Noguchi

Constructing scientific knowledge

How does a 'scientific fact' become recognized as a 'fact'? How does science 'construct knowledge' and how does language play a part in this? The answers are not simple because, as Gross (1990, pp. 206–7) observes, 'the sciences create bodies of knowledge so persuasive as to seem unrhetorical – to seem, simply, the way the world is'. Scientific discovery cannot be traced to a single text but occurs during the 'interpretation' of texts as they are retold in news articles, review articles, textbooks and popularizations' (Myers, 1990, pp. 102–3).

Bizzell vividly documents this interplay of texts to create an integrated awareness in her description of how she developed the concept of 'discourse community':

> I don't remember whether the concept of discourse community was 'my own idea'. I don't really believe that people have their 'own' ideas or 'own' them. The formulation of the concept in my review-essay was not taken from anywhere else in its present form, but it was certainly profoundly influenced by my reading in Kuhn, Fish, Richard Rorty, and the sociolinguists, and by discussions with Bruce Herzberg. ... And in turn, it would seem that this essay has influenced the work of the cognitivists who now define their research as 'socio-cognitive' ... and it has influenced the work on discourse conventions done, for example, by scholars in writing across the curriculum.
>
> (Bizzell, 1992, pp. 17–18)

This is an interesting example not only because it suggests the dynamics of interaction between an individual and a discourse community, but also because it shows how the 'review-essay' integrates prior work and influences subsequent developments.

The review-essay is a genre that serves as 'a forum for the synthesis of ideas' (Noguchi, 2006, p. 16) and a means by which what is to be considered a 'fact' can be presented to a wider community. It is, in other words, a 'debut genre' for a fact. The thinking on this emerged from research on 25 review articles published in a scientific journal in 1993 and the present work revisits this concept of 'reviewing' science as a step in constructing knowledge in disciplinary fields. Here the citation records of the 25 review articles in the above-mentioned study are examined. A citation record is usually a list (but can be a 'map' as described below) of other articles that have cited the article in question; this information is available via several online sources. The more an article is cited, the greater impact it has on the work of other scientists and, therefore, on its field.

This study has two parts. The first is an examination conducted on the citation records of 25 reviews from the *Proceedings of the National Academy of Sciences* (*PNAS*), published in 1993, over the 15 years since their publication to find whether or not they are viewed as repositories of tacit knowledge to be used as the basis of further research. The second part reconsiders the process of reviewing science because the information 'deluge', mentioned in the previous work (Noguchi, 2006), has now turned into an information 'explosion' in terms of quantity as well as momentum. It will be argued that reviewing science continues to be important in guiding its development but that the review article may be in the process of being replaced by other genres and modes of information dissemination.

Materials and methods

The 25 *PNAS* reviews considered in the present study were carefully examined and clarified into four categories by Noguchi (2006), showing that different subgenres could be identified within the science review article genre: (1) *history reviews* describing the background of a field or research focus and its current position; (2) *status quo reviews* giving the background of a field or research, with descriptions of relevant phenomena and important technologies; (3) *theory reviews* describing background and relevant phenomena as well as presenting a theory or a model to explain or classify the phenomena; and (4) *issue reviews* presenting a phenomenon or technology and pointing to some problem or issue involving it and then offering a solution. It would be interesting

Table 2.1   Number of citations in the top five review articles

Year	1993–95	1996–98	1999–01	2002–04	2005–07	2008	Total*
Issue 1	68	57	43	39	19	5	231
Issue 2	3	11	9	18	63	24	128
Issue 3	21	27	28	16	7	2	101
Theory 1	0	31	32	20	13	3	99
Theory 2	4	49	27	12	6	1	99

*Total number of citations from Pub Med Central and HighWire Press citation sites (16 November 2008).

to find out whether the citation rates differ with the type of review article.

Citation records were obtained from online sources, which list only those from high-impact, readily available journals. In other words, the actual number of citations is likely to be greater than the figures presented in Table 2.1, which gives the number of citations per three-year periods for the five top-cited review articles. Due to space concerns, the other reviews were not subjected to detailed analyses. Their citations ranged from 1 to 83 times per review, with 12 reviews being cited 11 to 83 times and the remaining eight being cited from 1 to 9 times. These figures were filtered manually by downloading all citations listed from online sources and categorizing them by year. From 1993 to 2008 (June), the six issue reviews averaged 81 citations per review, the six theory reviews averaged 46.5 citations, the four history reviews 27.3 citations and the nine status quo reviews 26.1 citations. One of the issue reviews was based on a speech and had only one citation. If it was removed from the calculation, the five issue reviews averaged 97 citations per review. Clearly, the issue reviews were the better cited.

Table 2.1 shows that the top three most cited reviews were issue reviews followed by two theory reviews. ISSUE 1, 2 and 3 refer to issue reviews by Blenis (1993), Ames *et al.* (1993) and Temin (1993), respectively. THEORY 1 and 2 refer to theory reviews by Anderson (1993) and Bennett and Scheller (1993), respectively. The issue reviews showed a relatively high percentage of opinion statements when compared with the other types of reviews (Noguchi, 2006, p. 158). One of the expert informants commented that 'there was a need for someone to summarize and synthesize it [a large body of literature]...to move the field forward'. The issue reviews may have been more frequently cited because this is what they seem to be trying to do, that is, as stated by the informant, 'change people's thinking' (Noguchi, 2006, p. 113).

As can be seen in Table 2.1, all of these five reviews continue to be cited in 2008. ISSUE 1 reached a peak of 35 citations in 1994, the year after its publication and 21 citations were achieved in 2000. ISSUE 2 averaged 2.6 citations per year from 1994 to 2003, when it dropped to zero. However, from 2004 to 2008 (November), the number jumped to about 20 citations per year. ISSUE 3 averaged ten citations per year until 2000, but the number fell, especially from 2004, averaging two per year. THEORY 1, after registering no citations until 1996, had a clear peak in 1998 of 28 citations. THEORY 2 showed an increase from 1996, peaking in 1998. Now, let us take a closer look at these reviews and how they are being cited.

Correlating citation patterns and research field activity

The peaks of citation activity appear to be related to research trends in the individual fields of research. For example, ISSUE 1 shows a peak in 1994 and a look at the abstract of the original review article offers an explanation for this:

> An explosion of new information linking activation of cell surface signal initiators to changes in gene expression has recently emerged. The focus of much of this information has centered around the agonist-dependent activation of the mitogen-activated protein (MAP) kinases. ... These signaling proteins may participate in the regulation of a variety of cellular processes.
>
> (Blenis, 1993)

Blenis concludes that:

> As indicated by the title of this review, there is great risk in trying to describe the ever-expanding, complex signaling network involved in the regulation of MAP kinases. ... Further characterization of the tyrosine kinase/Ras-mediated activation pathways regulating the MAP kinases and RSK is awaited with interest and yes, the map will become even more complex.

Citation data show that Blenis had accurately predicted what would subsequently occur in this research field. In 2008, it continues to be cited as giving definitive information about this topic (it is Ref. 6 in the following quote): 'RSK2 contains two distinct kinase domains, both of which are catalytically functional (reviewed in Refs. 6, 7)'.

ISSUE 2 had 24 citations in 2008 and 63 in the previous three-year period from 2005 to 2007. It will be discussed in detail below.

ISSUE 3 was cited in 6–13 articles per year between 1994 and 2003 but the numbers dropped from 3 to 2 from 2004. The author was one of the discoverers of retroviruses, which are related to diseases such as AIDS (Noguchi, 2006, p. 220). This review was cited as presenting tacit knowledge from the year after its publication, when it appeared as a citation in the first sentence of a paper by Zhang and Temin (1994), per-haps because Temin was a co-author. A 1995 paper by Parthasarathi *et al.* cites it three times in the Discussion section to support specific points. In 1998 (Mikkelsen *et al.*), it appears in the second sentence of the Intro-duction section, indicating its citation for the general background of the paper. In the 2008 paper by Archer *et al.*, it is the first reference of 37:

> The causative agent of AIDS, HIV, exhibits a high rate of evolution as a direct result of the error-prone nature of reverse transcriptase and its tendency to switch between RNA templates [1, 2].

Interestingly, the two other 2008 papers cite ISSUE 3 in the Discussion section to support specific points. This may be because Chakravarti *et al.* (2008) discuss a technique for amplifying DNA sequences while Gayral *et al.* (2008) reports work on plant viruses. These studies are branching out into areas beyond the HIV-related work covered in ISSUE 3.

THEORY 1 showed a distinct citation peak in 1998. This was the year when Anderson (1998) wrote another review entitled 'The caveolae membrane system', which has been cited more than 180 times, with ten citations in the first six months of 2008. The reason for this peak can be surmised from what Anderson states in the 1998 review:

> The cell biology of caveolae is a rapidly growing area of biomedical research. Caveolae are known primarily for their ability to transport molecules across endothelial cells, but modern cellular techniques have dramatically extended our view of caveolae.... Specific diseases attack this system ... Trying to understand the full range of functions of caveolae challenges our basic instincts about the cell.

Anderson is using these reviews to synthesize what is happening and is also trying to expand the body of tacit knowledge of the field.

THEORY 2 is cited in 1993 by Aalto *et al.* in the Discussion section for specific support, but by 1997 appears in the Introduction section

(Lauber *et al.*, 1997) and in 1998 (David *et al.*) as one of the three initial citations laying the basis for the paper. THEORY 2 continues to be cited in various sections of recent papers as it is used to support diverse studies extending into areas such as the molecular biology of the cell, pharmacological therapy and biomedical research.

Examining ISSUE 2 citations more closely

The ISSUE 2 review, which has been the most frequently cited of the five reviews from 2004 to the present, will now be considered in more detail. The *PNAS* citation page offers a citation map to visually present the relationship of a paper to others citing it. As can be seen from Figure 2.1, ISSUE 2 shows what looks like a network of connections of the top ten citing articles, which in turn are the most highly cited themselves from the list of articles citing ISSUE 2. In this case, the *Science* review by Wallace in 1999 is a major one as this review itself attracted the most citations among papers citing ISSUE 2.

For a closer look at how the citing of ISSUE 2 was done, its presentation in the *Science* article by Wallace (1999) and the most recent citations were examined in more detail (information is reported from articles to which the author had access through the interlibrary loan network). Before proceeding, the citation formats used in the references need to be explained as they differ with the journal. Some journals assign numbers to the references in the order in which they appear. In such a case, a smaller number indicates that the citation appeared early in the text, usually in the Introduction section, if the paper were reporting research. On the other hand, a larger number near the end of the listing would indicate that the citation came in the Discussion section. Other journals list the references alphabetically according to the first author's family name. In such cases, the specific section or paragraph in the text in which ISSUE 2 was cited is given.

The Wallace review (1999), using a numbered citation listing, cites ISSUE 2 as the 74th of 101 citations. It is one of three citations in the first sentence of the third paragraph of the fifth section (of a total of six sections) on 'Somatic mtDNA mutations in aging and cancer'. This suggests that the Wallace review simply considers the ISSUE 2 review as one of many similar papers in the field, that is, it is not cited at the beginning of the paper as presenting background knowledge. Instead, it appears near the end of the paper.

However, in papers citing ISSUE 2 in 2008, a different image emerges. Of the 15 papers, access to 12 allowed their detailed examination. Nine

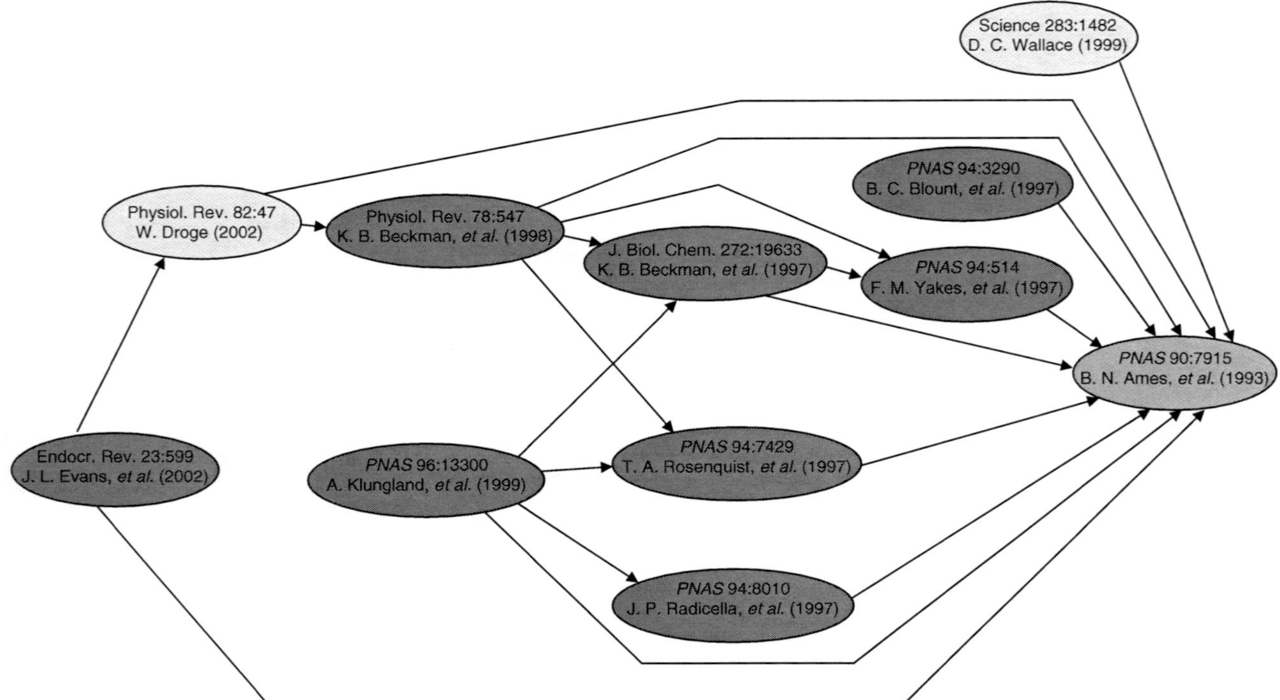

Figure 2.1   Network of citations of ISSUE 2 review from *PNAS* citation map (HighWire Press 2008)

refer to ISSUE 2 in the introduction to the paper, four within the first or second sentence. This shows that the ISSUE 2 review is now viewed as presenting general tacit knowledge because the first few sentences of a scientific journal paper describing research usually present the background of the field. As can be seen from the following examples, citation of the ISSUE 2 review appears either alone or with other references in the first sentence of the paper, being the citation with the lowest number in two of the cases:

Example 1 (Citation no. 1 of 31)

Oxidative stress generated from oxidant by-products of normal cellular metabolism or exogenous sources such as smoking plays a key role in tumorigenesis, causing oxidative DNA damages (1–3).

(Xie *et al.*, 2008)

Example 2 (Citation no. 1 of 68)

Iron, although central to human health, is the keystone in many human diseases. Excess iron can contribute to the formation of reactive oxygen species, leading to protein, lipid, and DNA damage (1).

(Sammarco *et al.*, 2008)

Example 3 (Methods Online, citation no. 8 of 32)

Damage to DNA plays an important role in many biological processes, such as mutagenesis, carcinogenesis and aging (7–10).

(Wang *et al.*, 2008)

Despite its recognition as a review presenting tacit knowledge, one paper displays an interesting citation pattern. Jones *et al.* (2008) refer to ISSUE 2 in both the Introduction and Discussion sections in a specific manner, unlike the general manner in which it was cited in examples (1) to (3). Oddly, the first citation does not appear until the fifth paragraph of the Introduction section.

Example 4 (Citation no. 27 of 50)

This increased post-thymic persistence may further jeopardize T cell function by allowing for the accumulation of oxidative damage to cellular DNA (24), mitochondria (25, 26), and lipid membranes (27), while simultaneously compromising the cellular maintenance and repair pathways that counteract such insults (27, 28).

(Jones *et al.*, 2008)

This section is what Swales (1990) would categorize as the niche-making move of a research paper. The authors, after presenting the background and known literature, proceed to point out gaps in the knowledge that their research is expected to fill. Rather than being cited in a general manner, as shown in examples (1) to (3), ISSUE 2 is being used to support one specific feature (lipid membranes). ISSUE 2 is also cited in the sixth paragraph (of eight) in the Discussion section, together with other papers, to support the argument of the authors, again for its specific effect on lipids:

Example 5

This loss of equilibrium has been shown to damage DNA (24), interfere with mitochondrial function (25, 26), and alter the lipids of the plasma membrane (27).

(Jones et al., 2008)

ISSUE 2 is again used to offer specific, rather than general, support in the Wong *et al.* (2008) paper in which it is cited in the penultimate paragraph of the Discussion section. It is cited to support the argument that: 'Subsequent accumulation of ROS-damaged DNA is a critical event during carcinogenesis and aging (2).'

Another specific citation instance of ISSUE 2 comes in one of the 2008 research articles (Ruder *et al.*). It is mentioned after an explanation on the use of databases and online searching.

Example 6

We searched PubMed database for all articles published in English from January 1966 through October 2006 with evidence relating to OS, antioxidant status and female fertility. Search terms included conception, conception delay, ROS, early pregnancy loss, antioxidant, OS, ovarian aging and infertility. We reviewed the abstract of the identified articles to determine if the article met the scope of our review. The reference lists of articles included in our review were also examined for additional potential articles.

(Ruder et al., 2008)

In the second sentence of the subsequent paragraph, ISSUE 2 is mentioned in a very specific manner:

Example 7

OS induces lipid peroxidation, structurally and functionally alters protein and DNA, promotes apoptosis, and contributes to the risk of chronic diseases like cancer and heart disease via effects on redox status and/or redox-sensitive signaling pathways and gene expression.

(Ames *et al.*, 1993)

This sentence does not occur in the Introduction section but in Materials and Methods section, suggesting that it is still necessary to cite ISSUE 2 in support of the selected techniques even 15 years after its original publication.

These citations in which the ISSUE 2 review is used for both general and specific support show that it is still considered to be relevant in conveying tacit knowledge and useful in supporting details.

Comparing reviews by ISSUE 2 first author and a research paper

The first author of the ISSUE 2 review, Bruce Ames, is a renowned biochemist who invented the Ames test (Ames *et al.*, 1973), which is used for the simple and inexpensive testing of the mutagenic potential of compounds. Ames also appears to be a good mentor, publishing as a co-author and sponsoring papers for publication in *PNAS*, which until 1994, required membership or 'communication' by a member for publication. The review, in the original 25, was co-authored with Mark K. Shigenaga and Tory M. Hagen. The three also published a review in 1994 entitled 'Oxidative damage and mitochondrial decay in aging'. Online citation research of this review shows that it has been cited about 73 times since its publication and continues to be cited at a pace of 2–3 times a year, with three citations as of 30 June 2008. This is less than the 119 citations registered for the ISSUE 2 review being focused on here, but is much higher than that for a *PNAS* article also published in 1994 by Chen and Ames, entitled 'Senescence-like growth arrest induced by hydrogen peroxide in human diploid fibroblast F65 cells'. This paper has been cited only 18 times with the most recent being once in 2007 and previously in 2005. As the research field is similar and Ames is a co-author of all three papers, the main difference concerns whether or not the paper is a research report or a review. The tendency seems to be for reviews to both attract more citations and have longer citation lives.

Re-examining the role of the review article in the construction of scientific knowledge

A survey of all *PNAS* issues available online reveals that while there were 23 review articles published in 1996, the number dropped to seven in

1997 and ranged from 1 to 4 from 1999 to 2007. This drop in the number of reviews is probably due to a journal policy change from one that required membership or sponsorship by an Academy member for publication to a 'direct submission track' from December 1995.

The current Information for Authors states that *PNAS* accepts research reports describing original research; feature articles that are in-depth research reports with 'exceptional breadth and are written at the invitation of the Editorial Board'; commentaries, also written by invitation, which 'call attention to papers of particular note'; and perspectives, also written by invitation, which 'present a viewpoint on an important area of research' and 'discuss current advances and future directions'. This last category is targeted at nonspecialists. *PNAS* also publishes colloquium papers and letters commenting on recent research articles. As can be seen, the category of 'reviews' has vanished from the list. What seems to have happened is that the functions of the review articles observed in 1993 have been parcelled out into feature articles, commentaries and perspectives, which like the review articles, are written upon invitation from the editors. The feature article, introduced in 2007, is described as follows:

> In this issue of *PNAS*, we are launching a new category of Direct Submissions. The Feature Article series highlights research articles at the forefront of science, truly innovative work of exceptional significance. These articles are held to the highest editorial standards with rigorous and anonymous peer review for all submissions. As with all research articles in *PNAS*, Feature Articles should appeal to specialists in the field but be generally accessible as well. Feature authors may use a slightly longer format than a regular research article so that they can fully develop and present their findings. Feature Articles may be highlighted with Commentaries, press coverage, or cover taglines, and provide an opportunity for all scientists to submit innovative, in-depth research to *PNAS*.
>
> (Schekman, 2007)

What seems to emerge is a new 'genre' that has some of the characteristics of a review article but can even include features that can appeal to the mass media. This may be an indication that the pace of developments in science and technology is too fast for the writing of reviews or that the Web-connected world of today demands more audience-friendly and readily accessible information dissemination. In order to evaluate the importance of review articles, which may now be a genre in flux, we need to take a look at information dissemination today, especially in the sciences.

Coping with information overload

The term 'information explosion' perfectly captures the fact that we are now overwhelmed with new information on a daily basis. Despite the scale of this information, the University of California Berkeley's School of Information Management and Systems (SIMS) is trying to quantify this explosion and their 2003 report states that for the Web alone, the volume of information tripled to 167 terabytes between 2000 and 2003. One terabyte is equivalent to 10^{12} bytes of information, and the entire print collections of the US Library of Congress amounts to 10 terabytes.

This information explosion is, of course, also affecting science and technology. To help manage this flood of information, there are many databases and search engines to support academic work, such as Web of Science, Scirus, GoPubMed and Google Scholar. However, while these tools can make it easier to find articles related to one's field of study or research, they do not offer evaluative, synthesizing and consolidating support. The question then arises of how this type of support can be obtained.

One possibility, albeit controversial, is via weblogs or blogs. Perhaps not blogs by individuals but by scientific communities, as stated by Schmidt of the NASA Goddard Institute of Space Studies Columbia University, and co-founder of RealClimate.org in *Nature Geoscience* (Schmidt, 2008, p. 208):

> With the importance of science in policy decisions being more apparent than ever, our ability to do science and enhance its relevance in public life relies on the community's willingness to engage, inspire and inform. Blogs are one way to do that, and they can excel at providing the context that is so often missing in other media. Not every scientist needs to have one, but maybe every scientific field does.

Schmidt's comment points to a very important reason for the accessibility of scientific information: its influence on policy decisions that can affect the general public.

The process of a scientific discovery becoming a part of the tacit knowledge of a field suggests a movement from the research report to popular acceptance via a 'coming-of-age' point within the scientific community. Today, however, with the rapid dissemination of information via Web sources, there seems to be a short circuit from the lab to the popular media, which can sometimes be problematic.

An example of how things can go wrong occurred in 2006, when two reports on stem cell research by researchers from a group based in South Korea were retracted by the reputable journal *Science* (2006). Fraudulent data in the papers had eluded discovery by *Science* editors and nine peer reviewers. As the implications of stem cell research carry great importance in medical fields, these papers had attracted wide publicity and media coverage. The first author, Hwang was even named by *Time* magazine as one of the 'People who mattered 2004'. Also, the publication of his papers in *Science* enabled Hwang to garner at least US$27 million to support his research together with prestigious titles and positions. Commenting on the debacle, Altshuler, who scrutinized the data, stated that 'studies are rarely accepted as dogma until they're replicated...a distinction often lost on the general public – and sometimes other scientists – amid the hype that envelops firsts' (Couzin 2006, p. 24). If the construction of scientific knowledge process discussed at the beginning of the present paper had been more carefully followed, then the information in the Hwang paper would probably not have created such a sensation until its data had been more carefully scrutinized by the scientific community. In the final analysis, as posted by Clarke (2008) on the *Nature* blog,

> The gold standard comes when the community as a whole says, 'Hey, cool, I can use this'. The paper is cited. The techniques are used. Science advances. Eventually, what was in the paper becomes part of the tacit knowledge assumed by reviewers.

While Clarke, an editor at *Nature*, is referring to the role of blogs in the communication of scientific knowledge, she is also describing a view of the process of knowledge construction. The importance of the work being cited and used to advance science is what leads to the production of tacit knowledge. As stated by Schmidt (2008), responsible blogging may be one way to deal with the information explosion and help guide the construction of knowledge.

Conclusion

This paper has examined the 'reviewing' of science and its role in the construction of scientific knowledge. Examination of the citation records of 25 review articles that were published about 15 years ago revealed that the reviews cited the most and over the longest period of time (some even being cited currently) were those that discussed issues or theories in the field, rather than those that were describing history or status quo. This suggests that identifying issues and proposing theories help guide the process of knowledge construction. The citation volume appears to be related to the research trends in the field with the number of citations increasing as the level of activity rises and also to the expansion of research fields.

The review article itself appears to be undergoing metamorphosis. The number of reviews in *PNAS* dropped sharply after 1996, with a shift to different types of papers. The newest, the feature article, could be characterized as a review that is more media-friendly, that is, more accessible to both specialists and a wider more general audience (Schekman, 2007). This may be in keeping with the rapidity of information dissemination today. With the explosive increase in the volume of information, scientists still need ways to manage the information relevant to their work. More usage of the citation mapping shown in Figure 2.1 is likely to occur and 'review-type' articles dealing with more specifically defined areas and sections of research activity should allow quick and manageable overviews of certain aspects of research.

Another new way to review science is via blogs, not by private individuals, but by professional institutions and reputable individuals such as editors of well-known scientific journals. What remains true is that there is a need for some way to identify 'the gold standard' (Clarke, 2008) and continue the construction of a body of knowledge that can inform responsible public policy decisions and support the development of science.

References

Aalto, M. K., Ronne, H. and Keranen, S. (1993) 'Yeast Syntaxins Sso1p and Sso2p Belong to a Family of Related Membrane Proteins That Function in Vesicular Transport', *The EMBO Journal*, XII, 11, 4095–104.

Ames, B., Lee, F. and Durston, W. (1973) 'An Improved Bacterial Test System for the Detection and Classification of Mutagens and Carcinogens', *Proceedings of the National Academy of Sciences*, LXX, 782–86.

Ames, B. N., Shigenaga, M. K. and Hagen, T. M. (1993) 'Oxidants, Antioxidants, and the Degenerative Diseases of Aging', *Proceedings of the National Academy of Sciences*, XC, 7915–22.

Anderson, R. G. W. (1993) 'Caveolae: Where Incoming and Outgoing Messengers Meet', *Proceedings of the National Academy of Sciences*, XC, 10909–13.

Anderson, R. G. W. (1998) 'The Caveolae Membrane System', *Annual Review of Biochemistry*, LXVII, 199–225.

Archer, J., Pinney, J. W., Fan, J., Simon-Loriere, E., Arts, E. J., Negroni, M. and Robertson, D. L. (2008) 'Identifying the Important HIV-1 Recombination Breakpoints', *The Journal of Virology*, LXXXII, 13, 6697–710.

Bennett, M. K. and Scheller, R. H. (1993) 'The Molecular Machinery for Secretion is Conserved from Yeast to Neurons', *Proceedings of the National Academy of Sciences*, XC, 2559–63.

Bizzell, P. (1992) *Academic Discourse and Critical Consciousness* (Pittsburgh and London: University of Pittsburgh Press).

Blenis, J. (1993) 'Signal Transduction via the MAP Kinases: Proceed at Your Own RSK', *Proceedings of the National Academy of Sciences*, LXXX, 5889–92.

Chakravarti, D. and Mailander, P. C. (2008) 'Formation of Template-Switching Artifacts by Linear Amplification', *Journal of Biomolecular Techniques*, XIX, 184–88.

Chen, Q. and Ames, B. N. (1994) 'Senescence-like Growth Arrest Induced by Hydrogen Peroxide in Human Diploid Fibroblast F65 Cells', *Proceedings of the National Academy of Sciences*, XCI, 4130–34.

Clarke, M. (2008) 'Role of Blogs in Communicating Scientific Knowledge', Peer-to-Peer at nature.com, http://blogs.nature.com/peer-to-peer/2008/04/role_of_blogs_in_communicating.html, date accessed 12 May 2008.

Couzin, J. (2006) '…And How the Problems Eluded Peer Reviewers and Editors', *Science*, CCCXI, 23–4.

David, D., Sundarababu, S. and Gerst, J. E. (1998) 'Involvement of Long Chain Fatty Acid Elongation in the Trafficking of Secretory Vesicles in Yeast', *The Journal of Cell Biology*, CXLIII, 5, 1167–82.

Gayral, P., Noa-Carrazana, J.-C., Lescot, M., Lheureux, F., Lockhart, B. E. L., Matsumoto, T., Piffanelli, P. and Iskra-Caruana, M. L. (2008) 'A Single *Banana Streak Virus* Integration Event in the Banana Genome as the Origin of Infectious Endogenous Pararetrovirus', *The Journal of Virology*, LXXXII, 13, 6697–710.

Gross, A. (1990) *The Rhetoric of Science* (Cambridge, Massachusetts: Harvard University Press).

HighWire Press (2008) http://www.highwire.stanford.edu/cgi/citemap?id=pnas%3B90%2F17%2F7915, date accessed 28 June 2008.

Jones, S. C., Clise-Dwyer, K., Huston, G., Dibble, J., Eaton, S., Haynes, L. and Swain, S. L. (2008) 'Impact of Post-Thymic Cellular Longevity on the Development of Age-Associated CD4 + T Cell Defects', *The Journal of Immunology*, CLXXX, 4465–75.

Lauber, M. H., Waizenegger, I., Steinmann, T., Hwang, H. I., Lukowitz, W. and Jürgens, G. (1997) 'The Arabidopsis KNOLLE Protein Is a Cytokinesis-specific Syntaxin', *The Journal of Cell Biology*, CXXXIX, 6, 1485–93.

Mikkelsen, J. G., Lund, A. H., Duch, M. and Edersen, F. S. (1998) 'Recombination in the 59 Leader of Murine Leukemia Virus is Accurate and Influenced by Sequence Identity with a Strong Bias toward the Kissing-Loop Dimerization Region', *The Journal of Virology*, LXXII, 9, 6967–78.

Myers, G. (1990). *Writing Biology: Texts in the Social Construction of Scientific Knowledge* (Madison, Wisconsin: The University of Wisconsin Press).

Noguchi, J. (2006) *The Science Review Article: An Opportune Genre in the Construction of Science* (Bern: Peter Lang).

Parthasarathi, S., Varela-Echavarri, A., Ron, Y., Preson, B. D. and Dougherty, J. P. (1995) 'Genetic Rearrangements Occurring during a Single Cycle of Murine Leukemia Virus Vector Replication: Characterization and Implications', *The Journal of Virology*, LXIX, 12, 7991–8000.

PubMed Central (2008) http://www.pubmedcentral.nih.gov/, date accessed 30 June 2008.

Ruder, E. H., Hartman, T. J., Blumberg, J. and Goldman, M. B. (2008) 'Oxidative Stress and Antioxidants: Exposure and Impact on Female Fertility', *Human Reproduction*, XIV, 4, 345–57.

Sammarco, M. C., Ditch, S., Banerjee, A. and Grabczyk, E. (2008) 'Ferritin L and H Subunits are Differentially Regulated on a Post-transcriptional Level', *Journal of Biological Chemistry*, CCLXXXIII, 8, 4578–87.

Schekman, R. (2007) 'Introducing Feature Articles in PNAS', *Proceedings of the National Academy of Sciences*, CIV, 16, 6495.

Schmidt, G. (2008) 'To Blog or Not to Blog', *Nature Geoscience*, I, 208.

Swales, J. M. (1990) *Genre Analysis: English in Academic and Research Settings* (Cambridge: Cambridge University Press).

Temin, H. M. (1993) 'Retrovirus Variation and Reverse Transcription: Abnormal Strand Transfers Result in Retrovirus Genetic Variation', *Proceedings of the National Academy of Sciences*, XC, 6900–3.

Wallace, D. C. (1999) 'Mitochondrial Diseases in Man and Mouse', *Science*, CCLXXXIII, 5407, 1482–88.

Wang, W., Lee, G. J., Jang, K. J., Cho, T. S. and Kim, S. K. (2008) 'Real-time Detection of Fe·EDTA/H_2O_2-induced DNA Cleavage by Linear Dichroism', *Nucleic Acids Research*, XXXVI, 14, doi:10.1093/nar/gkn370.

Wong, S. H. K., Shih, R. S. M., Schoene, N. W. and Lei, K. Y. (2008) 'Zinc-induced G2/M Blockage is p53 and p21 Dependent in Normal Human Bronchial Epithelial Cells', *American Journal of Physiology-Cell Physiology*, CCXCIV, C1342–49.

Xie, Y., Yang, H., Miller, J. H., Shih, D. M., Hicks, G. G., Xie, J. and Shiu, R. (2008) 'Cells Deficient in Oxidative DNA Damage Repair Genes Myh and Ogg1 are Sensitive to Oxidants with Increased G_2/M Arrest and Multinucleation', *Carcinogenesis*, XXIX, 4, 713–21.

Zhang, J. and Temin, H. M. (1994) 'Retrovirus Recombination Depends on the Length of Sequence Identity and Is Not Error Prone', *The Journal of Virology*, LXVIII, 4, 2409–14.

3
Literature Reviews in Applied PhD Theses: Evidence and Problems

Paul Thompson

Introduction

In this chapter some features of literature reviews within an academic genre are discussed, that of the PhD thesis, in a corpus of PhD literature review chapters. The approach taken is a corpus analytic one, starting with information about the frequency and range of nouns in the corpus, and then investigating how and for what purposes some of the most frequent nouns are used in the texts, in order to identify and exemplify characteristics of PhD literature reviews.

The corpus contains chapters from 24 British theses, with six each from four different applied disciplines, those of Agricultural Botany, Agricultural Economics, Food Science and Technology, and Psychology. The aim of the study is to explore the nature of literature reviews by examining the patterns in which some of the most frequent nouns in the corpus appear, in order to establish what is distinctive about the literature review as a (sub)genre and to identify some of the strategies that are used in these reviews.

Reviews in general are typically critical evaluations of something, written for a purpose, or purposes (a criterial feature of a genre according to Swales 1990) and my aim is to identify what those purposes are and some of the rhetorical means by which writers achieve their purposes. Nouns are the most frequent part-of-speech in academic written registers (Biber, 2006, pp. 47–8), with over 50 per cent of noun uses belonging to the semantic category that Biber terms 'abstract/process nouns'. These highly frequent nouns often occur in lexicogrammatical patterns (Hunston and Francis, 2000), which are distinguished here from lexical bundles (Biber *et al.*, 1999) – lexicogrammatical patterns are built around a combination of lexical item and grammatical class, allowing variation (e.g., it + BE + (ADV+) ADJ + that is a sequence which allows one or more adverbs to appear before the adjective, and which also allows for different forms of the lemma BE, as in *it was absolutely crucial that*), whereas a lexical bundle is a multiword lexical chunk (*it is important that*). Exploration of nouns and the lexicogrammatical patterns that they typically appear in within literature reviews is expected to provide an insight into what these texts are about, not in terms of topic, but in terms of what the core concepts or processes are, what functions the lexicogrammatical patterns perform within a broader rhetorical purpose and how these concepts or processes are evaluated. From a list of the most frequent nouns in the corpus of literature reviews, I will pick out nouns which are frequent in general language use, and are also used across the four disciplines, and then discuss the roles that these nouns play.

Rhetorical organization and purposes
of literature reviews

As British PhD theses usually are not published, the review of literature in such texts is less public than the other review genres explored in this book. The review can be as substantial, however, and, in a sense, it can carry greater importance and greater risk for the writer. A PhD thesis is a document produced for assessment purposes and the reception of the text will determine whether the writer is to be judged worthy of the award of a doctorate. Typically, the thesis writer will have spent at least three years working on the research and the writing of the thesis, and the thesis acts as the single text that is presented to the examiners for assessment. The success of a doctoral student's research over a long period of time depends on how the examiners evaluate the final written product. The writer of the literature review is therefore required both to evaluate and also to be evaluated, a feature of the social context of the genre that distinguishes it from other review genres such as the book review. Furthermore, the summative evaluation of the thesis is highly formalized, in the form of a *viva voce* examination, or a public defence. In this examination, it is expected that the thesis will provide evidence that the writer can lay claim to be an authority in the area of research, and also that the writer has a sufficiently critical perspective and knowledge of the theories, concepts and current state of knowledge in that area of research.

One distinctive feature of a literature review in a thesis or dissertation is that it is part of a larger text, and therefore should properly be viewed as a *sub-genre* rather than a genre in its own right. Literature reviews normally act as a foundation for the research that is to follow (in the thesis), placing the work within an historical, theoretical and possibly social or other context (depending on the nature of the research). Typically, the review summarizes the findings or arguments of related studies and places the work of others in a light that will reveal deficiencies or strengths in that work. The review may also provide discussion and definition of key concepts. These are performed with an awareness that the immediate audience (the examiners) are looking to identify any gaps in detail, logic or coverage, and the writer therefore must be prepared to defend all statements, while also demonstrating an ability both to write in a style appropriate to the discipline and to establish a tone of authority.

Ridley (2008, p. 7) identifies two main approaches to the integration of literature reviews within a thesis: *dedicated* and *recursive*. In the former case, the literature review takes the form of a single chapter often with the heading 'Literature review', or a set of chapters that have topic-related headings. In the latter type, the thesis reports a set of studies, with several chapters each providing an account of one or more studies, often in the form 'Introduction – Methods – Results – Discussion' (IMRD). In each of these chapters it is common to find a short review of literature for each study in the introduction. PhD theses have been observed to follow different patterns of organization however (Thompson, 1999; Ridley, 2000); and, as Swales (2004, p. 110) observes, they constitute a genre that is 'in a state of considerable flux'. There are topic-based theses in which separate chapters deal with different topics connected to an overall theme, and there are strongly theoretical theses in which the bulk of the text is devoted to development of a theory, or a theoretical model. In some theses there may not even be a distinct literature review, particularly in literature-based subject areas such as History and Literature.

Where distinct literature review chapters do exist, they tend, in terms of rhetorical organization, to resemble an 'Introduction' chapter in that they follow a CARS model (Swales, 1990): they establish a territory, establish a niche and then occupy that niche. In some cases the chapter labelled 'Introduction' in the thesis acts as the literature review chapter as well (see section below for details of such texts in the corpus for this study), but they are not necessarily the same structurally. Kwan (2006)

Table 3.1   A move structure for the thematic units in literature review chapters (Kwan, 2006, p. 51)

Move 1 *Establishing one part of the territory of one's own research* by:

- Strategy A: surveying the non-research-related phenomena or knowledge claims
- Strategy B: claiming centrality
- Strategy C: surveying the research-related phenomena

Move 2 *Creating a research niche* (in response to Move 1) by:

- Strategy A: counter-claiming
- Strategy B: gap-indicating
- Strategy C: asserting confirmative claims about knowledge or research practices surveyed
- Strategy D: asserting the relevancy of the surveyed claims to one's own research
- Strategy E: abstracting or synthesizing knowledge claims to establish a theoretical position or a theoretical framework

Move 3 (optional) *Occupying the research niche* by announcing:

- Strategy A: research aims, focuses, research questions or hypotheses
- Strategy B: theoretical positions/theoretical frameworks
- Strategy C: research design/processes
- Strategy D: interpretations of terminology used in the thesis

---

compared the moves in literature review chapters in doctoral theses to those identified by Bunton (2002) in his move analysis of PhD thesis introductions and developed a move model for the literature review chapter as shown in Table 3.1.

Kwan observes that the strategies do not necessarily all occur, nor do they always occur in sequential order in the way suggested by Table 3.1. The moves can also be recursive as is suggested by the naming of Move 1 (Establishing one part of the territory of one's own research), which allows for the possibility that the writer will establish one part after another in different theme-oriented sections of the chapter. Move 3, as indicated, is optional as this move and its strategies may already have appeared in the Introduction chapter if that is a separate chapter. What is evident from this model is that the main purpose of the literature review is to map the territory and then establish what the gap in present knowledge is. The corpus-informed linguistic analysis of the literature reviews that follows will demonstrate ways in which language is used for these purposes.

The corpus

This chapter reports on an investigation of literature reviews in PhD theses in four different disciplines, using the Reading Academic Text (RAT) corpus. This corpus is a collection of PhD theses and research articles written by staff and students at the University of Reading. The PhD thesis portion of the corpus contains 35 theses, in a variety of disciplines. The four disciplines represented in the corpus used in this study are Agricultural Botany, Agricultural Economics, Food Sciences and Technology and Psychology: for each discipline, six theses will be studied. The choice of disciplines investigated here is determined by availability (i.e. the four disciplines in which there are sufficient texts available in the RAT corpus) but what can be said is that the theses included are mainly applied research, primarily using approaches from the life sciences, but with social science approaches used in the case of Agricultural Economics.

Previous research on the RAT corpus has revealed that in the area of citation practices (Thompson, 2001, 2005), there is clear variation across disciplines and these findings are in accordance with those of Hyland (2000). In addition, there is variation between theses within a discipline and this paper will argue that it is necessary not only to recognize disciplinary differences but also fundamental differences in conceptualization of research and of knowledge (cf. Hyland, 2006).

For this study, it was decided to take a single chapter from each of the 24 theses. As indicated above, the concept of a literature review in a PhD thesis can vary from discipline to discipline, and there can also be differing degrees of conventionalization of rhetorical organization from one sub-discipline to another. In some cases, it may be conventional to have a separate dedicated chapter in a thesis titled 'Literature review' or 'Introduction' while in others it is not (those following a recursive pattern or those without distinct reviews of literature). Where there appeared to be more than one chapter that contained a substantial review of literature, a chapter that appeared to present a general review of literature was chosen.

Table 3.2 provides information on the chapters selected for inclusion in the corpus. In many cases the choice was relatively simple: the chapter chosen was either entitled 'Introduction' and was followed by a chapter called 'Materials and Methods' or equivalent (Ridley's

Table 3.2 Details of the chapters selected for analysis as literature review chapters

Discipline	Details of chapters *(the identifiers for the theses are made up of an abbreviation of the discipline name and a unique identifier)*
Agricultural Botany (AgBot)	4 'Introduction' chapters, 1 'Literature Review' chapter, and 1 introductory chapter called 'Sunflower' (AgBot2)
Agricultural Economics (AgEcon)	AgEcon1: C2 'The Classification of Marketing Systems' AgEcon2: C1 'Agricultural Research in the UK' AgEcon4: C3 'Exchange rates and trade' (described by the author as 'a literature survey') AgEcon5: C3 'Theory' AgEcon7: C2 'Agriculture and nitrates' AgEcon8: C5 'Economics and the provision of disease control information'
Food Science and Technology (FoodSci)	5 'Introduction' chapters, 1 'Literature Review' chapter
Psychology (Psy)	5 'Introduction' chapters, 1 'Literature Review' chapter

'dedicated' literature review chapter), or by a series of chapters reporting studies in an IMRD sequence.

The problematic cases were all in the Agricultural Economics sub-corpus, except for one Agricultural Botany thesis (AgBot2). This is a thesis that is as much about the development of new research techniques as it is about the phenomena investigated, and thus has theoretical and technical discussions in each chapter, which are based in review of related literature. The chapter chosen provides the background to the area of investigation and an overview of approaches taken to date. In the case of the AgEcon theses, it was possible in three cases to identify what the authors took to be the literature review chapter from statements that they made in the text, as follows:

A final objective of the [chapter] is to provide a platform for the theoretical and practical analyses proposed in chapters three through six. (AgEcon1)

In this chapter a literature survey of the impact of exchange rates on agricultural commodity trade in developing countries is conducted. (AgEcon4)

A literature review of sorts is integrated within chapter 3. (AgEcon5)

In the cases of AgEcon2 and AgEcon7, the chapters were chosen on the basis that the contents appeared to provide a theoretical, research and historical background to the topics, while in the case of AgEcon8 there were several chapters which might have been selected as the thesis is an extended argument drawing on literature throughout. However, the fifth chapter was chosen as it appeared to offer the broadest survey of literature, serving to provide background.

Information about the size of each chapter is presented in Table 3.3. These chapters, as can be seen, vary in length considerably, from 2,213 to 24,494 words, but this also needs to be considered in relation to the length of the whole thesis, as the length of theses represented here varies from 9,708 to 96,644 words (the shortest of these, FoodSci1, is a highly visual text, presenting information through tables and figures,

Table 3.3   Word counts for the chapter included in the corpus for this paper, and for the whole thesis

	Lit. review chapter	*Whole thesis*	*Percentage*
AgBot1	3,228	18,452	17.5
AgBot2	3,286	38,992	8.4
AgBot3	6,444	31,390	20.5
AgBot4	5,426	28,072	19.3
AgBot5	6,855	38,738	17.7
AgBot7	2,717	14,774	18.4
AgEcon1	2,213	75,691	2.9
AgEcon2	7,833	39,336	19.9
AgEcon4	7,726	55,219	14.0
AgEcon5	24,494	96,644	25.3
AgEcon7	8,424	41,917	20.1
AgEcon8	10,132	77,349	13.1
FoodSci1	3,998	9,708	41.2
FoodSci2	9,317	34,783	26.8
FoodSci3	5,376	17,088	31.5
FoodSci4	12,022	46,986	25.6
FoodSci5	8,845	33,742	26.2
FoodSci6	11,237	48,555	23.1
Psy1	16,320	72,955	22.4
Psy2	7,215	30,098	24.0
Psy3	11,744	45,232	26.0
Psy4	9,927	60,106	16.5
Psy5	11,377	57,591	19.8
Psy6	6,424	40,967	15.7

Table 3.4   Word counts for the literature review chapters by discipline

	Total in Lit. review chapters	Total in thesis	% of thesis	% of the Lit. review corpus
Agricultural Botany	27,956	170,418	16.4	13.8
Agricultural Economics	60,822	386,156	15.8	30.0
Food Science	50,795	190,862	26.6	25.1
Psychology	63,007	306,949	20.5	31.1

which are omitted from the word count). The final column indicates what percentage of the thesis the literature review chapter accounts for, and this ranges from 2.9 per cent to 41.2 per cent. The latter (41.2 per cent) is the introductory chapter in FoodSci1, and it is worth noting that the chapter in question begins with a declaration that much of the chapter had appeared in a review article published in a journal.

The word counts for each discipline are summarized in Table 3.4 where the word counts for the set of chapters in each discipline are presented along with information on the word counts for the whole theses. Then, in the third column a percentage figure is given to indicate how much of the entire thesis is accounted for by the literature review chapter. It can be seen that the theses in Agricultural Botany and in Food Science and Technology are considerably shorter. The theses in these two disciplines are, generally speaking, reports of experimental research, presenting in many cases a series of studies, in a recursive manner (i.e., chapters either consist of a single IMRD or a series of IMRD patterns).

Methods

The 24 chapters were first tagged for part-of-speech so that nouns could be extracted and quantified; also so that lexicogrammatical patterns could be searched for, both within the literature review corpus and within the BNC, through the Sketch Engine interface (http://www.sketchengine.co.uk/auth/). The BNC was used here as a reference corpus. Particular patterns were searched for in the tagged texts using regular expressions in the AntConc concordance programme, version 3.2.1w (Antony, 2007). For example, a regular expression was created to search for 'there + BE + (optional words) + evidence + to' so that instances such as *there is no direct empirical evidence to* can be captured, in addition to *there is evidence to*. Word lists were compiled in WordSmith Tools 5.0 (Scott, 2008). The output was then transferred to an Excel file which allowed further manipulation and sorting of the data to be performed.

It was important to ensure that lexical items had not only frequency but also range; in other words, that they not only appeared often, but also that they appeared in a large number of the texts in the corpus. To factor in the importance of range, a simple measure of combined frequency and range was created by multiplying the total number of occurrences of a given lemma in the corpus by the percentage of texts that the lemma appears in. For example, the lemma EFFECT (both 'effect' and 'effects') occurs 502 times in the corpus, and it appears in 20 out of the 24 texts, which is 83.3 per cent of the texts. The number of occurrences, 502, is multiplied by 83.3 to obtain an adjusted total of 418. This weighting gives more prominence to lemmas which have range and are used more widely.

Results and discussion

Frequency information

The frequency counts for the most common noun lemmas are shown in Table 3.5. While range is an important factor, it should also be observed that several of the nouns tend to congregate in certain texts more than others. For example, the lemma MODEL (which will be discussed below) occurs 343 times in the corpus, but the majority of occurrences are in four theses: AgEcon5, AgEcon8, FoodSci3 and Psy5. AgEcon5, which is an econometrics thesis and therefore highly mathematical, contains ten uses of the term 'production function approach' and 140 of 'function' (in its mathematical meaning). The predominance of certain nouns in certain theses is a result both of the topics treated in different theses (212 occurrences of RATE are in AgEcon4, which is a study of exchange rate mechanisms) and of the different approaches to knowledge creation in different disciplines. INFORMATION, for example, is a common noun in Agricultural Economics and Psychology, but relatively rare in the other two disciplines.

Table 3.5 The highest ranking noun lemmas on a combined frequency and range measure

Noun lemma	Occurrences	Texts	Adjusted measure
EFFECT	502	20	418.3
STUDY	430	18	322.5
RATE	341	21	298.4
LEVEL	320	22	293.3
SYSTEM	313	18	234.8
NUMBER	228	24	228.0
FACTOR	237	22	217.2
RESEARCH	285	18	213.8
PRODUCTION	242	20	201.7
CHANGE	335	19	195.4
USE	213	20	177.5
TIME	197	21	172.4
MODEL	343	12	171.5
RESULT	213	19	168.6
FUNCTION	233	16	155.3
APPROACH	192	18	144.0
VALUE	199	17	141.0
INFORMATION	192	17	136.0
CONTROL	175	18	131.3
INDIVIDUAL	216	14	126.0
PROBLEM	170	16	113.3
EVIDENCE	153	17	108.4
YEAR	153	20	108.4
MEASURE	190	14	108.4

Another important point to note, which is not evident from the figures in Table 3.5, is that the Agricultural Botany theses do not contain large numbers of the nouns shown in Table 3.5. The most frequent noun lemmas in Agricultural Botany are: SPECIES (123), WEED (103), PLANT (92), DISEASE (77), USE (76), CROP (59), SEED (52), PATHOGENS (52), PLANTS (48), NITROGEN (48) and CONTROL (47). These are the phenomena that are the subject of study in this discipline, and there is relatively little reference to the constructs and concepts of research in the Agricultural Botany literature reviews.

Evidence

From the list of the most frequent noun lemmas with a high measure of range, we will concentrate our attention on three nouns which are high frequency nouns in general English: EVIDENCE, PROBLEM and

Table 3.6 BNC rankings of the nouns in Table 3.4 (data from Leech, Rayson and Wilson, 2001)

BNC Rank position for noun lemma frequencies	*Lemma*
64	EFFECT
68	STUDY
80	RATE
58	LEVEL
14	SYSTEM
18	NUMBER
271	FACTOR
112	RESEARCH
240	PRODUCTION
48	CHANGE
67	USE
1	TIME
207	MODEL
65	RESULT
334	FUNCTION
221	APPROACH
119	VALUE
46	INFORMATION
102	CONTROL
316	INDIVIDUAL
23	PROBLEM
161	EVIDENCE
2	YEAR
394	MEASURE
409	DISEASE
208	DATA

MODEL. As can be seen in Table 3.6, these nouns rank, respectively, as 161st, 23rd and 207th in the list of frequent noun lemmas in the British National Corpus, which we can consider as representative of general British English use.

Our point of departure is an extract from one of the Psychology theses, Psy6. The passage given here as example (1) concerns preferences for tastes and smells and their origins, and it performs the function of creating a niche (Move 2 in Kwan's model):

(1) With regard to preferences for tastes, smells and foods it is commonly believed that what is exhibited early in life is in some way

related to later eating behaviour. However, evidence to support this view is lacking. Longitudinal studies of chemosensory function and hedonics remain to be done, and what data are available suggest the opposite; that very few human food preferences are 'hard-wired'. Taste and smell preferences appear to be highly dynamic and particularly context specific. Further, these preferences are responsive to shifts in social-environmental factors, and to psychobiological effects. With the exception of self-histories of food aversions, there is no evidence that specific taste and smell preferences formed early in life actually track into adulthood. On the other hand, many seemingly idiosyncratic food preferences of individual adults could have their roots in early childhood, suckling or even fetal experiences. Current knowledge is insufficient to either confirm, or disconfirm, such hypotheses at the moment. For a review of the ontogeny of human taste and smell preferences and their implications for food selection the reader is referred to Mela & Catt (1996). In summary, as Rozin (1991) concluded, 'If one is looking for variance to explain, the domain of preferences still offers a fertile field'. (Psy6)

Firstly, what is perhaps surprising for an extract from a literature review is that the role of references to the literature is not foregrounded. There are two citations in the final two sentences, but the dominant voice in this paragraph is that of the writer. This paragraph contains fewer citations than average (on average, one sentence in 3.8 in the corpus contains at least one citation, whereas in this paragraph there are two citations in ten sentences). Using the distinction between 'averral' and 'attribution' (Sinclair, 1988, cited in Groom, 2000), one can say that the majority of statements are averred. In a discussion of propositional responsibility, Groom (2000) argues that academic writers project a voice in their text through a complex interplay between averral, self-attribution and attribution. Academic writing requires what Fairclough (1992) has termed 'manifest intertextuality', the explicit reference to other texts through citation, but Groom argues that successful writing requires the projection of a clear voice and the adoption of a perspective on the part of the writer. This paragraph is evidence of a writer placing his or her voice above those of others.

Secondly, the role of EVIDENCE is noteworthy. The writer rejects two propositions on the basis that there is a lack of evidence and it is clear that propositions need to be supported by the existence of relevant evidence, if they are to be acceptable. The literature review in this thesis can be seen as, in many cases, guided by the evaluation of a set of propositions and as an assessment of how much evidence there is to support each proposition. In statistical terms, as shown in Table 3.5, the lemma EVIDENCE occurs 153 times in the corpus and it is 22nd in the noun frequency list, appearing in 17 out of the 24 texts. Inspection of the concordance lines for the word shows that it tends to feature in the pattern 'There is [x] evidence that/to' where there is an option to place a quantifying determiner before 'evidence' such as LITTLE, NO or SOME, or an adjective. This pattern accounts for over 30 per cent of the occurrences of EVIDENCE in the literature reviews, compared to less than 8 per cent in the BNC. Another pattern is 'The evidence [x] + VERB' where the verb tends to be SUGGEST or INDICATE.

EVIDENCE can come from DATA ('what data are available') and on this basis tentative conclusions can be drawn – they 'suggest' in this case because the data are limited, and in other parts of the corpus, they 'indicate'. As a result, hypotheses about the factors influencing taste and smell preferences cannot be confirmed because 'current knowledge is insufficient'. Both data and results are important sources of evidence in experimental research, and we find an example of the collocation of RESULT and SUGGEST in another text in the corpus:

(2) The results from these studies suggest that the effect of breast feeding is to delay the onset of allergic disease, and not to decrease the overall risk of becoming allergic during childhood. (FoodSci6)

Problem

The second noun lemma to be discussed is PROBLEM. An important pattern that PROBLEM appears in (determiner + adjective [optional] + PROBLEM + [optional postmodification] + auxiliary [optional] + BE + that/to) is shown in the following example:

(3) The major problem in breeding with a single source of resistance is that the pathogen will evolve rapidly to overcome it. For example, in North America up until 1980 there was only one race of downy mildew on sunflower, but within the space of ten years four new races had become prevalent (Gulya *et al.*, 1991). (AgBot2)

This pattern accounts for 14 per cent of the occurrences of PROBLEM in the literature reviews, four times more frequent than in the BNC where the pattern accounts for 3.5 per cent of the instances. As with EVIDENCE, PROBLEM is often followed by 'to' or 'that' clauses and expresses stance

(Biber, 2006) in that it indicates the status of the proposition that follows in the projected clause (it constitutes 'evidence' or 'a problem'). The two nouns are what Flowerdew (2003) terms 'signalling nouns' – the meaning of the nouns can only be made specific by reference to the context in which the noun occurs. The 'problem' in example (3) only becomes specific in the clause 'the pathogen will evolve rapidly to overcome it'. The theme position of 'problem' indicates the prominence of identifying problems and we find several instances in the corpus of sentences beginning with patterns such as 'The problem is to...' or 'One of the major problems is that...', where the pattern acts as an interpersonal orienting theme, and signals to the reader what the value of the following proposition is. Furthermore, these sentences tend to appear in paragraph initial position, as exemplified here:

(4) One long-term problem with continued indiscriminate herbicide use may be the selective resistance of weed species as referred to by Heitefuss (1986) and summarised by Froud-Williams (1988b). (AgBot3)

(5) An additional problem arising in many animal studies is how to maintain an equivalent energy intake when changing the natural eating habits of animals. (FoodSci2)

(6) A further problem is that classical conditioning theory predicts that conditioned responses will extinguish when they are no longer paired with a UCS, whereas in phobias the avoidance of the UCS does not lead to extinction of fear. (Psy5)

In addition to the observation that literature reviews in our corpus are concerned with discussion of evidence, therefore, we can also see that there is a focus on problems that are to be encountered in agricultural contexts, in the research work itself, or in existing theories/approaches. We may also observe that the placing of PROBLEM or EVIDENCE in sentence initial position, and particularly in paragraph initial position, marks the status of the information presented and is an assertion of the authorial voice, leading the reader through an account of what is known, what evidence there is to justify these knowledge claims, what limitations exist, and what problems there are to address.

Model

As observed above, the frequency of nouns in the corpus is often indicative of the types of research conducted by the doctoral students. The frequency of EVIDENCE is likely to be higher in studies that are empirical investigations, just as we can find that MODEL is highly frequent in theses that involve the development of conceptual or mathematical models. The lemma MODEL is the fourth most frequent noun in the corpus but the majority of occurrences are in four theses: AgEcon5, AgEcon8, FoodSci3 and Psy5. It is useful, at this point, to look at one of these and to illustrate the organization of the review as a way of showing how a literature review works. The heading for the section is 'Review of models to date', and the purpose of the writer is to briefly explain each model and to highlight the limitations of the existing models. These models are dealt with under two sub-headings: General Thermodynamic Models and Osmotic Pressure Virial Expansion Models. The limitations of each model in turn are presented as follows:

- It can only serve as a qualitative model since it lumps all the other system variables into a single parameter (Abbott *et al.*, 1990).
- This model does not account for the effect of the environment on the partitioning phenomenon.
- However, the model does not take into account salt-related effects on protein partitioning.
- The model is limited as it does not take into account salt-related effects on protein partitioning (Baskir *et al.*, 1989a).
- A limitation of the model is that protein molecular weight is not accounted for and the hydrophobicity of the protein has to be known.
- This makes the model difficult to apply over a wide range of systems without doing a large number of independent experiments. (FoodSci3)

The limitations and difficulties of each model are clearly stated with MODEL typically placed in subject theme position. Finally, the writer of FoodSci3 draws his review of the existing models to a close by pointing to the gap and to the need for better models:

(7) More quantitative models are needed which also work at high protein concentrations ... Profound limitations for the overall prediction of protein partition behaviour still exist in the modern models dealt with in this section, especially for partitioning in industrial PEG/salt systems. (FoodSci3)

The next section in the thesis outlines the requirements of such a model and it begins with the observation that the only work on such models to date is by the author himself, in a published journal article. What we see here is a strategic positioning of the writer, taking existing models one by one and indicating their limitations, then stating that a new model is required in order to address the gap in knowledge of the phenomena in question (and, interestingly, that the only person with experience of developing a model on the required lines is the writer himself!).

Conclusion

This chapter has proposed that some distinctive features of a literature review in a PhD thesis are that it:

- both evaluates and is evaluated;
- is a part of a larger text, and therefore should properly be viewed as a *sub-genre* rather than a genre in its own right;
- can be one chapter or can be part of several; and
- typically has the following moves: 'Establishing one part of the territory of one's own research', 'Creating a research niche' and the optional 'Occupying the research niche' (Kwan, 2006).

The three moves are fundamental to the rhetorical purpose of establishing a strong case for the work that is to come and on which the writer is to be evaluated. Through the exploration of the behaviour of three nouns in the corpus (EVIDENCE, PROBLEM and MODEL), we have observed how the writer's voice is the dominant voice in the text, how the writer takes a series of studies, models or theories in turn, to establish what is known but also what the limitations to knowledge and understanding are (the problems). We have also seen how the nouns are often used in lexicogrammatical patterns that help to structure the writer's message, by signalling to the reader what the value of the following proposition is. Patterns that were observed were:

1. DET + ADJ [optional] + PROBLEM + [optional postmodification] + BE + that/to
2. the + results/data + suggest/indicate + that
3. there + BE + ADV/ADJ [optional] + EVIDENCE + that/to

Within these patterns, variation is possible and lemmas other than those indicated could be inserted. For example, Pattern 3 could accommodate

DOUBT as in 'there is no doubt that' or DRAWBACK can be substituted for PROBLEM in Pattern 1 as in 'the main drawback of the enzymatic approach is that'.

There is variation too across the disciplines: for example, in Agricultural Botany, many of the most frequent nouns were subject-specific and referred to the subjects of study, and there was relatively little use of signalling nouns. However, it was not possible, due to space limitations, to examine the particular features of literature reviews in Agricultural Botany. Similarly, it was observed that certain nouns are more frequent in some disciplines than others, such as INFORMATION in Agricultural Economics and Psychology.

Finally, it is necessary to acknowledge some limitations to this study. First, the choice of chapters from Agricultural Economics was problematic because literature reviews spread across the thesis: the single chapter selected from AgEcon1 was too short and only represented 2 per cent of that thesis. It would have been better if a different chapter had been chosen, or a different thesis. Second, the theses in this corpus are all from applied disciplines and are not representative of work in non-applied areas. The high use of EVIDENCE and PROBLEM in the corpus texts is probably explained by the problem-based nature of applied subjects and the findings of this study need to be tested on texts from other disciplines.

References

Antony, L. (2007) *AntConc 3.2.1w*, http://www.antlab.sci.waseda.ac.jp/software.html, date accessed 10 November 2008.

Biber, D. (2006) *University Language* (Amsterdam: John Benjamins).

Biber, D., Johansson, S., Leech, G., Conrad, S. and Finegan, E. (1999) *Longman Grammar of Spoken and Written English* (London: Longman).

Bunton, D. (2002) 'Generic Moves in PhD Thesis Introductions' in J. Flowerdew (ed.) *Academic Discourse* (London: Longman), 57–75.

Fairclough, N. (1992) *Discourse and Social Change* (Cambridge: Polity).

Flowerdew, J. (2003) 'Signalling Nouns in Discourse', *English for Specific Purposes*, XXII, 4, 329–34.

Groom, N. (2000) 'Attribution and Averral Revisited: Three Perspectives on Manifest Intertextuality in Academic Writing' in P. Thompson (ed.) *Patterns and Perspectives: Insights into EAP Writing Practice* (Reading: CALS, The University of Reading), 14–25.

Hunston, S. and Francis, G. (2000) *Pattern Grammar: A Corpus-Driven Approach to the Lexical Grammar of English* (Amsterdam: John Benjamins).

Hyland, K. (2000) *Disciplinary Discourses: Social Interactions in Academic Writing* (London: Longman).

Hyland, K. (2006) 'Disciplinary Differences: Language Variation in Academic Discourses' in K. Hyland and M. Bondi (eds) *Academic Discourse across Disciplines* (Bern: Peter Lang), 17–48.

Kwan, B. (2006) 'The Schematic Structure of Literature Reviews in Doctoral Theses of Applied Linguistics', *English for Specific Purposes*, XXV, 1, 30–55.

Leech, G., Rayson, P. and Wilson, A. (2001) *Word Frequencies in Written and Spoken English: Based on the British National Corpus* (London: Longman).

Ridley, D. (2000) 'The Different Guises of a PhD Thesis and the Role of a Literature Review' in P. Thompson (ed.) *Patterns and Perspectives: Insights into EAP Writing Practice* (Reading: CALS, The University of Reading), 61–76.

Ridley, D. (2008) *The Literature Review: A Step-by-Step Guide for Students* (London: Sage).

Scott, M. (2008) *WordSmith Tools* 5.0, http://www.lexically.net/wordsmith/version5/index.html, date accessed 10 November 2008.

Swales, J. (1990) *Genre Analysis: English in Academic and Research Settings* (Cambridge: Cambridge University Press).

Swales, J. (2004) *Research Genres: Exploration and Applications* (Cambridge: Cambridge University Press).

Thompson, P. (1999) 'Exploring the Contexts of Writing: Interviews with PhD Supervisors' in P. Thompson (ed.) *Issues in EAP Writing Research and Instruction* (Reading: CALS, The University of Reading), 37–54.

Thompson, P. (2001) *A Pedagogically-Motivated Corpus-Based Examination of PhD Theses: Macrostructure, Citation Practices and Uses of Modal Verbs* (Unpublished PhD Thesis, University of Reading).

Thompson, P. (2005) 'Aspects of Identification and Position in Intertextual Reference in PhD Theses' in E. Tognini-Bonelli and G. Del Lungo Camiciotti (eds) *Strategies in Academic Discourse* (Amsterdam: John Benjamins), 31–50.

4
Back Cover Blurbs: Puff Pieces and Windows on Cultural Values

Helen Basturkmen

Introduction

The blurb on the back cover of a book has a strong promotional function aiming to entice readers to select the book in question. It offers fulsome praise, shuns negativity and is often edited by the publisher (Cronin and La Barre, 2005). Bhatia (2004) traces the historical development of the term 'blurb' back to the appearance in 1907 of a comic book jacket decorated with a drawing of the beautiful 'Miss Blurb' and subsequent definitions of the blurb as a 'flamboyant advertisement', a brief description functioning as a 'commendatory advertisement' and a 'puff piece' (p. 169). Blurbs are also sometimes referred to as 'advance praise' and according to Cronin and La Barre (2005) some US publishers explicitly label them as such on book covers. These writers entitled their own study of blurbs as an enquiry into 'patterns of puffery'.

All of the above descriptions suggest that the blurb is rather a superficial genre geared to extol the work (after all any blurb that is less than favourable would surely not be published). However, could it be that the blurb is more than just a sponsored piece of unabashed acclamation? Could it represent something deeper, something indicative of the assumed values of the readers?

This chapter argues that as well as being a rather superficial and blatant form of promotion (and thus of interest to applied linguists as a source of positive evaluation of an unmitigated nature), the blurb represents a cultural artefact and is of interest to applied linguists as a source of data by which to investigate the norms and values of the intended readership, the discourse community targeted by the work. The remainder of this chapter is divided into three main sections. The first section provides an introduction to the topic with a review of definitions of blurbs and an overview of research on this topic. This is followed by an investigation into blurbs contained in English as a Foreign Language (EFL) course books as a way of identifying the values of the English Language teaching community. The study is a content analysis of popular EFL course books in New Zealand at a specific point in time and it aims to show that key lexical items in the blurbs are representative of the values of the English Language teaching community in the local context. The final 'Conclusion' section suggests future research directions and an extended conceptualization of the communicative purpose of the blurb.

An overview of the blurb genre

The blurb has been variously defined in the literature. It combines description of the content and positive evaluation of the work and functions to influence the actions and judgements of the intended readership (Bhatia, 2004; Gea-Valor, 2005). Most writers take the term 'blurb' to refer to the text on the back cover of a book (Kathpalia, 1997; Basturkmen, 1999; Bhatia, 2004; Gesuato, 2007; Grupetta, 2008). However, as Gea-Valor (2005) notes, blurbs are increasingly being displayed on websites as well as the back covers of books. Cronin and La Barre (2005) understand blurbs to denote testimonials or endorsements on the back cover. Thus according to their definition, a book can have a number of 'blurbs', that is, testimonials. In this chapter, the term 'blurb' will be used to refer to the linguistic content of the back cover of books, content displayed in hard form (on the back cover or in the publisher's catalogue) or electronically in the Internet version of the latter. The blurb may or may not contain testimonies from leading figures in the field or from users of previous editions of the book.

For publishers, the cover and the back cover are seen as key marketing opportunities, a promotional site in which to persuade potential readers to select the work. Despite this perception, research into the use of blurbs by potential readers is limited. This lacuna led Grupetta (2008) to conduct a study investigating how readers used back cover blurbs. The study examined what use children made of back cover blurbs on works of fiction. The study found that a third of the children looked first at the back cover blurb (most looked first at the front cover image and title) and that nearly two thirds rated blurbs as very important in their decision making. Interestingly, most of the children preferred blurbs to have relatively vague content that did not give away too much of the story and very few considered themselves to be influenced by the celebrity endorsements in the blurbs.

The authorship of blurbs has also attracted consideration by analysts. Bhatia (2004) points out that it is not clear whether it is the writer of the book, the publisher or both who devise the blurb. Cronin and La Barre (2005) have considered the identity of blurb writers and conducted a study of blurbs on 450 books in business and history to see if there were 'serial blurbers' at work. However, they found little evidence for this in their study.

In applied linguistics one major area of investigation has been research into the rhetorical content and organization of blurbs, specifically investigation of moves in blurbs. In a study of the online blurbs of new releases (fiction and non-fiction) of four major publishing companies, Gea-Valor (2005) identified a three-move schema comprising Move 1 (Description), Move 2 (Evaluation) and Move 3 (About the author). Kathpalia (1997), while investigating moves in blurbs of books published internationally and in the local Singaporean context, found that works published in both these contexts drew on the same six-move schema (headline, justifying the book, appraising the book, establishing credentials, endorsements and targeting the market). A five-move schema is proposed by Bhatia (2004) in a description of academic works (headline, establishing the field, appraising the book, targeting the market and establishing credentials but not endorsements).

A second area of investigation in applied linguistics has been research into features of language use. A number of researchers have focused on the linguistic choices made by writers of blurbs. Gea-Valor (2005) identified key pragmatic functions (such as, complimenting) and micro-level features of discourse (such as, the use of imperatives, a pervasive feature of advertising discourse *per se*). Cacchiani (2007) investigated the range and frequencies of intensifiers (such as, *extraordinary, highly, really*). Such studies have focused on the promotional role of blurbs and how language is used in praising and complimenting the work.

A further line of enquiry has concerned possible variation in the genre. Cronin and La Barre (2005) compared the number of testimonials on the back covers of books published in two disciplines, business and history, and found that books on business had almost twice as many 'blurbs' as books on history. Kathpalia (1997) made a comparative study of blurbs on books published internationally and those published in the local Singaporean context. This cross-cultural comparison reveals that although the blurb writers in the Singaporean context used the same set of moves, differences were nevertheless apparent in how they sequenced and embedded the moves, how they used language to realize the moves (tending to prefer grammatical correctness to stylistically effective but grammatically deviant patterns) and the use of evaluation. With regard to the latter, Kathpalia (1997, p. 425) notes that 'evaluation of a book while associated with a particular move in the progression of the blurb often permeates throughout the blurb like spreading waves. However, in the local blurbs, the preference is to have a focused move indicating the value of the book rather than evaluative language that permeates the whole blurb'.

Gesuato (2007) investigated evaluations in blurbs on academic works in four fields (biology, engineering, education and linguistics) to find relatively little variation between the fields. The study revealed that evaluation occurred in 90 per cent or more of blurbs across the four fields, and the rate of occurrence was between 11 and 20 evaluations per work, with a similar range of entities being evaluated (including clarity, expertise, originality and relevance). It is perhaps not surprising that this study revealed little variation given the academic nature of all the works under review. Bhatia (2004), in an examination of two blurbs (one from a work of fiction and one from an academic work), found that although both blurbs shared the same communicative purpose (description and evaluation of the book) and drew on similar grammatical choices (e.g., both involved extensive use of nominal structures), they varied in terms of lexical choices, especially adjectives. The blurb for the work of fiction made a more extensive use of adjectives to evoke a fictional world of mystery and intrigue.

Blurbs as a window on cultural values

This section provides an analysis of blurbs for EFL course books and draws on a previous study by the author (Basturkmen, 1999). The study focuses on the values of the EFL teaching community in a particular context, New Zealand in 1998, and is based on a number of assumptions. The first is that language teaching, as well as being an intensely practical activity, is value-laden and that these values are reflected in the choices teachers and course developers make. One important choice is whether to use a course book and, if so, which course book to use. There are a number of commercially available course books and their use remains widespread. Teachers and course developers make a choice based on the fit between the work, the class or course and whether the work reflects the kind of pedagogy and ideas about teaching and learning that they embrace.

As new theories and perspectives about how languages are best learnt and taught emerge, course books come to reflect these ideas. Not all theories and perspectives are immediately and fully embodied into course book design, and course book developers vary in the extent to which these ideas are incorporated (Markee, 1997). Arbury (2008) investigated the extent to which findings from Second Language Acquisition (SLA) research were reflected in grammar activities in a selection of course books in use in New Zealand. The study revealed that some findings and theories from SLA but not others appear to have been incorporated into the works. However, this was an investigation of the actual contents of the course books, rather than the description and promotion of them in the blurbs.

The second assumption is that ELT course book blurbs are cultural artefacts, representing mainstream views of the ELT community at a particular point in time. The study draws on definitions of culture in the literature. These include Hofstede's (1984) definition of culture as a collective mindset and Agar's (1994) perspective of culture as an evolving entity that continuously selects components from other cultures as it sees fit. Course book blurbs provide a snap shot of the ideas and perspectives embraced in the work and offer a window on the perceived values of the teaching community.

This study is therefore an enquiry into the values the ELT community is likely to embrace or 'buy into'. Blurbs are designed to attract teachers to select the course book for use in class and are therefore written to address their needs as well as the values and expectations that publishers and course book writers perceive the teachers to hold. However, little research has been done on this site to identify aspects of pedagogy considered particularly important in the ELT community. Part of a teacher's role is decision making and amid the range of methods, types of language description and tasks, teachers act to determine the content, materials and activities for instruction. Their ideas about language teaching and learning are reflected in the choices they make. Thus course books provide a source of data for investigation of the values of the ELT community and this study sets out to examine these values as reflected in popular course books used in ELT in New Zealand.

Research into blurbs on ELT course books as a source of data on teachers' values has been limited. Todova (1997) examined descriptors in the blurbs on 28 language-teaching textbooks. The study found that although the prevailing trend at the time was for communicative language teaching, somewhat surprisingly, the great majority of the blurbs described the books as firmly based in grammar with only around half of the blurbs using the term *communicative* as a descriptor. Thornbury (2008) investigated concordances of the word *grammar* in a selection of British ELT publishers' catalogues to find that the catalogues consistently presented grammar as a system and set of grammar points and thus offered a conceptualization of grammar learning as atomistic and incremental.

Methodology

From a methodological point of view, the study has adopted a two-step procedure. The first stage is an investigation of the textual organization of blurbs. A small corpus of the back cover blurbs was developed comprising blurbs from the teachers' books of the seven ELT course books identified to be clear market leaders by the local leading distributor of ELT materials in Auckland, New Zealand's largest city, in 1998. (According to the distributor, only seven works were widely distributed in the community). One of the works was published locally and the other works were published internationally. See Appendix A for titles of works in the corpus. The blurbs were examined for moves and steps using the approach to genre analysis introduced by Swales (1990) and further developed by Bhatia (2004). A sub-corpus comprising the moves containing description of the content of the works were analysed using the software WordSmith Tools (Scott, 1998) for high frequency items and the concordances of these items were then examined qualitatively.

The second stage is a content analysis of the sub-corpus and identification of high frequency words and their collocations. It is a method for making 'replicable and valid inferences from data, in context ... the basic goal of which is to take a verbal, non-quantitative document and transform it into quantitative data' (Krippendorf, 1980, p. 14). It is a means of investigating the interests and values of a population to reach an understanding of 'the spirit of the age' (Berelson, 1971, pp. 90–1). (See Ryan and Russell (2000) for an overview of the aims and techniques involved in content analysis.)

Some words of caution are in order. Firstly, content analysts make inferences about a group (in the present study, the ELT community) on the basis of texts produced for it, not on the basis of texts produced by it. Secondly, although high frequency words are measures of attention, they are not an index of attention or how much attention and thus the importance that readers actually give to them is unknown (Krippendorf, 1980). The overall results are presented in the following section.

Moves and steps

The analysis reveals a four-move schema, which is shown in Figure 4.1. Move 1 identifies the market niche targeted by the present work and sets forth the product in terms of aims (Step A) and/or units of delivery

Moves *Communicative functions*	*Steps* *(The choices made by writers to achieve the purpose)*
Move 1 Identifies the market niche	Step A States aims of the work and/or Step B States units of delivery
Move 2 Identifies language teaching theory	Step A Explicit statement(s) of theory and/or Step B Provides contents solutions
Move 3 Presents credentials	
Move 4 Informs readers of other items in the course book package	

Figure 4.1   A model of move sequence in ELT course book blurbs

(Step B). Move 2 identifies the language teaching theory underpinning the work through making explicit theory claims about language and/or methodology (Step A) and/or offering content solutions (Step B), implicit understandings of the nature of language or how language learning comes about, for example, through task-based activities (see Figure 4.4 Move 2, Step B). Move 3 presents the credentials and expertise of the writer(s). Move 4 informs readers of other items in the course book package such as workbooks.

Not all moves or steps were present in all the blurbs. As shown in Table 4.1, Move 1 occurred in six cases and Moves 2 and 4 in all seven cases. Move 3 (establishing credentials) occurred in only three of the blurbs. This move thus appears to be optional. Move 2, Step A (explicit statements of theory) occurred in only three of the blurbs. However, Move 2, Step B (offering content solutions) occurred in all the blurbs. Four of the blurbs used both Steps A and B in Move 1 and three used both Steps A and B in Move 2.

High frequency words

The frequency of a word tends to denote the significance of the idea or concept it expresses and therefore suggests the value of that idea

Table 4.1   Occurrence of moves and steps in the corpus

	Occurrences		Occurrences
Move 1	6		
		Step A	4
		Step B	6
		Steps A & B	4
Move 2	7		
		Step A	3
		Step B	7
		Steps A & B	3
Move 3	3		
Move 4	7		

to the community that uses it. Examination of the explicit statements of theory (Move 2, Step A) revealed a narrow range of items: *communicative/communication* (four occurrences), *presentation and practice* (one), *controlled and freer practice* (one), *accuracy* (two), *fluency* (three), *traditional and recent approaches* (one) and *making learning interesting* (two). In the sub-corpus as a whole (Moves 1 and 2 from all seven blurbs), the most frequent words were *grammar/structure* (16 occurrences) and *learner/student* (15 occurrences). Words that occurred more often than seven times are shown in Table 4.2. The high frequency words have been further categorized into three main areas (instruction, language and learning).

Instruction

The largest semantic category was instruction. This is not surprising given that the texts were from course books and from versions of the course books targeting teachers. Most of the high frequency words in this category referred to the organization of the work (*syllabus, unit, section*) and types of pedagogical content (*activities, tasks, exercises*). Examination of the concordances of these items showed that *activities* and *tasks* were used in expressions denoting ideas about language learning processes (*task-based listening, problem-solving tasks, student-centred fluency activities*) but *exercises* were collocated with products for teaching (*workbook exercises, vocabulary building exercises*).

Language

The second largest category was language. The word *language* itself was used in a range of expressions but 5 of the 12 occurrences of this item

Table 4.2   Frequently occurring words in the corpus by category*

Instruction		
	unit	11
	material	11
	course	11
	activity	10
	class	8
	teach	8
	syllabus	7
	section	7
	exercise	7
	task	7
	Total	87
Language		
	grammar/structure	16
	English	12
	language	12
	vocabulary	8
	skills	7
	listening	7
	Total	62
Learning		
	student/learner	15
	study/learn	11
	Total	26
Other		
	use	13
	provide	12
	Total	25

* The use of learner in references to the type of learner targeted by the work, such as, young learners or adult learners were not included in the frequency count.

were in expressions suggesting a cognitive view of language learning (*detailed notes on language, revise specific language, the language review*). A cognitive view assumes language learning involves active mental processes and some level of conscious attention. See Figure 4.2.

The word *grammar/structure* was the most frequent item in the corpus. It was used in phrases referring to parts of the book itself (*Grammar Reference, summary of the units' main grammar points*), phrases that again suggest a cognitive view of learning. *Vocabulary* occurred less often (eight occurrences) and was almost consistently used in second place to grammar (*development of grammar and vocabulary, grammar and vocabulary units*). Other major parts of the linguistic system were mentioned

le for the course. Detailed notes on   **language** and methodology are accompanied
s clear guidance on using the material, **language** notes given help with potential
to supplement lessons, revise specific **language** and structures, and provide var
work things out for themselves and the **language** review provides a summary of th
grammar syllabus covers the essential   **language** at this level * extensive voca

Figure 4.2   Concordances of 'language' showing a cognitive view

less often or not at all. *Pronunciation* or *phonetics* was mentioned four times and *text* or *discourse* was not mentioned. Skills were mentioned seven times and included uses, such as, *multi skills* and *integrated skills*. *Listening* occurred frequently (seven occurrences). *Reading* and *speaking* occurred but not frequently and surprisingly *writing* was not mentioned at all.

Learning

The items *study/learn* occurred 11 times and *student/learner* 15 times. The latter were often used in phrases denoting an active learner role (*stimulate students to make their own observations, use of learners' own knowledge*). Figure 4.3 shows this with reference to the concordances of *student/learner*. To a lesser extent these same items were used in phrases indicative of a more passive learner role (*inform students about everyday life, designed to take students from*).

Figure 4.4 shows the schema used for the analysis of a work outside the corpus, a recent edition of the teacher's book for Interchange 3 (*New Interchange 3*) by Richards, Hull and Proctor (2005). This blurb incorporates all the moves and steps shown in Figure 4.1. It informs readers of the market niche (adults and young adult learners) and what the course book delivers (including up-to-date content and grammar practice). It provides explicit statements of theory (English is viewed as an international language and a communicative view of language

tivity highly original tasks stimulate   **students** to make their own personal cont
of vocabulary exercises that encourage **students** to activate their lexical knowl
ggested homework activities that help   **students** extend their classroom studies
rchange incorporates suggestions from **students** and teachers using the first ed
tunities to share opinions and ideas   **Student**-centred fluency activities * A
rcises. Grammar questions encourage   **students** to work things out for themselv
e interest of adult learners. * Use of   **learners'** own knowledge, experience and

Figure 4.3   Concordances of 'student/learner' showing an active role

---

Move 1
Step A *Interchange* Third Edition is a fully revised edition of *New Interchange*, the world's most successful English series for adults and young adult learner. **Step B** Each unit includes up-to-date content, additional grammar practice, and more opportunities to develop speaking and listening skills. The series incorporates suggestions from teachers and students all over the world. By keeping the best, and improving the rest, it remains the series that everyone has grown to know and love.

Move 2
Step A *Interchange* Third Edition is written in American English, but reflects the fact that English is the major language of international communication, and is not limited to any one country, region, or culture. The philosophy of the series is that English is best learned when used for meaningful communication.

Step B Key features

- A proven multi skills syllabus
- A focus on accuracy and fluency
- Contemporary, real-world topics
- Natural, conversational language
- Grammar in communicative contexts
- Task-based listening activities
- Fun, personalized speaking activities
- An updated pronunciation syllabus
- Frequent learner-centred progress checks
- A new self study listening section

Move 4
This section lists other items in the course book package including class audio programme and lab programme.

Move 3
This section describes each of the three authors in terms of experience, specializations and publications.

Figure 4.4   An illustration of the schema applied to *Interchange 3* (Richards, Hull and Proctor, 2005)

learning is presented). A range of content solutions (Move 2, Step B) are set out and highlighted through the use of bullet points. The content solutions indirectly point to aspects of a language teaching theory. Some of the content solutions can be related to ideas in second language acquisition. *Grammar in communicative contexts* suggests a view that grammar can be successfully acquired through communicative activities and/or situated use and *fun, personalized speaking activities* suggest a humanistic approach to language teaching. Not all items in this section can be directly related to ideas about language learning, however. *Natural, conversational language* can be related to a view of language and may indicate a view of conversation as the primary form of language.

Wmatrix (Rayson, 2008) has been used to compare the frequencies of words in this blurb to those in the written sampler of the British National Corpus. The comparison, based on log likelihood statistics, reveals a number of keywords, that is, words that are most distinctive in the blurb and which arguably represent the values this specific work wishes to appeal to. The keywords include *listening, grammar, communicative, learner-centred* and *fluency*. See Table 4.3.

The analysis of content in the blurbs in the corpus has offered a view into the assumed values of the ELT teaching community in New Zealand at this point in time. The community was understood to value practical solutions in preference to theoretical rationalization, value listening skills above other skill areas, view language as, at core, a set of grammatical structures and was expected 'buy into' practices derived from a cognitive theory of language learning.

The fact that the community would value practical solutions to teaching problems rather than theoretical positions was suggested by a number of findings. Less than half the blurbs contained explicit statements of the theoretical basis of the work (Move 2, Step A, explicit statements of theory). The blurbs invariably included Move 2, Step B, offering content solutions as the most extensive and prominent step

Table 4.3   Log-likelihood values: *Interchange* blurb compared to BNC written sampler*

Items	Interchange blurb		BNC written sampler		Log likelihood statistics in descending order
listening	3	1.88	31	0.00+	31.97
syllabus	2	1.25	1	0.02+	31.01
English	4	2.5	189	0.00+	30.80
grammar	2	1.25	4	0.00+	27.20
speaking	2	1.25	41	0.00+	18.67
communicative	1	0.62	0	0.00+	17.42
fluency	1	0.62	0	0.00+	17.42
learner-centred	1	0.62	0	0.00+	17.42
real-world	1	0.62	0	0.00+	17.42
task-based	1	0.62	0	0.00+	17.42
skills	2	1.25	74	0.01+	16.36
language	2	1.25	94	0.01+	15.42
activities	2	1.25	102	0.01+	15.10
communication	2	1.25	105	0.01+	14.99

* The items *interchange, series* and *edition* have been removed from the above list.

(see Figure 4.4). Connections between theory and practice were not part and parcel of the blurbs. Documents are interesting in terms of what is said as well as what is not said (Flick, 2007, p. 111).

It is possible that such connections are obvious to the ELT community and clear statements on this are simply unnecessary. Or, this gap may reflect a disassociation between theory and practice as perceived in the mindset of the community, and again reinforce the claim that the ELT community values practical solutions to teaching problems rather than theoretical considerations of the learning process. That the community would view language education as being concerned primarily with teaching grammatical structures and vocabulary was inferred from the fact that these items occurred frequently in the blurbs whereas other aspects of language, such as discourse and intonation, did not.

Listening was the most emphasized skill in the blurbs. This may reflect the importance of this skill in the teaching community. However, a more mundane explanation can also be suggested. Teachers may find it difficult to source good quality listening texts compared to written texts which are more readily available and publishers are aware that teachers turn to course books to provide this type of material. The practices the ELT community 'buy into' can be associated with a cognitive theory of language learning. For example, *grammar* and *language* had a tendency to co-occur with reference type items (e.g. language notes, grammar review units) indicative of a view of language learning as the development of a store of consciously acquired grammatical knowledge.

Conclusion and suggestions for future research

This chapter has shown that the back cover blurb has been considered from a number of different research perspectives. Some writers like Kathpalia (1997), Gea-Valor (2005), Cacchiani (2007) and Gesuato (2007) have considered the promotional role that the blurb plays and the use of devices for the purpose of 'fulsome praise' and evaluation. However, although the research has shown that such language use is a pervasive feature, what is not clear is how the intended readership receives this praise. Is it effective as a promotional tool or does its pervasiveness on back cover blurbs render it meaningless? Is it the number of evaluations that sways the would-be reader or the fulsomeness of the praise? Possibly neither the volume of evaluations nor the munificence of the praise are very important in the eyes of the intended readers, as was the case with celebrity endorsements reported in the study carried out by Grupetta

(2008). Further research is needed to investigate how readers respond to the promotional features of blurbs.

Two further lines of enquiry have been genre-based investigations of moves and steps and the question of variation. Although comparative moves have been identified, researchers (Basturkmen, 1999; Bhatia, 2004; Gea-Valor, 2005) have not agreed on the number of moves involved. This may not be surprising given that blurbs investigated in these studies have been from a range of types of works. Bhatia's (2004) preliminary investigation of the blurb on one work of fiction and one academic work indicated differences. Further more extensive research could investigate differences between blurbs on various types of work. The study of blurbs on ELT course books (Basturkmen, 1999) showed the context bound nature of the genre, especially the second move, the move detailing pedagogical content. Research is needed to examine blurbs on other types of pedagogically oriented texts to ascertain whether they too involve a similar move sequence.

The present chapter has considered blurbs as a means of understanding the values of the intended community/readership. The literature (Bhatia, 2004; Gea-Valor, 2005) has described the communicative purpose of the blurb as two-fold, to provide a description of the content and to promote the work. The latter has been largely construed to date as achieved by positive evaluations and glowing praise. However, I would suggest that this is only one means by which the promotional function is achieved and that it is not enough for the blurb to present the book in the most positive light.

The blurb also needs to appeal to the values of the intended readership. Unless the readers can see the connections between the content of the work and their own values, unless they can identify what is being put out on display with their own interests, they are unlikely to select the work however brilliant the content or the writer or however rich the praise. Unless the blurb succeeds in appealing to the values of its intended readership, it will surely not garner much interest. This chapter therefore suggests a broader understanding of the communicative purpose of the blurb to include the purpose of appealing to values.

Turning to the title of this chapter, 'Back Cover Blurbs: Puff Pieces or Windows on Cultural Values', the suggestion here is that although the puff is an obvious feature of blurbs, one that is very much on the surface of the discourse in the choice of positive adjectives, compliments and intensifiers, it is the more humdrum descriptive content that is the most significant promotional tool, and that potential readers form initial evaluations of the work more from reference to this than to the puff. Again, research into reader response might be able to provide insights into how readers actually make an evaluation of prospective works.

References

Agar, M. (1994) 'The Intercultural Frame', *International Journal of Intercultural Relations*, XVIII, 2, 221–37.

Arbury, J. (2008) *SLA and the Analysis of Language Teaching Materials* (Unpublished MA thesis, University of Auckland, New Zealand).

Basturkmen, H. (1999) 'A Content Analysis of ELT Textbook Blurbs: Reflections of Theory-in-Use', *Regional English Language Council Journal*, XXX, 1, 18–38.

Berelson, B. (1971) *Content Analysis in Communication Research* (New York: Hafner).

Bhatia, V. K. (2004) *Worlds of Written Discourse* (London: Continuum).

Cacchiani, S. (2007) 'From Narratives to Intensification and Hyperbole: Promotional Uses of Book Blurbs' in M. Davies, P. Rayson, S. Hunston and P. Danielsson (eds) *Proceedings of the Corpus Linguistics Conference, University of Birmingham, 27–30 July 2007*, http://www.corpus.bham.ac.uk/corpling proceedings07/paper/79_Paper.pdf, date accessed 10 December 2008.

Cronin, B. and La Barre, K. (2005) 'Patterns of Puffery: An Analysis of Non-Fiction Blurbs', *Journal of Librarianship and Information Sciences*, XXXVII, 1, 17–24.

Flick, U. (2007) *Doing Conversation, Discourse and Document Analysis* (California: Sage Publications).

Gea-Valor, M. L. (2005) 'Advertising Books: A Linguistic Analysis of Blurbs', *Ibérica*, X, 41–62.

Gesuato, S. (2007) 'Evaluation in Back-Cover Blurbs', *Textus*, XX, 1, 83–102.

Grupetta, C. (2008) 'Getting Them Hooked', http://www.thebookseller.com/in-depth/feature/70467-getting-them-hooked.html, date accessed 10 December 2008.

Hofstede, G. (1984) *Culture's Consequences: International Differences in Work-related Values* (California: Sage Publications).

Kathpalia, S. S. (1997) 'Cross-Cultural Variation in Professional Genres: A Comparative Study of Book Blurbs', *World Englishes*, XVI, 3, 417–26.

Krippendorf, K. (1980) *Content Analysis* (California: Sage Publications).

Markee, N. (1997) *Managing Curricular Innovation* (Cambridge: Cambridge University Press).

Ryan, G. W. and Russell, B. (2000) 'Data Management and Analysis Methods' in N. K. Denzin and Y. S. Lincoln (eds) *Handbook of Qualitative Research* 2nd edition (California: Sage Publications), 769–802.

Richards, J. C., Hull, J. and Proctor, S. (2005) *Interchange 3 (3rd edn.). Teacher's Edition* (Cambridge: Cambridge University Press).

Rayson, P. (2008) *Wmatrix: A Web-Based Corpus Processing Environment* (Computing Department, Lancaster University), http://www.ucrel.lancs.ac.uk/wmatrix/, date accessed 30 December 2008.

Scott, M. (1998) *WordSmith Tools* (Oxford: Oxford University Press).

Swales, J. (1990) *Genre Analysis: English in Academic and Research Settings* (Cambridge: Cambridge University Press).

Thornbury, S. (2008) 'McEnglish in Australia', http://www.Perso.wanadoo.es/sthornbury/McEnglish.htm, date accessed 10 December 2008.

Todova, E. (1997) 'Capulet and Montague – Reconciled and Ennobled: Recognising the Existence of a Balanced Approach with CLT', *Journal of Communication and International Studies*, I, 4, 127–34.

Appendix A

The corpus of blurbs:
New Zealand: A Language Survival Kit
New Headway English Course Intermediate Teacher's Book
Reward Intermediate Teacher's Book
Pre-Intermediate Matters Teacher's Book
New Interchange 1 Teacher's Book
True to Life Elementary Teacher's Book
Language in Use Intermediate Teacher's Book

Part II
Disciplinary Variation

5
Reporting and Evaluation in English Book Review Articles: A Cross-Disciplinary Study

Giuliana Diani

Introduction

This chapter explores a review genre – the book review article – that is something of a hybrid. It often appears in the book review section of academic journals yet differs from both book reviews and review articles. Its primary function is to evaluate the knowledge claims of other researchers in the context of their publications. This is clearly different from a book review which functions to evaluate a range of features of books (Hyland, 2000).

One identifying feature of the book review article is reporting the ideas that an author discusses in his or her book as a point of departure for the reviewer's development of an evaluative discourse.

The inclusion of explicit references to the work of others is widespread in academic writing (Swales, 1990; Tadros, 1993; Hyland, 2000; Thompson, 2005). This is also salient in book review articles. However, the particularity to note here is that reporting is not only used when referring to the reviewed book author's discourse through citation (e.g. 'Lightfoot concludes that'), but also to the reviewer's own positions as alternative views of the issues discussed ('I argue that'; 'I show that').

This leads to the complex interplay between 'averral' and 'attribution' (Sinclair, 1987). In Sinclair's terms, a text is made up of propositions that may be put forward by the writer (averrals) or attributed by the writer to some other person or entity (attributions). In terms of the present study, while averral opens up a space for the voice of the reviewer, attribution allows the introduction of 'the other' voices, whether of the reviewed book author or the discourse community.

In the light of this, the study presented in this chapter centres on a corpus-based analysis of reporting clauses. It focuses on English book review articles across the disciplines of linguistics, history and economics and examines the use of *that*-clause complementation, which project either others' ideas or those of the reviewer. The study proceeds by observing selected reporting verbs in terms of their frequency and capability to act as clues in the representation of 'consensus and conflict' in the genre considered (Hunston, 2004), that is, patterns of agreement and disagreement, as are typical in the reviewers' praise or criticism of the position of the reviewed authors. While I expect that the consistent use of reporting verbs reflects both the characteristics of the genre and the role it plays within the scientific community, I explore variation in their uses which reveals characteristics of these disciplines themselves.

About the book review article

The book review article is a site where reviewers offer a critical analysis of the ideas that an author discusses in his or her book (not necessarily a new one) as a springboard for a wider evaluation of them, comprising a discussion of the issues they raise and an appraisal of what this means for the community. As has been mentioned earlier, the most important realization of the reviewer's concern for referring to reviewed book authors' discourse is that of citation. The importance of citation can thus be seen in its prominent role of offering an important opportunity for reviewers to convey evaluation of the work of other researchers.

As is the case with all review genres, evaluation is a central feature, but this is presented as argument in the book review article. In examples such as extract (1) below, reporting the reviewed author's ideas allows the reviewer to provide evaluative commentary, and these evaluative elements act as signals of potentially argumentative sequences, more explicitly involving the reviewer in the argument:

> (1) At the end of chapter 3, which introduces the Chomskyan view of language acquisition as 'growth' of biological entities called 'grammars', *Lightfoot concludes* that language is an epiphenomenon, and that 'the notion of a language is not likely to have much importance if our biological perspective is taken' (74) .... *But Lightfoot has two real problems here.* The first may be more a problem of rhetoric than a substantive theoretical problem .... *While this first problem may*

be confusing for some inexperienced readers, the second problem seems to betray a confusion in Lightfoot's own thinking. (LIBRA)

The structure of the whole article is mostly based on an argumentative pattern. It is divided into the traditional sections of a research article: Introduction, Critique and Conclusion. The Introduction and the Conclusion are often very similar in structure to those of the research article, as shown in extract (2) below, taken from the Introduction section of a linguistics book review article, where the reviewer announces his perspective in reviewing the book author and indicates the structure of his argument. The Critique, representing the body of the article, is usually characterized by a highly cyclical structure: each single issue identified is discussed critically in a series of sections.

(2) *The narrative structure of my discussion is organized as follows: in section 2, I consider* a representative number of Postal's core arguments and their factual basis in some detail, and *argue* that, contrary to his substantive claims, there is nothing like congruence between the B-extractions on the one hand and the environments which tolerate attested RPs on the other. *In section 3, I review* a number of his assertions about the class of conjuncts which, following Lakoff (1986), Postal considers in connection with CSC violations and *argue* that here too, his proposal fails to take into account the full range of facts. In particular, *I show* that these conjuncts fail his own criteria for the identification of weak (in his terms, selective) islands, and that, in particular, there are good cases of extraction from antipronominal contexts within these conjuncts. *In section 4, a careful review* of Postal's critique of non-extraction RNR accounts shows that the weight of evidence does contraindicate an extraction treatment. (LIBRA)

Materials and methods

The analysis is based on three small comparable corpora of English book review articles in the disciplines of linguistics, history and economics. The following corpora were made use of:

- a corpus of 60 linguistics book review articles (LIBRA) published in six British and American academic journals spanning the years 1999–2001 (consisting of 359,000 words);

- a corpus of 45 history book review articles (HIBRA) published in five British and American academic journals spanning the years 1999–2001 (consisting of 206,089 words);
- a corpus of 24 economics book review articles (EBRA) published in six British and American academic journals spanning the years 2000–2003 (consisting of 167,239 words).

The present study makes use of sub-corpora extracted from each of the three disciplinary corpora. The three sub-corpora contain ten texts each, comprising 55,194 words in linguistics, 35,745 words in history, and 52,709 words in economics. All frequency data reported in this chapter will be presented as normalized figures, calculated per thousand words.

Grammatically, a reporting clause is generally introduced by *that*-clause complement, whose principal role is to report somebody's speech or thought (Biber *et al.*, 1999, p. 196). Consequently the present analysis of reporting verbs with *that*-clauses started from a search in each corpus for the word *that* using WordSmith Tools (Scott, 1998), and only instances where *that* was used to introduce a complement clause were selected. In particular, the only cases counted were those where the subject of the projecting clause was an individual, where the lexical verb presented the type of projecting and where the *that*-clause presented the projected idea or speech (*Lightfoot concludes that language is an epiphenomenon*). Although omission of the *that* complementizer is possible, research has shown that its retention is 'the norm in academic prose' (Biber *et al.*, 1999, pp. 680–83). A manual analysis of two of the most frequent reporting verbs in the corpora, *argue* and *suggest* confirmed this finding: only a few instances of them occurred without the complementizer. Thus, it was thought that this restriction would not alter the frequency data.

From the reporting clauses identified, the most frequent ten reporting verbs were selected. This list was examined item-by-item using a concordancer. This allowed an investigation of the use of these verbs in their textual contexts. In particular, the types of voice that were associated with these verbs were examined. The expression 'voice' is here intended as a form of reference to a source to which a proposition is attributed. For the type of voice, a distinction was made between self-projection – discussed by Hyland (2001, 2002a) in terms of self-promotion and establishing credibility – and other-projection. Self-projection includes direct reference to the reviewers, through the use of first person singular and plural pronouns (*I suggest that*). In the field of other-projection, we find all those identities that are explicitly introduced as distinct from the reviewer, 'third persons', and only instances where the 'third person' referred to a reviewed book author (*Lightfoot concludes that*) or the disciplinary community (*most historians still believe that*) were counted.

Finally, selected reporting verbs were studied from a semantic and pragmatic point of view. Particular attention was given to the lemmas *argue* and *suggest* and to the dialogic sequences they helped to create in the construction of the reviewer's evaluative argument, that is, Reporting^Agreement/Disagreement.

The analysis is both qualitative and quantitative, and it will also stress some problematic cases in the interpretation of corpus data. The overall results were discussed with a view to identifying the preferences for different reporting verbs among the three disciplinary communities under investigation and, hopefully, to revealing some of the genre-specific purposes which motivate those preferences.

Reporting verbs across disciplines

A preliminary overview: Exploring frequency data

Table 5.1 gives the quantitative data of the ten most frequent reporting verbs with *that*-clause complement used in book review articles and are presented comparatively across the three disciplines. The verbs are presented in lemmatized form.

Following Hyland's (2002b) threefold distinction of reporting verbs according to the process they perform – 'research', 'cognition',

Table 5.1 Most frequent ten reporting verbs with *that*-clause complement in book review articles by discipline (lemmatized) (per 1,000 words)

Linguistics (*LIBRA*)	*Freq.*	*History* (*HIBRA*)	*Freq.*	*Economics* (*EBRA*)	*Freq.*
argue	0.42	argue	1.14	argue	0.78
suggest	0.38	suggest	0.55	find	0.47
note	0.34	note	0.44	show	0.44
propose	0.33	describe	0.27	conclude	0.25
find	0.30	point out	0.25	think	0.17
show	0.27	discuss	0.22	believe	0.13
point out	0.20	show	0.22	suggest	0.11
say	0.18	believe	0.19	assume	0.09
discuss	0.11	say	0.19	say	0.07
claim	0.09	conclude	0.14	propose	0.06

'discourse' – the reporting verbs identified in the light of the preferred type of activity referred to across the disciplines have been analysed.

As revealed by Table 5.1, it turns out that the 'discourse' verb groups predominate across the disciplines (*argue, suggest, describe, point out, conclude, say, claim, discuss, propose*); in fact, 81.3 per cent of the top ten reporting verbs favour a 'discourse' verb in history, and although the percentage is lower in both linguistics (64.82) and economics (52.94), it is still substantial. Both economics and history also have appreciable numbers of 'cognition' verbs (*believe, think, assume*), amounting to 15.44 per cent of the top ten reporting verbs in economics and 5.69 in history.

Comparison of the 'discourse' verbs across the disciplines shows that the verb *argue* is the most frequent reporting verb in all three disciplines. More specifically, history displays a somewhat higher frequency than do economics and linguistics (1.14 occurrences per 1000 words vs. 0.78 and 0.42 respectively). Another discipline-related point is that the second most frequent verb for both history and linguistics is once again a 'discourse' verb, *suggest* (0.55 occurrences in history, 0.38 in linguistics), while for economics it is a 'research' verb, *find* (0.47). Although it appears from the most frequent forms found in each discipline that all three disciplines largely employed 'discourse' reporting verbs as the basis for the reviewer's arguments, the high frequency of a 'research' verb like *find* in economics (0.47 occurrences), in comparison with very low frequencies in linguistics (0.30) and in history (0.10), may reflect the fact that a very important type of reporting in the discipline also consists of statements simply reporting the findings of the reviewed author's research without evaluating marking, as it is to a much greater extent created through 'discourse' verbs:

> (3) *Lopez (2001) finds* that there is no difference between SV and other time series forecasts using conventional error statistics. (EBRA)

Unlike the verb *find*, the use of *show* suggests more than the neutral communication of reported information (Thomas and Hawes, 1994, p. 135). The verb enables the reviewer to construct a consensus with the reviewed author signalling a clear acceptance of the findings, as in extract (4) below, where the expression *revealing detail* constitutes positive evaluation:

> (4) *Dickson shows* in revealing detail that the differences between the totalitarian state established in the People's Republic during the

Mao era and the authoritarian state established in Taiwan during the Chiang Kai-shek era ... (HIBRA)

The predominance of 'discourse' verbs in all three disciplines in the book review article genre is in line with the results of Hyland (2002b) for research articles; he found that writers in the humanities and social sciences greatly favoured *argue* and *suggest*, followed by *find* and *show*. As noted by Hyland,

> The greater use of Discourse Act forms in the humanities and social sciences is more appropriate in an argument schema which more readily regards explicit interpretation, speculation, and complexity as accepted aspects of knowledge. These disciplines are typically more discursive and examine relationships and features that are more subject to contextual and human irregularities than those studied in the hard sciences. Writers in the soft disciplines therefore employed arguments that made greater use of Discourse Act forms which expedited the verbal exploration of such issues, facilitating qualitative arguments which rest on finely delineated interpretations and conceptualizations, rather than systematic scrutiny and precise measurement. (Hyland, 2002b, p. 126)

The clearest differences across the three disciplines, however, emerge when these 'discourse' verbs are studied with a view to their collocational behaviour, in particular focusing on the expressions that are chosen as the object of argument in the projected clauses introduced by these verbs.

Economics tends to associate these verbs with expressions of causal/final relations like *factor, reason* and *result* as well as with expressions of a high degree of abstraction from the real world: these are expressions of theoretical artifacts like *model, method, approach*. History, on the other hand, shows a clear preference for expressions referring to facts and their logic interpretation like *explanation, contribution, interpretation*. With regard to linguistics, what is 'discoursed' is mostly presented as *issue, problem, question, debate*.

The data can be explained, on the one hand, by the interest generally shown by economists for model-based reasoning, and, on the other, by historians in the interpretations of events, in exploring the relations that characterize them. Linguists, instead, seem to be inspired by an 'argumentative rhetoric'.

Reporting verbs and types of voice

The second phase of analysis concentrates on the concordance-based study of the occurrences for each of the reporting verbs listed in Table 5.1. The aim is to examine the voices as sources within disciplinary discourse that are associated with each verb: be that of the reviewer, in which case it is an 'averral' as realized through explicit reference to the reviewer by use of first person pronouns, or of 'third persons' (whether attributed to the reviewed book author or the disciplinary community).

The three voices (reviewed book author, disciplinary discourse community and reviewer) are respectively illustrated in extracts (5) to (7) below.

(5) As for the predictability of the semantic range of converted units, *Stekauer suggests* that meaning based on the basic features of the extralinguistic reality alluded to is more predictable in conversion than that based on the possible situations in which an item of the extralinguistic reality can be set. (LIBRA)

(6) For better or worse, *most historians still believe* that they are engaged in a search for reasons why things happened as they did. (HIBRA)

(7) Easterly focuses on correlations between economic performance and its hypothesized determinants, based on the most-often cited papers in this literature. *I would argue* that this is in fact the best use that can be made of these cross-country studies of growth. (EBRA)

A tabular representation of voices associated with each verb across the disciplines is given in Table 5.2.

A closer look at Table 5.2 reveals a number of interesting aspects across the disciplines. First of all, it can be noted that for all the top ten reporting verbs across the corpora, the most pervasive voice conveyed by their use is that of the reviewed book author ('*Stekauer suggests that*' in (5) above), amounting to 89.31 per cent in history, 77.20 in economics and 75.86 in linguistics. Since book review articles primarily function to evaluate the knowledge claims of other researchers, I would expect references to the reviewed author's ideas to be more frequent than those to the other voice, the disciplinary community.

It is striking, however, that these reporting verbs are not only associated with citation, but are also used for projecting the reviewer's own views (*I would argue that*). The substantial use of reporting verbs in

Table 5.2 Representation of voices associated which each verb by discipline (%)

Linguistics	Attr. RA	Attr. LDC	Aver.
argue	78.26	8.69	13.04
suggest	80.95	4.76	14.28
note	84.21	0.00	15.78
propose	77.77	16.66	5.55
find	47.05	11.76	41.17
show	93.33	0.00	6.66
point out	81.81	0.00	18.18
say	60.00	0.00	40.00
discuss	66.66	0.00	33.33
claim	80.00	0.00	20.00
History	Attr. RA	Attr. HDC	Aver.
argue	92.68	4.87	2.43
suggest	95.00	5.00	0.00
note	100.00	0.00	0.00
describe	100.00	0.00	0.00
point out	100.00	0.00	0.00
say	42.85	14.28	42.85
discuss	87.50	12.50	0.00
show	87.50	12.50	0.00
believe	75.00	25.00	0.00
conclude	100.00	0.00	0.00
Economics	Attr. RA	Attr. EDC	Aver.
argue	85.36	9.75	4.87
find	80.00	0.00	20.00
show	86.95	4.34	8.69
conclude	84.61	0.00	15.38
think	22.22	0.00	77.77
believe	57.14	0.00	42.85
suggest	83.33	0.00	16.66
assume	80.00	0.00	20.00
say	50.00	0.00	50.00
propose	100.00	0.00	0.00

Attr. RA: attributed to the reviewed book author
Attr. LDC: attributed to the linguistics discourse community
Attr. HDC: attributed to the historical discourse community
Attr. EDC: attributed to the economics discourse community
Aver.: averred by the reviewer

averrals with explicit markers of the presence of the reviewer by use of first person pronouns (18.62 per cent in linguistics, 17.64 in economics, 5.34 in history) suggests that there is a considerable need for reviewers to create a space for their own views. They exploit the reviewed book author or the discourse community to find a niche for their claims on the topic – for instance, by counter-claiming or pointing out gaps in existing research (including, of course, the reviewed book author's ideas under discussion). Extracts (8) and (9) illustrate this point:

(8) *Herman claims* that 'the vaunted separation between dramatic text and dramatic performance on verbal/non-verbal lines, are not quite as radical as they are seen to be' (p. 26). In contrast, *I suggest* that the difference is fundamental, especially from a pragmatic point of view. (LIBRA)

(9) Other scholars have discovered this newfound 'cult of heritage' and detected the expanding range of commemoration in our time. *David Lowenthal argued* that heritage is much less about 'grand monuments, unique treasures, and great heroes' and now 'touts the typical and the vernacular'. *Raphael Samuel*, who looked at this issue in England, *concluded* that heritage has become a 'nomadic' concept that is attached to almost anything including landscapes, country houses, family albums, and the museums of local football clubs.... The objective, *I suspect*, was not to reaffirm either tradition or democracy but to imagine a mythical nation drained of politics and inequality... Heritage did not exclude democratic or traditional aspirations, but it muted the attention they had once received.... *I would argue* that it is now scattered into a thousand preservation projects and commemorative sites that are frequently seen as part of a world that has disappeared never to return, rather than as part of a long-term quest for reason and justice. (HIBRA)

To elaborate on the discipline factor, the high occurrence of reviewer self-projection across the three disciplines may reflect the rhetorico-argumentative practices of the soft-knowledge domains in constructing an authoritative discoursal identity. A high-key representation of an authorial self helps to reinforce the conceptual structure of the discipline by presenting the soft-knowledge fields as 'typically more interpretative and less abstract... which means greater intervention in the argument is required and the writer's presence is necessarily stronger' (Hyland, 1999, p. 115).

However, these were not the only voices revealed by the analysis documented here. Indeed, there were a number of problematic cases concerning some occurrences, which could not be readily categorized under the three voices considered in the present study.

These cases are of four main types, although they might not be the only ones, considering that the analysis concerned fairly small corpora:

- polyphonic occurrences *strictu sensu* (cf. Bres and Verine, 2002), where the reviewer engages in internal dialogues without appearing overtly in the text (see example (10));
- instances serving as evidence of attribution introduced through generalized nominal categories referring to theoretical and textual constructs. Some examples of this are: *many studies, recent research, the most recent theories, some recent papers* as shown in example (11);
- attributions to an abstract reader (see example (12)) or 'people in general' (*one* in example (13));
- occurrences where verbs are not used with a reporting function as in example (14).

The following examples give some flavour of this:

(10) Strohm maintains that ... Yet, for all his efforts to persuade us of this, *it is hard to believe* that ... anything could have rivaled in impact the plague that in mid-century 'eliminated between one-third and one-half of the populace in one year.' (HIBRA)

(11) *Some recent papers have shown* that habit formation may help explain other empirical puzzles in macroeconomics as well. (EBRA)

(12) *Readers of this review might wish to argue* that it is unfair criticism to say that researchers who use simulations must be responsible for constructs that are a priori to their simulations. (LIBRA)

(13) In his afterword, however, Nora suggests that there may be an overabundance of memory and commemoration, particularly of World War II. Yet *one can argue* that what today looks like compulsive remembering may be the delayed result of decades ... (HIBRA)

(14) Thus, *Kammen noted the work of Thomas Hart Benton,* who in the 1920s undertook to paint murals of ordinary folks and their life-styles as a way of democratizing the larger imaginary of the nation itself. (HIBRA)

The variety of cases such as these provides a clear picture of the role played by reporting in the structure of the book review article. As we can see in the next section, the genre finds its distinctiveness in a combination of reporting and evaluation of the reported.

Reporting verbs and evaluation of the reported: The case of *argue* and *suggest* across disciplines

As rightly noted by Hyland,

> Report verbs do not simply function to indicate the status of the information reported, but the writer's position in relation to that information. The selection of an appropriate reporting verb allows writers to signal an assessment of the evidential status of the reported proposition and demonstrate their commitment, neutrality or distance from it. (Hyland, 2000, p. 38)

This is particularly evident in a genre like the book review article, where we have seen that there is a widespread occurrence of reporting verbs which imply a complex relationship between the views of the reviewer and those reported of the reviewed book author or the disciplinary discourse community.

As research has shown (Bondi, 1999), it is not always easy to distinguish signals of reporting framework from signals of evaluative framework of reported discourse. Some lexical elements can realize a modal as well as a reporting meaning, by expressing different degrees of adhesion to what is reported on the part of the reporter (e.g., the contrast between *show* and *claim*).

The question that arises from these observations is: is there any variation between the semantics of reporting verb and its pragmatic function? In seeking answers to this question, corpus evidence was looked towards, using two selected lexical items: the choice of lemmas to be analysed across disciplines fell on *argue* and *suggest* as they are the first two of the ten most frequent reporting verbs found in all three disciplines considered in the present study.

Argue across disciplines

The semantics of *argue* denotes construction of argument and conflict. Its definitions listed in the *Longman Dictionary of English Language and Culture* (1992, p. 51), for example, are 'express disagreement in words, often with strong feeling; quarrel; provide reasons for or against (something) clearly and in proper order'. *Argue* thus represents a lexical unit with an explicit argumentative meaning. It implies that a claim is made and that there is a response to the claim.

A pragmatic analysis of its occurrences did not show any significant variation between its semantics and its main discourse function, namely expressing disagreement. Extract (15) is an interesting example of this:

> (15) *He argues* that L.A.... Let us put aside the fact that *this assertion is probably disputable, because exaggerated*; it would be more satisfactory to present Los Angeles not as the first American city but rather as the ultimate one to 'separate decisively' from the European model. (HIBRA)

The fact that the reviewer starts his claim by saying 'this assertion is probably disputable, because exaggerated' makes his opposing view overt. The contrast with the reviewed author is achieved also through the claim that: 'it would be more satisfactory to present Los Angeles not as the first American city but rather...', where the conflict is high-lighted by the contrastive connector *but*. The expression *He argues that* clearly acts as both reporting framework and explicit signal of argumen-tative role: the statement of a claim on the part of the reviewed author. It seems to establish the premises for long sequences of argumentative dialogue between the reviewer and the reviewed author, although the force of elements signalling conflict may vary.

Let us now focus on the use of *argue* across disciplines. The results are presented in Table 5.3, where the percentages indicate the distribution of Reporting^Disagreement sequences with *argue* within the total of the verb occurrences in each discipline.

Looking at disciplines tendencies, it can be seen that linguistics dis-plays a somewhat higher frequency of negatively-evaluated attributions introduced by *argue* than economics and history do (46.09 per cent vs. 18.97 and 15.17 per cent respectively). The widespread use of *argue* in

Table 5.3 Distribution of Reporting^Disagreement sequences with *argue* by discipline (%)

Argue by discipline	*Reporting^Disagreement*
Linguistics	46.09
History	15.17
Economics	18.97

contexts of disagreement and at least potential conflict in linguistics corroborates the general picture emerging from other studies that linguistics texts are often more overtly argumentative than economics and history texts (Fløttum *et al.*, 2006, p. 261). Economists and historians are present, but in a rather careful way, while linguists are the most directly present and polemic authors.

Although the findings indicate that *argue* is used in contexts of disagreement between reviewer and reviewed book author, the analysis of concordance lines shows interesting exceptions. I find that the verb is also used in contexts of positively-evaluated attributions. Here are some examples:

(16) *Ullman correctly argues* that both Eltinge and the Long Beach scandals brought anxiety about effeminacy and masculinity to the fore. (LIBRA)

(17) *Herbst also argues interestingly* that this explains the absence of precolonial mapping in Africa. (EBRA)

By adding adverbial comment to the reporting verbs (*correctly* and *interestingly*), the reviewer gives evidence to support the reviewed author's point of view.

With regard to the discipline variable (see Table 5.4 below), the particularity to note here is that historians make much more use of the verb in positively-evaluated contexts compared to negative than linguists and economists do. History can be said to hold an essentially positive tone, since most attributions with *argue* carry positive evaluation (18.54 per cent vs. 15.17 per cent negative evaluation). On the whole, linguistics reviewers definitely tend to express much more disagreement, when compared to economists and historians, amounting to 46.09 per cent of all attributed statements introduced by *argue*, with agreement accounting for less than 5 per cent. By contrast, in economics

Table 5.4   Distribution of Reporting^Agreement sequences with *argue* by discipline (%)

Argue by discipline	*Reporting^Agreement*
Linguistics	4.94
History	18.54
Economics	15.52

book review articles the percentages for contexts of positively-evaluated and negatively-evaluated attributions introduced by *argue* are very similar, with slightly higher figures for disagreement than for agreement (18.97 per cent vs. 15.52 per cent).

Suggest across disciplines

Another lexicalization of argumentative procedures has been identified by its frequency across the corpora, *suggest*. According to the *Longman Dictionary of English Language and Culture* (1992, p. 1327), its definitions are 'mention as a possibility; state as an idea for consideration; propose; cause (a new idea) to appear or form in the mind'. The occurrences highlight that, though less explicitly argumentative, this verb signals a pragmatic function that is often associated with a claim. This can give rise to the expectation that there is a responsive move to the claim made. The data show that the reviewed author's reported opinions, when introduced by *suggest*, are often followed by a move in which the reviewer shows points of convergence or conflict. As we have seen for *argue*, the most interesting patterns across the corpora are those that involve 'passive moves' like agreement and disagreement (Stati, 1994), which represent a dialogic alternation of turns in the reviewer's evaluative argument, as shown in examples (18) and (19):

Reporting^Agreement

(18) *Susan Gail*, in her commentary on the final set of essays, *suggests* that the achievement of this goal might, in fact, be a consequence of the multisitedness of the analyses presented in the collection. *There is great merit in the observation* ... (LIBRA)

Reporting^Disagreement

(19) *Crosby seems to suggest* a special 'merchant' culture developing from the late Middle Ages through the Renaissance by contrasting the worldview of European nobles...with the worldview of the urban merchants (attentive to every penny), and then further *suggesting* that all other societies had values closer to those of Europe's nobles.... *But this is balderdash*, and comes of comparing apples and oranges. (HIBRA)

In example (18) the attributed statement introduced by *suggest* is evaluated positively. Through the choice of the wording *there is great merit in the observation*, the reviewer's consensus is straightforward. In (19), the

Table 5.5 Distribution of Reporting^Agreement and Reporting^Disagreement sequences with *suggest* by discipline (%)

Suggest by discipline	Reporting^Agreement	Reporting^Disagreement
Linguistics	7.23	8.09
History	38.00	21.00
Economics	22.64	16.98

expression *but this is balderdash*, instead, signals the reviewer's explicit disagreement with the reviewed author's statement, and the conflict is highlighted by the contrastive connector *but*.

With regard to the distribution of positively-evaluated and negatively-evaluated attributions introduced by *suggest* across disciplines, we may note that there are clear similarities between the results found for *argue* and those for *suggest* in linguistics and history. As shown in Table 5.5, once again linguistics shows a marked preference for negative evaluation of attributed statements introduced by *suggest* (8.09 per cent vs. 7.23 per cent positive evaluation), while history for positive (38 per cent vs. 21 per cent). An interesting difference appears in economics, where it makes considerably more use of positive evaluation than negative (22.64 per cent vs. 16.98 per cent). Quite the reverse is true for *argue*, even though negative evaluation has only slightly higher figures than positive (18.97 per cent negative evaluation vs. 15.52 per cent positive). This seems to mean that there is still some reluctance for economics reviewers to commit themselves to direct criticism. The small amount of occurrences of negative evaluation does not mean, of course, that there is little argumentation in the articles. It just means that the economics reviewer hesitates to involve him- or herself in this form of direct criticism; a certain prudence is favoured with regard to the use of disagreement.

Conclusions

This study on reporting and evaluation in book review articles has revealed that for the three disciplines under examination there is a considerable use of reporting clauses with a *that*-clause complement in contexts where the reviewer's position is at issue. Interestingly, the analysis has shown that reporting is not only used in referring to the reviewed book author's discourse through citation, but also to the reviewer's own views on the issues discussed. By choosing first person pronouns as the grammatical subjects, reviewers make their clear personal commitment to the proposition advanced. Reporting clauses which project the reviewer's own ideas thus offer an important opportunity for reviewers to position themselves within their disciplinary community by presenting their opinions in a way which will make them most likely to be accepted.

In terms of disciplinary preferences for the choice of reporting verbs, the study has produced some tendencies rather than highly conspicuous differences across disciplines. On the whole, we have seen that all three disciplines are characterized by frequent use of reporting verbs of 'discourse' groups (*argue, suggest, claim, discuss, conclude, propose, say*), thus confirming Hyland's (2000, p. 37) claim that 'the greater use of argumentative reporting verbs in the soft fields reflects the more discursive character of these disciplines'.

As for selected reporting verbs that characterize the three disciplinary corpora, like *argue* and *suggest*, the analysis has revealed that they give privilege to dialogic sequences in which a plurality of opinions by the reviewed author is introduced and then supported or contrasted with the reviewer's own (i.e. denoting agreement or disagreement). Significant differences in the distribution of these patterns have been found across disciplines. The findings have been interpreted in relation to the epistemological ethos of the disciplines.

Because of the small corpora used in this study, there are of course limitations to the generalizability of the results. To begin with, reporting verbs can undoubtedly be studied with regard to the voices they are associated with in a fruitful way, provided a more all-inclusive amount of data is considered than in this preliminary study, and the categorization of data is refined so as to include other voices that were only indicated here as more problematic data. In addition, comparative analysis with other disciplines may be worthwhile.

References

Biber, D., Johansson, S., Leech, G., Conrad, S. and Finegan, E. (1999) *Longman Grammar of Spoken and Written English* (London: Longman).

Bondi, M. (1999) *English across Genres: Language Variation in the Discourse of Economics* (Modena: Il Fiorino).

Bres, J. and Verine, B. (2002) 'Le Bruissement des Voix dans le Discours: Dialogisme et Discours Rapporté', *Faits de Langue*, XIX, 159–70.

Fløttum, K., Dahl, T. and Kinn, T. (2006) *Academic Voices* (Amsterdam: John Benjamins).

Hunston, S. (2004) ' "It Has Rightly Been Pointed Out …": Attribution, Consensus and Conflict in Academic Discourse' in M. Bondi, L. Gavioli and M. Silver (eds) *Academic Discourse, Genre and Small Corpora* (Rome: Officina Edizioni), 15–33.

Hyland, K. (1999) 'Disciplinary Discourses: Writer Stance in Research Articles' in C. Candlin and K. Hyland (eds) *Writing: Texts, Processes and Practices* (London: Longman), 99–121.

Hyland, K. (2000) 'Academic Attribution: Interaction through Citation' in K. Hyland *Disciplinary Discourses: Social Interactions in Academic Writing* (London: Longman), 41–62.

Hyland, K. (2001) 'Humble Servants of the Discipline? Self-Mention in Research Articles', *English for Specific Purposes*, XX, 3, 207–26.

Hyland, K. (2002a) 'Authority and Visibility: Authorial Identity in Academic Writing', *Journal of Pragmatics*, XXXIV, 8, 1091–112.

Hyland, K. (2002b) 'Activity and Evaluation: Reporting Practices in Academic Writing' in J. Flowerdew (ed.) *Academic Discourse* (London: Longman), 115–30.

Scott, M. (1998) *WordSmith Tools* (Oxford: Oxford University Press).

Sinclair, J. McH. (1987) 'Mirror for a Text', Manuscript. (Published 1988 *Journal of English and Foreign Languages*, Hyderabad, India, 15–44).

Stati, S. (1994) 'Passive Moves in Argumentation' in S. Čmejrková and F. Stícha (eds) *The Syntax of Sentences and Text* (Amsterdam: John Benjamins), 259–71.

Swales, J. (1990) *Genre Analysis: English in Academic and Research Settings* (Cambridge: Cambridge University Press).

Tadros, A. (1993) 'The Pragmatics of Text Averral and Attribution in Academic Texts' in M. Hoey (ed.) *Data, Description, Discourse* (London: HarperCollins Publishers), 98–114.

Thomas, S. and Hawes, T. P. (1994) 'Reporting Verbs in Medical Journal Articles', *English for Specific Purposes*, XIII, 2, 129–48.

Thompson, P. (2005) 'Aspects of Identification and Position in Intertextual Reference in PhD Theses' in E. Tognini-Bonelli and G. Del Lungo Camiciotti (eds) *Strategies in Academic Discourse* (Amsterdam: John Benjamins), 31–50.

6
Discipline and Gender: Constructing Rhetorical Identity in Book Reviews

Polly Tse and Ken Hyland

In review genres the control of evaluative resources is central to both effective writing and authorial identity. The ways in which writers judge others' work and express these judgements in their texts not only signals what they think, but also who they are, displaying both their status as disciplinary insiders and their individual competences and values. In other words, and in an important sense, we are what we write, and what we write in review texts is a discursive construction of self through evaluation. In this chapter we explore the role of gender and discipline in the performance of such an academic identity by examining a corpus of reviews, written by men and women, in the contrasting fields of philosophy and biology.

Identity, gender and academic discourse

While a complex and multifaceted issue, identity is increasingly seen as something that we actively and publicly accomplish through discourse (e.g., Hatch, Hill and Hayes, 1993; Ivanič, 1998), and therefore a practice which is oriented to community as much as individuality. In its broadest sense, *identity* refers to 'the ways that people display who they are to each other' (Benwell and Stokoe, 2006, p. 6): a social performance achieved by drawing on appropriate linguistic resources. It is through our use of community discourses that we claim or resist membership of social groups, that is, we define who we are in relation to others by constructing ourselves as credible members of a particular social group (Bakhtin, 1986). Essentially, institutional contexts privilege certain ways of creating meanings and so encourage the performance of certain kinds of professional identities. Powerful discourses, such as those authorized by academic disciplines, therefore act to restrict the rhetorical resources participants can bring from their past experiences and constrain what they might take from those made available by the context. A key dimension of such prior experience, and therefore a possible factor in shaping the individual's projection of an authorial identity, is that of gender.

Some commentators have pointed to the agonistic and aggressive nature of much academic writing in English and suggested that this represents a 'gendered discourse' which reflects masculine values of competition, rationality and objectivity (e.g., Frey, 1990; Belcher, 1997). This 'masculinist epistemology' (Luke and Gore, 1992, p. 205) is said to force both male and female academics to adopt a masculine style of writing, or at least to present versions of themselves in their writing which correspond to imposed gender identities. It also privileges male values and disadvantages women, who tend to favour a more facilitative and conciliatory interaction style (Kirsch, 1993). For Cameron (2007), however, such views draw on the doubtful belief that men and women 'speak different languages'; a monolithic conception of patriarchy popularized in the work of Tannen (1990), Gray (1992) and others and critiqued by Cameron as the 'Myth of Mars and Venus'. This focus on male–female styles tends to minimize gender intra-group differences and inter-group overlaps, neglecting the context of local meanings and the ways that language use helps shape gender, rather than the other way around.

In fact, evidence for gender-preferential discourses in academic contexts has been mixed. Flynn (1988) and Rubin and Greene (1992) found that female undergraduates employed a more affiliative style of argument than men, while Roen and Johnson (1992) observed that females used more positive evaluative items in student peer reviews, and that these compliments were more personalized, contained more intensifiers and attended far more to the gender of the addressee. While such results may support a view of different verbal cultures, Lynch and Strauss-Noll (1987), Francis *et al.* (2001) and Rubin and Greene (1992) found little difference in the use of assertion in the written argument patterns of male and female students.

These studies of gendered interaction are inconclusive partly because few studies actually look at written texts, or only examine students' writing, which often display different patterns to those of experts (e.g., Crammond, 1998). It is also unclear whether all male writers are advantaged and females discomfited by the use of adversarial rhetorical practices. Such generalizations simply violate our understandings of discourse and our experiences of academic writing. Moreover, a preoccupation with bipolar conceptions of academic writing exaggerates difference and leads to the reification of gender roles as fixed and static practices. In this polarizing perspective, then, any individual acts of self-representation can only appear as either socially determined or aberrant. Seeing identity as constituted through 'performativity' or the repeated performance of gendered norm rather than as reflecting essentialized categories of masculinity and femininity gives more respect for individual agency. Similarities in male–female discourse might therefore be taken as evidence for broader normative constraints in academic discourse and the effects of tight restrictions on the options of writers. Robson *et al.* (2002), for example, believe that assertive and conflictual expressions of argument may be a general feature of academic discourse, employed by both men and women.

We now turn to look at some of these issues in more detail, first sketching out our approach before examining how male and female academics use evaluative features in book reviews.

Corpus and approach

Our corpus consists of 56 reviews of single-authored academic books in leading journals in philosophy (Phil) and biology (Bio) together with interviews with reviewers and editors in those fields. We collected 14 reviews by males in each discipline (seven of books with male authors and seven with female authors) and 14 reviews by females in each discipline (again, seven of books with male authors and seven with female authors). These texts produced an electronic corpus of 61,000 words as shown in Table 6.1. The more discursive philosophy reviews were two and a half times longer than the more focused biology reviews with males producing texts about 10 per cent longer overall, perhaps

Table 6.1 Book review corpus by gender and discipline

Gender	Discipline		Totals by gender
	Phil	Bio	
Female review female	11,432	4,469	15,901
Female review male	9,419	3,690	13,109
Male review female	10,657	4,455	15,112
Male review male	12,733	4,089	16,822
Totals by discipline	44,241	16,703	60,944

underlining the view that men give more opinions, occupy more inter-actional space and contribute more in public discourses (e.g., Tannen, 1994).

We computer searched these sub-corpora for explicit features of eval-uation drawing on previous studies of metadiscourse and stance by the authors (Hyland 2001, 2005a, b; Hyland and Tse, 2004) as well as those found from a close reading of the texts themselves. We then orga-nized these features into broad categories depending on their evaluative functions as follows:

- *Hedges* signal the writer's reluctance to present propositional infor-mation categorically (e.g., *might, possible, perhaps*).
- *Boosters* express certainty and emphasize the force of propositions (e.g., *definitely, clearly, it is evident*).
- *Attitude markers* express the writer's appraisal of propositional infor-mation, conveying surprise, obligation, agreement, importance and so on (e.g., *amazingly, it is disappointing, even x*).
- *Engagement markers* explicitly address readers, either by selectively focusing their attention or by including them as participants in the text through second person pronouns, imperatives, questions and asides (Hyland, 2001) (e.g., inclusive *we, let's, note that*).

The textual analyses were supplemented by semi-structured interviews with three reviewers and one editor from each discipline. These focused on the participants' views on evaluative language, their understandings of disciplinary constraints, and opinions on argument and gender.

Overall patterns of evaluation

Analysis of these features indicates something of the extent of evalua-tion in these reviews with almost 2,800 examples overall, or about 50 per review. Table 6.2 shows that men and women make use of broadly similar resources, with males employing more evaluative devices in each category, with the exception of attitude markers. Analysis of the sub-corpora, presented in the four right hand columns, suggests that both males and females employ more features when reviewing female authors.

The importance of creating a shared evaluative context through engagement markers and hedges is evident in all the reviews. *Engage-ment markers* such as imperatives, inclusive pronouns and questions, for

Table 6.2 Evaluation categories by gender (per 1,000 words)

	All Reviewers		Females		Males	
	Female	*Male*	*Rev F*	*Rev M*	*Rev F*	*Rev M*
Engagement Markers	13.2	15.3	15.1	10.9	15.9	14.7
Hedges	9.8	11.0	10.9	8.5	11.1	10.8
Attitude Markers	9.1	8.5	8.9	9.2	9.3	7.8
Boosters	7.0	9.0	6.7	7.3	9.0	9.0
Totals	38.1	43.8	41.6	35.9	45.3	42.3

instance, help underline an appeal to scholarly solidarity and communal understandings (1); while *hedges* serve to tone down the author's judgemental authority (2):

(1) *Notice that* since non-substances must mention substances in their definitions they are not primary things on the criteria of Z 4. This is a useful point to keep in mind, when *we* try to understand why Aristotle says in chapter 5 that non-substances do not have essences strictly speaking. (Female Phil)

What counts as 'making sense', or as an explanation or answer to questions that biologists take as central? What is the 'making sense' process, and in particular what role do models, mathematics, mechanics, and metaphors play? How do *we* know when biologists have succeeded – at what? Keller organizes her book around the thesis that there is no simple answer to these questions. (Female Bio)

(2) *Some* readers *might* yet be surprised by some features of this project: John Stuart Mill looms larger here than Aristotle, and the neo-Kantian flavor is strong. (Female Phil)

There are also *some* samples (Spain, Hungarian Gypsies, Zulus) that *appear to* display no sex difference in 2D:4D, which *suggests* that in some populations the ratios do not vary with prenatal androgen exposure. (Male Bio)

Generally, both male and female writers employed similar patterns of evaluation in their texts and conducted their interactions with readers in similar ways. We might say, then, that the discursive construction of an appropriate authorial identity in this genre involves a decidedly interpersonal stance with relatively high frequencies of attitudinal lexis, hedged evaluation and explicit engagement with readers.

Gender patterns in evaluation

Perhaps surprisingly, males used about 15 per cent more evaluative features overall, with hedges, boosters and engagement markers particularly prominent in their writing. These are all features of a personal and engaging style more usually associated with female discourse (Holmes, 1988).

Boosters, or items used to reinforce arguments and express conviction, represent the widest gender differences in the corpus, and our results here echo those of Crismore *et al.* (1993) and Francis *et al.* (2001) who found that men used more boosters in academic writing than women. Our concordance data also supports studies by Johnson and Roen (1992) and Herbert (1990) which found that females mainly used boosters to intensify praise, fully committing themselves to their positive evaluations of a book:

> (3) Chapter 5, entitled 'The Variable Environments of Evolutionary Relevance', brings up some *very* interesting points concerning hominid mothering in the Pleistocene and Neolithic... (Female Bio)

> In an *extremely* readable and coherent style, Thomas integrates biology, politics, social concerns, and economics... (Female Bio)

> Wedin's interpretations are *extremely* detailed and dense, and they contain many subtle points, which are worthy of admiration and thought. (Female Phil)

Males, in contrast, were more likely to use boosters to underpin their confidence in their judgements, often framing these evaluations with a personal pronoun. Self mention is an explicit intrusion into the text to stamp a personal authority onto one's views and this was a strategy employed far more by male reviewers, imparting a strong opinion to the evaluation:

> (4) This was particularly noticeable in the areas with which *I was most familiar*, where *I also found* occasional unsupported statements that *I believe* were incorrect. (Male Bio)

I have absolutely no doubt that Whitford's understanding of these seemingly simple, but (in reality) amazingly complex systems is among the most comprehensive in the world community of desert ecologists. (Male Bio)

I believe Kennett's original framing of the problem to be extremely useful. However, unlike her, *I believe* that it sets things up aptly to draw a skeptical conclusion regarding the distinctions offered by folk-theory. (Male Phil)

The only feature more common in the female's reviews was expression of attitude, particularly regarding the overall coverage, argument and value of the book, and the experience, reputation and ability of its writer:

(5) Rosalind Hursthouse has written *an excellent book*, in which she develops a neo-Aristotelian virtue ethics that . . . (Female Phil)

The *beauty* of Janice Moore's volume is that it combines this *compelling* natural history with a *clear-eyed critical skepticism, challenging conventional wisdom* as it explores the ways that . . . (Female Bio)

I found this book rather *repetitive*, and Barlow's knowledge of evolutionary theory a little *naive*. (Female Bio)

These expressions of inscribed appreciation are commonplace in our texts and indicate how reviewers judge target texts according to community-based codes of intellectual and rhetorical performance.

The male writers' greater willingness to make bold statements, boost their arguments and generally take a more confident and uncompromising line might be seen as a consequence of seniority rather than be attributed to some abstract gendered behaviour. After all, few women hold chairs in these fields, oversee research labs or sit on important committees, as several of our informants commented:

Yes scientists are mainly male . . . the imbalance is even greater when you go up the ladder . . . It's hard because part of being confident depends on how you're perceived. You know, many people think women are not as good in writing that kind of 'factual' report. I know this perception is wrong but it affects how you see and present yourself. (Female Bio interview)

Unfortunately there is a huge gender imbalance in professional philosophy. The observation that men use more 'I' and are more assertive

> may be due to the hierarchical thing that the women feel that they have to be more careful or less assertive and this has to do with masculine aggressivity. (Male Phil interview)

The reluctance of women to make the same use of boosters, self mention and engagement markers may therefore, at least in part, be related to the dominance of men in higher career positions. But not all informants concurred that this influenced writers' rhetorical decisions or promoted a masculine writing culture. This biologist is an example:

> Status makes a difference, gender doesn't. They're all scientists, they are not men and women. But yes this field is so male-dominated that some women might try twice as hard as men to project a style of a so-called professional poker face scientist because they feel they need to somehow. (Male Bio interview)

Overall, our findings support Francis *et al.*'s (2001) contention that the academic writing of men and women exhibits far more similarities than differences. The power of the genre to constrain behaviour and influence practice, however, may be underpinned by, and itself support, more gendered social structures. While women are increasingly active in these fields, both philosophy and biology are traditionally masculine domains where men hold the most senior positions. The predominant discourse patterns and modes of argument that define these disciplines are therefore shaped by communities which are largely male and might therefore support the performance of particular professional identities. These speculations about the expectations of rhetorical interaction receive some support from our disciplinary data, which we turn to in the next section.

Gender, discipline and evaluation

Table 6.3 compares the ways that male and female reviewers used evaluation by discipline, with differences in each feature in the final column of each discipline. It is clear from this, admittedly relatively small data set, that language uses by males and females show greater similarity *within* each discipline and more variations *between* the disciplines.

Clearly, engagement, hedging and boosting are all evaluative features more common in philosophy than biology, reflecting the more visible role of the agent in the soft knowledge fields. In research writing,

Table 6.3   Gender use of metadiscourse in individual disciplines (per 1,000 words)

Gender	Philosophy			Biology		
	Female	*Male*	*+− F/M*	*Female*	*Male*	*+− F/M*
Engagement Markers	14.7	17.2	−2.5	9.3	10.1	−0.8
Hedges	11.0	11.4	−0.4	6.9	9.8	−2.9
Attitude Markers	8.8	8.3	0.5	9.8	9.1	0.7
Boosters	7.3	9.6	−2.3	6.1	7.4	−1.3
Totals	41.8	46.5	−4.7	32.1	36.4	−4.3

rhetorical practices are closely related to the ways the disciplines create knowledge, with philosophers taking a more explicitly involved and interpretive approach compared with the biologist's greater reliance on shared background understandings and proven methods (Hyland, 2000). These rhetorical conventions are also apparent in review genres, with the scientists exhibiting a relatively greater preference for impersonality. These generalizations need to be qualified, however, and are worth examining in more detail.

Evaluation in philosophy reviews

The greater use of engagement markers and boosters by the male reviewers is the most obvious gender difference in philosophy and, on closer analysis, this seems to relate to very different ways of conceptualizing argument between the genders in this discipline.

The reviews written by male philosophers are conspicuous in the extent to which they are invested with an explicitly committed and engaged stance. This is a personal and intrusive discourse which presents an individual voice proclaiming ideas and meeting objections head-on with conviction and a clear acceptance of responsibility, as in these examples:

(6) This is *almost certainly too weak* an account, for *it fails* to rule out chance coincidences of judgment and motivation. This problem *may be* avoidable by appeal to a more complex pattern of possibilities, however *I believe* that any moderated account of the disposition to exercise control will run into a *serious* difficulty, as follows. (Male Phil)

> *My only quarrel* with Baker's presentation of her material (the book
> is *generally very well written* and as *clear as the subject matter permits*)
> is that *I find here and there a certain carelessness* in her use of logical
> concepts. (Male Phil)

Bloor (1996) has called this directly challenging mode of philosophical debate 'mind-to-mind combat'; a style which assumes that the best
way to investigate ideas is to subject them to extreme opposition. While
hedged, the use of hedges and first person here place the writer and
his views squarely in the text to leave readers in no doubt of where he
stands, confronting and challenging readers and expecting more from
them in terms of agreement and engagement.

In contrast, our data show that many female philosophers employ a
very different rhetorical style, shaping their evaluations to construct a
reasonable and scholarly persona, which encodes both praise and criticism of a target book as an outcome of logical reasoning. This approach
emphasizes another side of philosophy, demonstrating respect for values of rationality and logic by careful exemplification and coherent
analysis.

> (7) *Since* Walzer argues that there are competing interpretations of the
> meanings of social goods (e.g. health care as a need or as a commod-
> ity), he can justify his own interpretations of these meanings only as
> interpretations; *nevertheless*, he continues to seek consensus as if his
> interpretations or the principles he thinks are implied in them are
> the universally shared and correct ones. *An additional problem* is that
> he seems to have no critical stance from which to object to society's
> present principles of justice, *since* they may be grounded on a socially
> accepted interpretation of the social goods they are used to distribute.
> (Female Phil)

Essentially, this is an approach which sets out ideas in a way that
displays both reasoning and an appreciation of the reader's likely knowledge and understanding. The writer manages the argument towards
a consensus, guiding readers by anticipating their likely reactions
and needs.

Clearly, both approaches represent effective and appropriate ways of
arguing in philosophy, and both are available to men and women,
but our analyses show a clear gender preference for these choices.
Nor are these differences merely inventions of the analysts' fevered

imaginations. Several of our informants also pointed to these different gender-preferred argument repertoires:

> Argument is central in our field, but there are different ways to do it … clarity and logic is most valued in the field and it is relatively easy to learn how to write clearly and logically than to forcefully express something, because it only takes more practice to write clearly, but it may involve changing your own personality if you want a battle. I prefer to work twice as hard on plain logical and coherent presentation if I want to convince. When peaceful discussion would do why do you want to fight? It sounds too aggressive and I don't like it. Some men do, they think a philosopher's job is to fight. (Female Phil interview)

> It really gets to the arguments … They are creatures of criticisms. They all think it is their jobs to point out errors, or somebody else's opinions are wrong. There is some feminist critique on some 'adversarial style', and these women complain there is too much conflict and too competitional … but some of those guys their mind might be like kick-boxers, they just want to show they are the smartest and shut one up and be the boss. (Male Phil interview)

So, philosophy offers practitioners different options in constructing arguments which seem to spill into patterns of reviewing with males tending to favour a more explicitly personal style of evaluation and females adopting a carefully reasoned one.

Evaluation in biology reviews

Gender differences in the use of evaluative features are generally much narrower in biology, with only hedges employed significantly more by one group. This gender variation in hedging is interesting and appears to be related to both gender preferences and to the different role that reviews serve in biology.

In philosophy, books are the main vehicle for advancing scholarship and presenting original research. The carefully argued engagement with recurring problems of philosophy correspond to what Becher and Trowler (2001) call a 'rural research area' where topics are less narrowly focused, slower moving and less competitively researched. Biology, in contrast, is a more fast moving and competitive environment where advances are made at such a rapid pace that journal articles are the key means of reporting and negotiating knowledge. Books, therefore, tend to assemble already codified knowledge rather than disseminate new work, and are written to reinforce existing paradigms. Most of the books that are reviewed in biology are therefore intended for student readers, and as a result reviewers often tend to focus on visible production and stylistic features rather than fine points of argument. It is this which mainly distinguishes these reviews from the more argumentative philosophy examples and which helps account for some of the rhetorical choices in evaluation.

Interestingly, it was the male reviewers who were more likely to engage with the research methodologies and underlying theories of the reviewed texts, taking on the writer's argument more directly than the female reviewers. This more argumentative stance meant that the writers gave greater attention to weighing the pros and cons of the reviewed author's position and to navigating a route through complex contradictions and alternatives. Like the philosophers, this explicit evaluation of the authors' ideas encouraged rhetorical choices of personal involvement, helping to explain the frequencies of features shown in Table 6.3.

Closer analysis of the texts, moreover, revealed that many of these more critical and evaluative reviews by males were of books written by other men. While the frequencies are too small and allow only speculative comments (just seven texts in each combination of gender of the reviewer and the reviewed writer), concordance patterns suggest in particular that male reviewers used far more hedges in reviewing the books of other males, toning down the strength of their evaluations:

(8) Although he wanders freely through an eclectic selection of images and ideas, he *could perhaps* have done more to explore new ground. (M-review-M Bio)

That omission ignores what is *likely to be* a significant component of genetic medicine in this era of genomes and proteomes, and it results in a *rather* skewed consideration of the relative merits of the three alternative frameworks for policy formulation. (M-review-M Bio)

It was *a bit of* a tedious read due to the level of detail, the *somewhat* artificial breakdown of topics by chapter, and the nature of models in general. Because of the amount of detailed discussion it was *often* difficult to see the forest for the trees. (M-review-M Bio)

Hedging in these texts, then, mainly helped writers to mitigate their critical evaluation of a book's content, reducing the face threat of a more direct condemnation (Hyland, 2000).

The less critically evaluative stance of female reviewers not only meant far fewer hedges in the female biology corpus, but also that those they did use were deployed in a different way, often to redress the impact of the book's argument on readers, rather than the impact of the criticism on the author:

> (9) I expect *some* readers *would* enjoy the multidisciplinary treatment... (F-review-F Bio)

> So although readers *might* be horrified by what they see... (F-review-M Bio)

> A sceptical reader with even a modicum of expertise in the use of statistics *may* feel uneasy about all these tests that sometimes compare... (F-review-F Bio)

> Even with the warning that it is not a scholarly book, biologists *might* find themselves shocked by other aspects, if they are not familiar with the genre. (F-review-M Bio)

These very different uses suggest that the conventions of the discipline help persuade male biologists to express their criticisms of reviewed books tentatively, particularly as the very short length of these reviews prevent them from appealing to experimental evidence for support.

Another area where disciplinary conventions seem to override gender differences is in the use of engagement markers. Reviewers in both these fields take some trouble to reach out to readers and include them in the writer's enthusiasm for the topic of the book or a verdict on it. The fact that engagement markers are less frequent in other genres (e.g. textbooks and research articles) in biology, however, seems to make them all the more striking when they occur in these short reviews. Inclusive pronouns and questions, in fact, are extremely common in the biology reviews, sucking the reader into the writer's argument:

> (10) What counts as 'making sense', or as an explanation or answer to questions that biologists take as central? What is the 'making sense' process, and in particular what role do models, mathematics, mechanics, and metaphors play? How do we know when biologists

> have succeeded – at what? Keller organizes her book around the thesis that there is no simple answer to these questions. (Bio)

> The fallacy of course is that nature may have equipped *us* to desire certain things not necessarily to achieve them. *Our* taste for sweets is the obvious example. There is no reason to believe that the Pleistocene hunter-gather was any happier without sweets than *we* are with unlimited access, as eating too much sweets leads to obesity and related health problems. *We* seem to be miserable either way. (Bio)

These choices help writers to construct a specific cultural and institutional context by predicting how readers are likely to react to their arguments. It reflects the fact that evaluation is always based on a prior evaluation of audience so the writer can meet readers' expectations of inclusion while simultaneously positioning them to accept particular interpretations.

Overall, however, we see in these texts how important reviews can be to writers who may see them as an opportunity to state their own views rather than simply evaluate those of others. Reviews are highly visible and offer their writers a rhetorical platform to signal their allegiance to a particular orientation or group, and proclaim a position without engaging in the long cycle of inquiry, review and revision involved in a research. We have seen, however, that this is an opportunity largely taken by men reviewing the books of other men. Once again, this may be because of men's position in the field rather than any masculine proclivity for dominance and self-assertion, as one female biologist puts it:

> I think it might be related to the keen competition between labs and the fact that principal investigators in these labs are mainly male. They may feel it is their responsibility to respond to each other's findings, even if they can't be certain, to promote an active image of their labs and to show other competing labs that they're not ignorant of the issues. You know that people who control grants are aware of what's going on, whether you have something interesting to contribute to the field or not, if anyone is doing similar work as you're doing… maybe women are less likely to be in charge so don't feel as much need to respond to ideas. (Female Bio interview)

The linguistic and rhetorical choices in these reviews may therefore reflect something of the intense competition for funding, influence and esteem between male dominated labs and research groups as writers construct a professional identity for themselves.

Conclusions

This study of evaluation in book reviews supports current research, which suggests that there is no one-to-one relation between gender and language. Our analysis gives greater space for individual agency and challenges perspectives which stress an 'essentialist' view of gender: a view which reifies language behaviour and gives a fixed identity to groups. While there is some evidence here that men may be more inclined to take a more argumentative line in their evaluations, it is difficult to link these to an abstract conception of competitive and aggressive male discourse traits. Instead we find multiple relations and meanings cross-cut by discipline and seniority. Social forces structure the identity options available to individuals and we see in these texts something of how disciplinary practices shape the options that writers bring to the writing task.

To be persuasive, writers need to connect with a community value system, making rhetorical choices which evaluate both their propositions and their audience. This means that in order to understand what counts as effective evaluation every instance has to be seen as an act socially situated in a disciplinary or institutional context. But while the version of self that will be rewarded may be constrained by disciplinary conventions in this way, individual agency is not eliminated. Identities are not totally determined and the unique history of an individual's encounters with texts gives them the possibility of recombining available options in their own ways.

As they write, academics draw on a repertoire of possible identities based on their experiences, purposes and conceptions of self, which interact with the conventions of the genre. Our diverse experiences and memberships of overlapping communities, including those of class, ethnicity and gender influence how we understand our disciplinary participation and how we want to interact with our colleagues in the performance of a professional academic identity. However, while gender is an important component of our lived experience, it is unlikely to be a determining influence on our academic writing. The ways in which men and women use a language, in other words, are not fixed by their gender but constructed, negotiated and transformed through social practices informed by particular social settings, relations of power and participation in disciplinary discourses.

References

Bakhtin, M. (1986) in C. Emerson and M. Holquist (eds), *Speech Genres and Other Late Essays* (University of Texas, Austin, TX V: McGee, Trans).

Becher, T. and Trowler, P. (2001) *Academic Tribes and Territories: Intellectual Enquiry and the Culture of Disciplines*, 2nd edn (Milton Keynes: SRHE/Oxford University Press).

Belcher, D. (1997) 'An Argument for Non Adversarial Argumentation: On the Relevance of the Feminist Critique of Academic Discourse to L2 Writing Pedagogy', *Journal of Second Language Writing*, VI, 1, 1–21.

Benwell, B. and Stokoe, E. (2006) *Discourse and Identity* (Edinburgh: Edinburgh University Press).

Bloor, T. (1996) 'Three Hypothetical Strategies in Philosophical Writing', in E. Ventola and A. Mauranen (eds), *Academic Writing: Intercultural and Textual Issues* (Amsterdam: John Benjamins), 19–43.

Cameron, D. (2007) *The Myth of Mars and Venus* (Oxford: Oxford University Press).

Crammond, J. (1998) 'The Uses and Complexity of Argument Structures in Expert and Student Persuasive Writing', *Written Communication*, XV, 2, 230–68.

Crismore, A., Markkanen, R. and Steffensen, M. (1993) 'Metadiscourse in Persuasive Writing', *Written Communication*, X, 1, 39–71.

Flynn, E. (1988) 'Composing as a Woman', *College Composition and Communication*, XXXIX, 423–35.

Francis, B., Robsen, J. and Read, B. (2001) 'An Analysis of Undergraduate Writing Styles in the Context of Gender and Achievement', *Studies in Higher Education*, XXVI, 3, 313–26.

Frey, O. (1990) 'Beyond Literary Darwinism: Women's Voices and Critical Discourse', *College English*, LII, 5, 507–26.

Gray, J. (1992) *Men Are from Mars, Women Are from Venus* (New York: Haper-Collins).

Hatch, J. A., Hill, C. A. and Hayes, J. R. (1993) 'When the Messenger Is the Message: Readers' Impressions of Writers' Personalities', *Written Communication*, X, 4, 569–98.

Herbert, R. K. (1990) 'Sex-Based Differences in Compliment Behaviour', *Language in Society*, XIX, 1, 201–24.

Holmes, J. (1988) 'Paying Compliments: A Sex-Preferred Positive Politeness Strategy', *Journal of Pragmatics*, XII, 3, 445–65.

Hyland, K. (2000) *Disciplinary Discourses: Social Interactions in Academic Writing* (London: Longman).

Hyland, K. (2001) 'Bringing in the Reader: Addressee Features in Academic Articles', *Written Communication*, XVIII, 4, 549–74.

Hyland, K. (2005a) *Metadiscourse. Exploring Interaction in Writing* (London: Continuum).

Hyland, K. (2005b) 'Stance and Engagement: A Model of Interaction in Academic Discourse', *Discourse Studies*, VII, 2, 173–91.

Hyland, K. and Tse, P. (2004) 'Metadiscourse in Academic Writing: A Reappraisal', *Applied Linguistics*, XXV, 2, 156–77.

Ivanič, R. (1998) *Writing and Identity: The Discoursal Construction of Identity in Academic Writing* (Amsterdam: John Benjamins).

Johnson, D. M. and Roen, D. H. (1992) 'Complimenting and Involvement in Peer Reviews: Gender Variation', *Language in Society*, XXI, 1, 27–57.

Kirsch, G. (1993) *Women Writing in the Academy: Audience, Authority, and Transformation* (Carbondale and Edwardsville: Southern Illinois University Press).

Luke, C. and Gore, J. (1992) 'Women in the Academy: Strategy, Struggle, Survival', in C. Luke and J. Gore (eds), *Feminisms and Critical Pedagogy* (New York: Routledge), 192–210.

Lynch, C. and Strauss-Noll, M. (1987) 'Mauve Washers: Sex Differences in Freshman Writing', *English Journal*, LXXVI, 1, 90–4.

Robson, J., Francis, B. and Read, B. (2002) 'Writers of Passage: Stylistic Features of Male and Female Undergraduate History Essays', *Journal of Further and Higher Education*, XXVI, 4, 351–62.

Roen, D. H. and Johnson, D. M. (1992) 'Perceiving the Effectiveness of Written Discourse through Gender Lenses: The Contribution of Complimenting', *Written Communication*, IX, 435–64.

Rubin, D. and Greene, K. (1992) 'Gender-Typical Style in Written Language', *Research in the Teaching of English*, XXVI, 7–40.

Tannen, D. (1990) *You Just Don't Understand: Men and Women in Conversation* (New York: William Morrow).

Tannen, D. (1994) *Talking from 9 to 5: How Women's and Men's Conversational Styles Affect Who Gets Heard, Who Gets Credit, and What Gets Done at Work* (New York: William Morrow).

7
Phraseology and Epistemology in Academic Book Reviews: A Corpus-Driven Analysis of Two Humanities Disciplines

Nicholas Groom

Introduction

The aim of this chapter is to identify relationships between phraseology and epistemology in the discourses of two humanities disciplines, history and literary criticism. The empirical focus of the chapter will be on two large computerized corpora of book review texts compiled from academic journals in these two disciplines. Using the tools and methods of corpus-driven linguistics (Tognini-Bonelli, 2001; Hunston, 2002; Sinclair, 2003, 2004), I will show how one of the core epistemological values of history and literary criticism as humanities disciplines is reflected in a range of notable phraseological features in the peer review genres represented by these two corpora.

Phraseology and epistemology

For the purposes of this chapter, *phraseology* will be defined in general terms as 'the preferred way of saying things in a particular discourse' (Gledhill, 2000, p. 1) and more specifically as 'the tendency of words to occur, not randomly, or even in accordance with grammatical rules only, but in preferred sequences' in attested language data (Hunston, 2002, p. 137). In other words, phraseology will be seen as a social rather than a psychological phenomenon, which manifests itself in the form of conventionalized linguistic sequences that occur in texts produced at different points in time by different speakers or writers within a given discourse community.

The term *epistemology* is also to be understood in social terms in this chapter. That is, it will be used to refer not to philosophical questions about the nature of knowledge in general, but to the ways in which knowledge is conceptualized, produced and reproduced within particular discourse communities.

Disciplinary discourses as knowledge domains: Becher's model of epistemological variation

The idea that conceptions of knowledge and approaches to knowledge creation might vary in significant and systematic ways across the academic disciplinary spectrum is not a particularly controversial one. Rather, the problem for researchers has traditionally been one of how to describe this variation in a comprehensive and coherent way. Over the last two decades, the theoretical model proposed by the higher education researcher Tony Becher (1989, 1994; Becher and Trowler, 2001) has proved to be by far the most popular solution to this particular descriptive conundrum. Indeed, Becher's model has become so widely accepted that it now constitutes the de facto standard account of epistemological variation in academic discourse research (e.g. Parry, 1998; Hyland, 2000, 2007; Groom, 2005; North, 2005; Holmes and Nesi, forthcoming).

Much of the appeal of Becher's model derives from its elegant division of the academic disciplinary spectrum into four broad 'knowledge domains', as presented in Figure 7.1.

Disciplinary grouping	Nature of knowledge
Pure sciences (e.g. physics): 'hard-pure'	Cumulative; atomistic (crystalline/tree-like); concerned with universals, quantities, simplification; resulting in discovery/explanation.
Humanities (e.g. history) and pure social sciences (e.g. anthropology): 'soft-pure'	Reiterative; holistic (organic/river-like); concerned with particulars, qualities, complication; resulting in understanding/interpretation.
Technologies (e.g. mechanical engineering): 'hard-applied'	Purposive; pragmatic (know-how via hard knowledge); concerned with mastery of physical environment; resulting in products/techniques.
Applied social sciences (e.g. education): 'soft-applied'	Functional; utilitarian (know-how via soft knowledge); concerned with enhancement of [semi-] professional practice; resulting in protocols, procedures.

Figure 7.1   Becher's four 'knowledge domains' (Source: Becher, 1989)

As can be seen, the epistemology of the 'soft-pure' knowledge domain of the humanities, upon which we will be focusing in this chapter, is characterized as *reiterative* (i.e. concerned with revisiting perennial questions and reinterpreting previously existing data), *holistic* (i.e. interested in analysing phenomena as organic wholes and in tracing the interconnections that structure them), and *concerned with particulars, qualities [and] complication* (i.e. oriented towards the elaboration of detailed, subjective and complex accounts of phenomena, and thus towards the deconstruction of broad generalizations). All of these specific epistemological dispositions are seen as contributing in complementary ways to the wider goal of developing broader and deeper understandings of known phenomena.

These characterizations are intuitively very appealing, but at the same time there are a number of important questions surrounding them that have yet to be fully addressed. What do the epistemological precepts sketched out by adjectives such as *cumulative, reiterative, purposive* and *functional* look like as text? Do such precepts have any clearly distinguishable phraseological manifestations at all? If so, are they broadly the same in all disciplines within a given knowledge domain, or do individual disciplines within a particular knowledge domain have their own unique ways of expressing them? And if not, wherein lies their validity? My aim in this chapter is to open these questions up for discussion, and it is through a comparative phraseological analysis of two corpora of book reviews in two different disciplines that I propose to do so.

Clearly, a full analysis of the four knowledge domains presented in Figure 7.1 would be well beyond the limited scope of this chapter. Indeed, it will not even be possible within this chapter to conduct a comprehensive phraseological investigation of any one of the domains mapped out above. For reasons of space, then, the analysis presented in this chapter will be restricted to just one knowledge domain, the 'soft-pure' domain of the humanities, and to just one of the core epistemological properties that Becher's model imputes to that domain: the property of reiterativeness.

The book review genre as an object of analysis

Once a somewhat neglected genre in academic discourse studies, the book review is now increasingly seen as playing an important role in the discursive construction of disciplinary knowledge, and thus as constituting an important locus of disciplinary discourse research (Motta-Roth, 1998; Moreno and Suárez, 2008). Firstly, it performs the valuable function of summarizing the content of newly published books, thereby disseminating this content to researchers who might otherwise lack the time or resources to become apprised of it. Secondly, and perhaps most obviously, book reviews evaluate new contributions to disciplinary knowledge, thereby contributing in a very direct and explicit way to the ongoing process of negotiating what counts or does not count as valid knowledge and practice within a given discipline. Finally, the book review genre constitutes 'an alternative forum in which academics can set out their views... without engaging in the long cycle of inquiry, review and revision involved in a full-length paper' (Hyland, 2000, p. 43). As such, book reviews also provide an important platform for graduate students, early career researchers and scholars working in resource-poor contexts, who might otherwise find it difficult to add their own voices to current debates in their own specialist fields.

In summary, then, the book review genre plays a vital role in helping to define and redefine the core epistemological values of particular disciplinary discourses, and thus makes an ideal object of empirical analysis for the purposes of this chapter. Indeed, some of the strongest evidence in support of this chapter's basic premise – that phraseology and epistemology are indissolubly interlinked – comes from previous studies of the book review genre, as we will see in the next section.

Evaluation and epistemology in book reviews

The empirical basis for Becher's model of epistemological variation as presented earlier in this chapter is described in a series of papers published during the 1980s, one of which includes an analysis of published book review texts in two fields, history and sociology (Becher, 1987). Becher found that while the history reviews in his sample were typically very positive and genteel in their evaluations, reviews in sociology were much more likely to be highly critical and contentious. Becher relates this greater degree of critical rancour to the greater importance of theoretical and methodological allegiances in sociological research, compared with the avowedly 'atheoretical' *modus operandi* favoured by many historical researchers.

Although rather ad hoc and informal, Becher's analysis is significant insofar as it leads him to hypothesize that there are systematic correspondences 'between the epistemological properties of [a] subject and the language used to evaluate the research generated within it' (Becher, 1987, p. 264). This claim has been taken up and explored in more detail and with much more methodological rigour by Hyland (2000).

Focusing on evaluative speech acts across eight different disciplines, Hyland found marked quantitative and qualitative differences between disciplines belonging to 'soft' knowledge domains (in Becher's terms) on the one hand, and 'hard' knowledge disciplines on the other. Specifically, reviewers in the soft fields studied by Hyland were more critical than were their counterparts in the hard fields, and much more inclined to engage in detail with the substantive content of the books under review.

Hyland notes that these differences reflect the different roles of published books in soft and hard fields, and that these different roles in turn are indicative of more fundamental divergences in epistemological orientation. Full-length books are important in soft disciplines because their format is well-suited to the kinds of comprehensive and detailed discussion favoured in these fields. In hard disciplines, in contrast, books are less a forum for the discussion of new ideas than they are a vehicle for the transmission of agreed facts, especially to novices and non-specialists – hence the greater focus in hard science reviews on presentational issues such as the clarity of diagrams or the quality of indexing.

While Becher (1989) and Hyland (2000) focus more on the content of evaluations in book reviews than they do on the characteristic linguistic forms that such evaluations take, supporting evidence of a more explicitly phraseological nature is provided in a recent study by Groom (2005). Using the same two corpora that will be studied later in this chapter, Groom analysed the kinds of evaluative meanings made by the 'introductory *it*' grammar patterns *it* + **link verb** + **adjective** + **that-clause** and *it* + **link verb** + **adjective** + **to-infinitive clause** (Francis *et al.*, 1996) in book reviews in the disciplines of history and literary criticism. This study identified similarities as well as differences in the datasets obtained from each corpus, although only the differences provided strong indications of underlying epistemological values. Of these, perhaps the most striking examples are provided by the pattern variant *it seems*. In history book reviews, introductory *it* patterns beginning with *it seems* are more likely to evaluate claims in terms of their likelihood or factual correctness:

(1) **It seems clear**, though Muirhead has not been able to find conclusive evidence, that anti-Semitic feeling impeded his promotion.

(2) Given the imbalance in conventional forces in Europe at the time, **it seems unlikely** that British and American troops were much more than expensive hostages.

In literary criticism, in contrast, these patterns are much more likely to offer a negative evaluation of the judgement of the person making the claim:

(3) His claim is well-taken, but **it seems odd** to make such a claim about a poem rhetorically aimed at the 'fit though few'.

(4) Surely, the history of readings of 'To Autumn' bears out Bennett's point that the political has been repressed by its readers, but **it seems overingenuous** to suggest that this is a function of the poem's 'strategic silencing' of such concerns.

Observations such as these suggest marked differences in epistemological comportment even among disciplines within the same knowledge domain. Whereas historical argumentation seems to be oriented firmly towards the impersonal evaluation of claims, or of the evidence upon which claims are based, it seems that in literary criticism 'the quality of [the critic's] whole sensibility is up for judgement' (Bazerman, 1981, pp. 378–79).

This chapter aims not only to contribute to the strand of analysis reviewed above, but also to extend it in one important respect. Whereas previous studies have tended to focus more or less exclusively on the characteristic ways in which disciplinary knowledge claims are evaluated in book reviews, my analysis also aims to take the language of the disciplinary knowledge claims themselves into account. My hypothesis is that disciplinary content meanings, such as *the imbalance in conventional forces in Europe at the time* or *the poem's 'strategic silencing' of such concerns* in examples (2) and (4) above, are just as likely to be expressed in phraseological form as evaluations are, and are thus just as likely to reflect and reproduce discipline-specific epistemologies. The problem, of course, concerns how such phraseologies are to be extracted from corpus data. A solution to this methodological problem will be introduced in the next section.

From closed-class keywords to semantic sequences

Although perfectly valid on its own terms, the deductive, 'corpus-based' methodology used in Groom (2005) is less than ideal for the purposes of this chapter, for the simple reason that it involves specifying objects for concordance analysis on an *a priori* basis. While it is entirely feasible to draw up a prespecified list of features for studying some linguistic phenomena (evaluation being a case in point), it is much more difficult to imagine how one would go about compiling an *a priori* list of phraseologies expressing the epistemological property of reiterativeness. What is needed instead, then, is a more inductive, 'corpus-driven' approach (Tognini-Bonelli, 2001), in which the initial process of selecting items for qualitative concordance study is delegated to a computer algorithm.

The inductive approach selected for the present study is keywords analysis (Scott and Tribble, 2006). Keywords analysis centres on the qualitative concordance analysis of a set of words which have been identified by a computational procedure as being statistically significant, or 'key', in a specialized corpus, when compared against a larger and more general reference corpus.

Whereas most keywords analysts focus principally or exclusively on the nouns, verbs and adjectives in a given keywords list, I will follow Gledhill (2000) and Groom (2007) in focusing exclusively on words belonging to 'closed' grammatical classes (e.g. conjunctions, determiners, prepositions and pronouns). As I have argued in more detail elsewhere (Groom, forthcoming), this strategy is much more promising than it might at first seem. First of all, closed class words are by far the most frequent words in any corpus (in English, at least), so an analysis of the phraseological properties of even a small selection of such words will guarantee coverage of a substantial proportion of a corpus. Furthermore, obtaining such a subset by means of a statistical keywords analysis means that the researcher can be reasonably confident that the words in question are significantly associated with that corpus, and thus by extension with the disciplinary discourse that the corpus represents.

Most importantly of all, conducting exhaustive quantitative and qualitative analyses of random concordance samples of closed-class keywords allows the researcher to identify and make statements about 'semantic sequences' (Hunston, 2008), recurrent sequences of meanings, individual instances of which may have very different surface realizations, but which nonetheless exhibit sufficient underlying regularity to be classified as instances of the same phraseology. To illustrate, consider examples (5) to (7) below, which come from a corpus linguistic study of research articles in history and literary criticism (Groom, 2007):

(5) a tidal wave of conservative loyalism

(6) masculine images of cigar smoke and stiff wool

(7) the problem of punctuation

On the face of it, these three phrases have nothing in common beyond their basic structural properties as postmodified noun phrases with *of* as their central linking preposition. As such, they would not be identified as instances of the same phraseology (or indeed as phraseological at all) by automated procedures such as lexical bundle analysis, which searches for repetitions of strings of exactly the same orthographic word-forms (e.g. Biber *et al.*, 2004; Hyland, 2008; Oakey, 2009). However, the high degree of surface variation in these three phrases belies the fact that exactly the same sequence of semantic elements underpins all three of them. Specifically, the noun phrase that follows *of* describes an abstract or concrete phenomenon of some kind, and the noun phrase that precedes *of* conceptualizes that phenomenon in a particular way. *Conservative loyalism* is being conceptualized as *a tidal wave*; *cigar smoke and stiff wool* as *masculine images*; and *punctuation* as a *problem*.

Groom (2007) interprets this CONCEPTUALIZATION + *of* + PHENO-MENON sequence as an indicator of epistemological reiterativeness, and notes that it accounts for 12 per cent of all instances of *of* in a corpus of history research articles, and an even more impressive 24 per cent of all instances of *of* in a comparable corpus of research articles in literary criticism. Given that *of* is the second most frequent word in both of these corpora, these are very significant observations indeed.

We will return to these findings later on in this chapter. For the moment, the key point to note is that, although they are not the easiest type of phraseology to identify, semantic sequences are nevertheless a particularly useful focus for corpus linguistic studies of specialized discourses because they are empirical observations of 'what is often said' in these discourses (Hunston, 2008, p. 272). Accordingly, semantic sequences will form the central focus of the analysis to be reported in the remainder of this chapter.

Corpora, keywords and concordance analysis

An overview of the two computerized corpora to be studied in this chapter is given in Table 7.1. As can be seen, HistRev (the history book reviews corpus) and LitRev (the literary criticism book reviews corpus) are of unequal size and composition. This being the case, all quantitative comparisons in the analysis that follows will be based on normalized figures, which describe the number of times a feature occurs (or is estimated to occur based on the analysis of a sample of the data) per million words in each corpus.

Table 7.1   Basic composition data for HistRev and LitRev

	HistRev	*LitRev*
Word tokens	3,200,810	1,011,238
Texts	4,017	685
Sources	American Historical Review	Essays in Criticism
	English Historical Review	Early Modern Literary Studies
		Journal of Modern Literature
		Nineteenth Century Literature
		Romanticism on the Net
Sample period	1999–2003	1994–2003

Keyword lists were obtained by comparing each corpus separately against the 90-million-word written component of the British National Corpus. This 'discourse-external' mode of comparison was preferred over other possible comparison types, in order to allow any similarities as well as differences that might exist between the two corpora to appear. (Comparing HistRev and LitRev against each other or against an external reference corpus of book reviews spanning a range of academic disciplines would strongly bias the analysis towards the identification of differences or unique features.)

Table 7.2   Distribution and frequency per million words of key prepositions across HistRev and LitRev

	HistRev	*LitRev*
against	672	not key
among	752	371
as	9,598	12,082
between	1,698	1,833
beyond	252	290
by	6,159	not key
despite	362	234
in	24,357	23,618
of	47,087	49,533
through	1,001	1,064
throughout	280	259
upon	not key	568
within	699	713

The keywords procedure described above identified 48 closed-class keywords in total. (Full lists of these keywords, together with frequency data and statistical keyness scores, can be found in Groom, 2007). As space does not permit a discussion of all of these items in this chapter, it is necessary to select a subset of keywords for closer study here. *En bloc*, the 13 prepositions identified by the keywords procedure constitute the largest grammatical word class in the data as a whole, and thus present themselves as an obvious candidate group for analysis. Furthermore, previous studies using a closed-class keywords methodology to study specialized discourses have found prepositions to provide particularly fertile points of departure for concordance-based analysis (cf. Gledhill, 2000; Groom, 2007; for theoretical discussion see Hunston, 2008). Accordingly, the discussion that follows will be based on an analysis of the 13 key prepositions listed in Table 7.2.

Principal findings of the study

Phraseologies describing reiterative epistemological processes, or indicating the importance of such processes, were found to be a substantial feature of the concordance data for 5 of the 13 statistically key prepositions listed earlier. (The other prepositions were found to be relevant to different epistemological values suggested by Becher (1989), but for reasons of space cannot be discussed here.) I will begin by looking at by far the most frequent of these, *of*.

One of the most frequent semantic sequences emerging from the concordance data for *of* in both HistRev and LitRev is one that was introduced earlier in this chapter, CONCEPTUALIZATION + *of* + PHENOMENON. As argued in Groom (2007), this phraseology gives very clear indications of the importance of reiterativeness within the epistemologies of both history and literary criticism. In book reviews, it most commonly serves to conceptualize phenomena as discipline-specific issues, problems, questions or themes. In some instances, it is clear from the context provided by the concordance line that a phenomenon is being conceptualized as such for the first time:

(8) Borer explores *the question of how Vietnam and Afghanistan affected the legitimacy of the superpower governments at home.* (HistRev)

(9) Increasing publication in book form and electronic media makes women's texts more widely available, posing *the question of 'what to make of this emerging body of material'.* (LitRev)

In other cases the reviewed author is presented as returning to an already well-established question, issue or theme in the discipline, although as examples (11) and (12) below indicate, positive evaluations are often bestowed upon scholars who approach these issues in a fresh or novel way:

(10) James Tracy tackles *the perennial problem **of** war finance*. (HistRev)

(11)[Stevenson] extends *the idea **of** the phallic sublime* to the androgynous sublime. (LitRev)

(12) Josephine A. Roberts addresses *the issue **of** voice* from a different angle. (LitRev)

This notion of reiterativeness as reconceptualization is also strongly present in the concordance data obtained for the key preposition *as*. These data contain a substantial number of sequences that indicate how a disciplinary phenomenon has been, or could be, conceptualized, either by the author or book under review, or by other members of the disciplinary discourse community in question:

(13) She portrays French public opinion in 1945 *as* driven by a thirst for three kinds of justice. (HistRev)

(14) The failure of Caliban's education can be seen *as* a failure to erase a repressed legacy. (LitRev)

(15) Rejecting standard portrayals of Sicily *as* simply a backward society caught up in feudal mentalities, Riall focuses on the negative impact of 'modernizing' reforms. (HistRev)

As with the CONCEPTUALIZATION + *of* + PHENOMENON sequences discussed above, the important point to note here is that the conceptualizations offered by such phraseologies in both disciplines are by definition subjective and interpretative, and thus highly contestable. There are many other ways in which French public opinion in 1945 or the failure of Caliban's education could be conceptualized. Indeed, the whole point of the sequence in example (15) above is to indicate that a 'standard' (and perhaps somewhat patronizing and simplistic) conceptualization of Sicily is being challenged by the fresh interpretation offered by the book under review.

This notion of reiterativeness as a matter of challenging disciplinary orthodoxies emerges even more strongly from the data for *against*, one of the two prepositions found to be key in HistRev only. My concordance analysis suggests that in around 15 per cent of all instances, this word participates in semantic sequences that present the argument (or a part of the argument) of the book under review as being opposed to some form of disciplinary orthodoxy:

(16) Her picture of prostitution in the expensive brothels goes *against* the popular view that they were dens of shame and sin. (HistRev)

(17) It argues directly *against* the long-established and influential Soviet interpretation that the Time of Troubles was predominantly a war between social classes over the development of serfdom. (HistRev)

(18) Gill is candid about presenting 'a defense counsel's brief' *against* the accusations that have typically been rendered against Eddy. (HistRev)

Similar observations to the above can also be made in the case of *beyond*. A substantial proportion of the data for this keyword in both corpora consists of sequences that describe or evaluate a person or thing (usually the author or book under review) as crossing disciplinary boundaries of various kinds, either by challenging disciplinary orthodoxies or opening up new ways of thinking about perennial questions in a given field of study. As can be seen in examples (19) and (20) below, such interpretative radicalism is usually evaluated in positive terms:

(19) McFarlane brings to the forefront important issues of narrative representation and gender identification *beyond* the traditional scope of gay studies. (LitRev)

(20) This is a crucial insight . . . Its widespread adoption would enable historians to go *beyond* the established preoccupation with formal institutions, usually those of central government, and to incorporate the informal agencies and unofficial agents of state power. (HistRev)

Indeed, the same kinds of sequence are also used to evaluate negatively those authors who do not fulfil this apparent epistemological remit:

(21) I was hoping that the author would offer some new insights or perspectives that would go *beyond* those already available. (LitRev)

(22) Though at times Brewer's book moves tentatively *beyond* previous scholarship, basically it rearranges the known picture and in no substantial way supersedes earlier work. (LitRev)

Comparable negative evaluations are also found in the concordance data for upon, a word that is only key in LitRev. Here, the cardinal sin is one of relying too heavily on secondary sources:

(23) Snider's treatment…relies rather too heavily *upon* contemporary critical theory and not enough upon close analysis of the texts. (LitRev)

(24) His account of the course of the addiction is unduly reliant *upon* Molly Lefebure's 1974 biography. (LitRev)

The data for upon also provide evidence of a more positive kind that value is attached (in literary criticism at least) to work that makes some form of critical break with the past. For example, about 4 per cent of all instances refer to emphatic arguments that are framed in contrast to antecedent work or received wisdom of some kind. This semantic sequence nearly always features a form of the verb *insist*:

(25) Awareness of the (mis)uses to which the figure of Thoreau has been put…leads Buell finally to insist *upon* the Henry David Thoreau who read in order to write. (LitRev)

(26) This book acknowledges the mediated nature of Romanticism as an-always-already theorized concept, yet it also insists *upon* the mediated state of theoretical 'metacommentary' that delivers Romanticism to us. (LitRev)

Upon also participates in sequences that evaluate a new book as casting new light on established issues:

(27) …using the letters sent between James and his favorites to shed light *upon* the relationships within which they were produced. (LitRev)

or as providing opportunities for critical reflection and reappraisal:

(28) The essays also provide occasion to reflect *upon* some of the difficulties inherent in bibliographical analysis. (LitRev)

(29) Michael Gamer's fine study addresses this need while it reflects *upon* and organizes those reassessments. (LitRev)

Summary and discussion of findings

The foregoing analysis has successfully identified a wide range of phraseologies expressing reiterative epistemological meanings in both corpora. The present research has also been successful in its aim of incorporating phraseologies expressing disciplinary content meanings as well as evaluative meanings into the analysis. Indeed, content sequences such as CONCEPTUALIZATION + *of* + PHENOMENON and PHENOMENON + *as* + CONCEPTUALIZATION occur far more frequently in both corpora than do the evaluative phraseologies revealed through analyses of the prepositions *against, beyond* and *upon*. Both groups are clearly important, nonetheless, as each one provides a different perspective on reiterative knowledge making practices in these two humanities discourses. Evaluative phraseologies highlight the idea that new knowledge creation in the humanities often involves challenging disciplinary shibboleths and crossing disciplinary boundaries. Content phraseologies bring to the fore the ways in which humanities scholars create new conceptual entities and subject those recognized conceptual entities to constant processes of reassessment and reformulation.

Table 7.3 provides quantitative and distributional data for each of the main groups of semantic sequences identified in HistRev and LitRev. The very high frequency figures obtained for many of these sequences in both corpora suggest that the values expressed by these phraseologies

Table 7.3 Frequency and distribution of 'reiterativeness' phraseologies across HistArt and LitArt

Keyword	Semantic sequence group	Frequency per million words	
		HistRev	*LitRev*
against	'Challenging Orthodoxy'	100	–
as	'Conceptualization'	2,303	4,349
	'Addition'	1,152	1,329
beyond	'Crossing Disciplinary Boundaries'	93	180
of	'Conceptualization'	6,121	8,421
upon	'Insisting'	–	23
	'Reflecting'	–	17
	'Illuminating'		2
	'Over-relying'		2
TOTALS		9,769	14,323

are fundamental to the epistemology of both disciplines. However, the figures in Table 7.3 also show that eight of the nine groups of semantic sequences identified above occur even more frequently in LitRev than they do in HistRev. This is very much in line with Groom's (2007) phraseological analysis of research articles in the same two disciplines.

Although these substantial quantitative differences do not in themselves prove that reiterative phraseologies are more characteristic of the discourse of literary criticism than they are of the discourse of history, they do certainly invite us to formulate such a claim as a working hypothesis to pursue in further studies. It will be interesting to find out whether phraseologies associated with other epistemological values sketched out in Becher's model (such as 'holism' or a 'concern with particulars') are also biased towards a particular discipline, or whether they are more equitably distributed.

Notwithstanding the clear quantitative and qualitative differences between the two corpora noted above, it is also important to acknowledge that the present research has also identified significant continuities between the two datasets, if only at a relatively high level of generality. If nothing else, these phraseological commonalities do seem to provide empirical support for the idea that disciplinary discourses can be divided into broad knowledge domains, and to that extent can be thought of as having certain shared epistemological characteristics. While this does not mean that we can therefore claim to have identified 'the phraseology of the humanities', it does suggest that we may have begun to think about academic discourses in a rather different way: not as discrete and disconnected entities, but as complex networks of family resemblances (cf. Wittgenstein, 1953; Swales, 1990; Taylor, 2000).

Conclusions

This chapter has conducted a small-scale study of the relationship between phraseology and epistemology in two humanities disciplines. By focusing on a small group of prepositions, the analysis presented in this chapter has been able to identify a range of phraseological features that describe or indicate the essentially reiterative nature of knowledge creation in two humanities fields, history and literary criticism.

As this chapter has restricted itself to the analysis of one epistemological property within one knowledge domain, it is not possible at this stage to offer any firm or detailed conclusions about the precise nature of the relationship between phraseology and epistemology in the humanities, let alone in the disciplinary discourses of the academy as a whole. Nevertheless, I would argue that the chapter has been broadly successful in four important respects. Firstly, it has provided clear empirical support for the claim that phraseology and epistemology are inextricably interlinked, and that the former provides a window on the latter. Secondly, the results of the present analysis allow us to predict that there will be both continuities and differences in the phraseological profiles of different disciplines within a given knowledge domain. Thirdly, the chapter has demonstrated that the book review genre is an excellent forum for work that seeks to identify and analyse these continuities and differences. Fourthly and finally, the chapter has demonstrated both the value of closed-class keywords analysis as a general methodology for corpus-driven discourse analytic work, and the central importance of semantic sequences as an object of analysis in such work.

There are a number of ways in which the work done in this study can be further developed. It could be expanded by conducting analyses of the other humanities values identified in Becher's model. It could also be extended to the analysis of other word classes not discussed in this chapter, and beyond that to studies of phraseology and epistemology in other knowledge domains and other academic genres. Clearly, and to paraphrase Stubbs (1986), all of this is will be a matter of very prolonged and very detailed fieldwork. But while the challenges laid out in this research agenda are admittedly very great, I hope that this chapter has gone at least some way towards demonstrating that the descriptive and theoretical rewards of carrying out such an agenda will be even greater.

References

Bazerman, C. (1981) 'What Written Knowledge Does: Three Examples of Academic discourse', *Philosophy of the Social Sciences*, XI, 3, 361–87.

Becher, T. (1987) 'Disciplinary Discourse', *Studies in Higher Education*, XII, 3, 261–74.

Becher, T. (1989) *Academic Tribes and Territories: Intellectual Enquiry and the Culture of Disciplines* (Milton Keynes: SHRE/Open University Press).

Becher, T. (1994) 'The Significance of Disciplinary Differences', *Studies in Higher Education*, XIX, 2, 151–61.

Becher, T. and Trowler, P. (2001) *Academic Tribes and Territories: Intellectual Enquiry and the Culture of Disciplines*, 2nd edn (Buckingham: The Society for Research into Higher Education and Open University Press).

Biber, D., Conrad, S. and Cortes, V. (2004) ' "If You Look at…": Lexical Bundles in University Teaching and Textbooks', *Applied Linguistics*, XXV, 3, 371–405.

Francis, G., Manning, E. and Hunston, S. (1996) *Collins COBUILD Grammar Patterns 1: Verbs* (London: HarperCollins).

Gledhill, C. (2000) *Collocations in Science Writing* (Tübingen: Gunter Narr.).

Groom, N. (2005) 'Pattern and Meaning across Genres and Disciplines: An Exploratory Study', *Journal of English for Academic Purposes*, IV, 3, 257–77.

Groom, N. (2007) *Phraseology and Epistemology in Humanities Writing: A Corpus-Driven Study* (Unpublished PhD Thesis, University of Birmingham, UK).

Groom, N. (forthcoming) 'Closed-Class Keywords and Corpus-Driven Discourse Analysis' in M. Scott and M. Bondi (eds) *Keyness in Text* (Amsterdam: John Benjamins).

Holmes, J. and Nesi, H. (forthcoming) 'Verbal and Mental Processes in Academic Disciplines' in M. Charles, S. Hunston and D. Pecorari (eds) *Academic Writing: At the Interface of Corpus and Discourse* (London: Continuum).

Hunston, S. (2002) *Corpora in Applied Linguistics* (Cambridge: Cambridge University Press).

Hunston, S. (2008) 'Starting with the Small Words: Patterns, Lexis and Semantic Sequences', *International Journal of Corpus Linguistics*, XIII, 3, 271–95.

Hyland, K. (2000) *Disciplinary Discourses: Social Interactions in Academic Writing* (London: Longman).

Hyland, K. (2007) 'Different Strokes for Different Folks: Disciplinary Variation in Academic Writing' in K. Fløttum (ed.) *Language and Discipline Perspectives on Academic Discourse* (Newcastle: Cambridge Scholars Publishing), 89–108.

Hyland, K. (2008) ' "As Can Be Seen": Lexical Bundles and Disciplinary Variation', *English for Specific Purposes*, XXVII, 1, 4–21.

Moreno, A. I. and Suárez, L. (2008) 'A Study of Critical Attitude across English and Spanish Academic Book Reviews', *Journal of English for Academic Purposes*, VII, 1, 15–26.

Motta-Roth, D. (1998) 'Discourse Analysis and Academic Book Reviews: A Study of Text and Disciplinary Cultures' in I. Fortanet, S. Posteguillo, J. C. Palmer and J. F. Coll (eds) *Genre Studies in English for Academic Purposes* (Castelló de la Plana: Publicacions de la Universitat Jaume I), 29–58.

North, S. (2005) 'Disciplinary Variation in the Use of Theme in Undergraduate Essays, *Applied Linguistics*, XXVI, 3, 431–52.

Oakey, D. J. (2009) 'Fixed Collocational Patterns in Isolexical and Isotextual Versions of a Corpus' in P. Baker (ed.) *Approaches to Corpus Linguistics* (London: Continuum), 142–60.

Parry, S. (1998) 'Disciplinary Discourse in Doctoral Theses', *Higher Education*, XXXVI, 3, 273–99.

Scott, M. and Tribble, C. (2006) *Textual Patterns: Key Words and Corpus Analysis in Language Education* (Amsterdam: John Benjamins).

Sinclair, J. McH. (2003) *Reading Concordances* (Harlow: Pearson Education).

Sinclair, J. McH. (2004) *Trust the Text: Language, Corpus and Discourse* (London: Routledge).

Stubbs, M. (1986) 'A Matter of Prolonged Field Work: Notes toward a Modal Grammar of English', *Applied Linguistics*, VII, 1, 1–25.

Swales, J. (1990) *Genre Analysis: English in Academic and Research Settings* (Cambridge: Cambridge University Press).

Taylor, G. (2000) 'The Generic and the Disciplined: Can Universal and Particular Be Reconciled?' in G. Crosling, T. Moore and S. Vance (eds) *The Learning Dimension: Proceedings of the Third National Language and Academic Skills Conference* (Melbourne: Monash University), 156–62.

Tognini-Bonelli, E. (2001) *Corpus Linguistics at Work* (Amsterdam: John Benjamins).

Wittgenstein, L. (1953) *Philosophical Investigations* (Oxford: Blackwell).

Part III

Cross-Linguistic Variation

8
(Non-)Critical Voices in the Reviewing of History Discourse: A Cross-Cultural Study of Evaluation*

Rosa Lorés Sanz

Book reviews: an evaluative genre?

In the last few years book reviews have become central to the exploration of academic genres. But, how evaluative is this evaluative genre? Much has been said and written about evaluation. This 'elusive concept' (Bondi and Mauranen, 2003, p. 269) has been approached from a variety of perspectives and under a myriad of labels (e.g. evaluation, modality, stance, appraisal) that overlap, combine or separate in different ways. Thompson and Hunston (2000, p. 5) offer us a definition of evaluation which reads as follows: '[evaluation is] the broad cover term for the expression of the speaker or writer's attitude or stance towards, viewpoint on, or feelings about the entities or propositions that he or she is talking about'. Defined in this way evaluation covers not only attitude and modality, but also the values ascribed to the entities and propositions which are evaluated. Such broad conceptualization is advantageous for the study undertaken here, because it allows us to observe not only how the relationship writer-reader is constructed and maintained but also what the writers' disciplinary community value-system is and how it is manifested in language.

When focusing on evaluation in academic writing, again a number of labels emerge, most commonly 'academic criticism' (Salager-Meyer and Alcaraz Ariza, 2003) or 'academic conflict' (Burgess and Fagan, 2002; Fagan and Martín Martín, 2002–03; Salager-Meyer *et al.*, 2003; *inter alia*). Most recently, the concept of 'evaluative act' (Suárez, 2006) and, subsequently, 'critical act' (Moreno and Suárez, 2008a, b) has been developed, which complements previous approaches to the analysis of evaluation (e.g. Hyland, 2000) by establishing functionality – rather than grammaticality – as the criterion for identification of evaluative units. The cross-cultural standpoint which interests us here has been adopted to explore differences for instance, between Chinese and English (Bloch and Chi, 1991; Taylor and Chen, 1991), between English, French and Spanish (Salager-Meyer *et al.*, 2003), between English and French (Salager-Meyer *et al.*, 2005), between English and Italian (Giannoni, 2006), and, very exhaustively, between Spanish and English (Salager-Meyer and Alcaraz Ariza, 2003; Suárez, 2006; Moreno and Suárez, 2008a, b). Moreover, evaluation has also been analysed in academic book reviews from a cross-disciplinary perspective (Motta-Roth, 1998; Hyland, 2000; Tse and Hyland, 2006).

The research presented here intends to contribute to the cross-cultural analysis of this evaluative academic genre. In particular, the present study aims to explore to what extent the same disciplinary community (that of historians) use book reviews (BRs) for the same purposes when working in two different languages, Spanish and English and, therefore, in two different cultural contexts. Or rather, whether the linguistic/cultural factor influences the critical profile of BRs when dealing with the same discipline. To draw conclusions on this respect the present study will first explore the degree to which both positive and negative evaluative acts are used in history BRs in English and Spanish, and then the distribution of those evaluative acts along the texts in both contexts of use, following the move structure of BRs described by Motta-Roth (1998). A distinction is made between positive acts, in which praise towards the text or an aspect of it is expressed, and negative acts, which evaluate the text or an aspect of it in negative terms. The quantitative results yielded from this contrastive study will then be read in the light of the data provided by a group of specialized informants. My aim here is to assess whether a different degree of use of positive and negative evaluative acts and a different distribution of these acts along the texts can be explained in the light of different expectations and different conventions in the two linguistic communities where history BRs are given shape.

Corpus and method

For the purposes of the present study, a corpus of 60 BRs (30 in English and 30 in Spanish) was collected to make up what is understood to be a comparable corpus (Connor and Moreno, 2005; Moreno, 2008).

Therefore, all the BRs under study were complied with the following conditions:

- they were book reviews, and not book notes or book commentaries;[1]
- they were successful pieces of writing in the sense that they had been published in prestigious journals (see below for the selection of journals);
- they were published between the years 2000 and 2007;
- the texts within each subcorpus were comparable in length;
- all the BRs were single-authored;
- all the BRs were written by different authors;
- all the BRs referred to just one book. Reviews of edited books, coordinated books or proceedings from conferences were discarded;
- only reviews of books dealing with topics ascribed to contemporary history were selected; and
- all the book reviewers contributing to the journals in English were affiliated to British institutions, and all those contributing to the Spanish journals were affiliated to Spanish institutions.

Complying with the criteria mentioned above, the BRs were selected from three different journals in each language (ten BRs per journal). To ensure comparability of readership and quality, their inclusion in the European Reference Index for the Humanities (ERIH) of the European Science Foundation was checked as was their similarity in rank.[2]

The English journals comprised:

English Historical Review (Oxford Journals, ranked A in ERIH)
History of European Ideas (Elsevier, ranked B in ERIH)
History Workshop Journal (Oxford Journals, ranked A in ERIH)

The Spanish journals comprised:

Cuadernos de Historia Contemporánea (Universidad Complutense de Madrid, ranked B in ERIH)
Hispania: Revista Española de Historia (Consejo Superior de Investigaciones Científicas, ranked A in ERIH)
Pasado y Memoria (Universidad de Alicante, ranked B in ERIH)

The corpus collected amounted to a total of 87,092 words. An effort was made to select BRs that were of comparable size. This was partly achieved within each subcorpus, as texts exceedingly long or short were discarded. However, it was found that history BRs were considerably longer in English than in Spanish. Thus the total number of words of the English subcorpus is 52,351 words (1,745 words per text on average) versus 34,741 words in the Spanish subcorpus (1,158 words per text on average). The fact that we were not dealing with comparable corpora in terms of extent was accounted for in the methods by normalizing results per 1,000 words.

To carry out the study proposed, a previous tagging needed to be made of each evaluative act – or 'critical act' – defined by Moreno and Suárez (2008a, b) as 'positive or negative remarks on a given aspect or sub-aspect of the book under review in relation to a criterion of evaluation with a higher or lower degree of generality' (2008b, p. 18). Thus defined, we are able to build on previous and very useful conceptualizations of evaluative units (see Hyland, 2000, 'praise and criticism') and we manage to avoid the limitations that identification based on the lexicogrammar might impose. In this way, evaluative acts are identified, following Moreno and Suárez (2008a, b), not as grammatical units but as functional units, that is, any structural unit, irrespective of its lexicogrammatical configuration, that contains both the (sub)aspect commented upon and what is said about it. Here are some examples which illustrate the way in which the tagging of critical acts was carried out:

Example 1

[1+] *Esa visión poligonal, que es en sí misma un interesante trazado del marco de conjunto para este tema durante todo el siglo,* [2+] *se realza extraordinariamente por la forma en que se traen a colación las citas de los discursos de los académicos en la segunda parte del trabajo.* [Such polygonal vision, which in itself is an interesting description of a general approach to this topic throughout the century, is made extraordinarily prominent by the way in which quotations of the academics' speeches are introduced in the second part of the book] (HSP1)[3]

Example 2

[1+] *Prof. Ringer's stylistic clarity is particularly welcome here,* [2-] *even if continued insistence on Weber's singular causal analysis' has an air of the emperor's new clothes about it.* (HWJ6)

As illustrated in examples (1) and (2), two evaluative acts can cluster within the limits of just one sentence: two positive acts in example (1) and one positive and one negative in the case of example (2). These instances show that it is essential for the correct counting of evaluative acts in the present study to discard the sentence as the unit of analysis and to establish functional criteria at the time of identifying units of praise and criticism. In fact, although the concept of evaluative act solves part of the problem, we still need to take into account that 'evaluation is a product not of lexicogrammar, but of discourse, and that a single evaluative item is often ambiguous until supported by other items that make the same point' (Thetela, 1997, p. 102).

Discrimination between positive and negative acts was carried out according to my own interpretative skills. Ambiguous or non-obvious cases were measured against the interpretation provided by two informants, one Spanish, one British, both of them specialists in the field of contemporary history. Findings on the quantitative side were then interpreted in the light of the answers to a questionnaire, which was submitted to all the 60 book reviewers whose texts were selected and the editors of the six journals chosen for the present study. Twelve book reviewers (six British and six Spanish) and three editors (two British and one Spanish) provided the information requested, a sample large enough to shed light on some of the quantitative findings gathered.

The critical profile of BRs in English and Spanish: results

In order to explore the degree and distribution of use of evaluation, all the positive and negative acts were identified in the 60 BRs which make up the corpus, yielding the following results:

Table 8.1 Positive and negative evaluative acts in British and Spanish history BRs. Normalized frequencies per 1,000 words and raw numbers in brackets

	Positive	*Negative*
British BRs	5.88 (308)	3.24 (170)
Spanish BRs	9.3 (326)	0.97 (34)

The following graph illustrates the (un)balance in both subcorpora between positive evaluation and criticism:

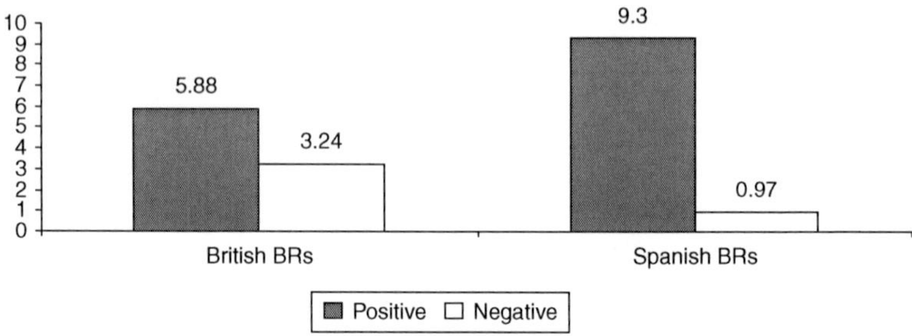

Graph 8.1 Positive and negative evaluative acts in British and Spanish history BRs. Normalized frequencies per 1,000 words

The data obtained after the normalization of evaluative acts (positive and negative) per 1,000 words in the two subcorpora show that, in general terms, there are similar frequencies in the total use of evaluative acts in both subcorpora: 9.17 in British BRs and 10.27 in Spanish BRs. That is, Spanish and British academics make their BRs evaluative to similar degrees. We also observe that in both texts positive evaluation is more frequent than negative evaluation: but this is as far as similarities go.

Differences, however, are quite relevant. To start with, there is a much greater imbalance between positive and negative evaluative acts in Spanish BRs than in the British texts, where the frequency of negative acts is quite substantial. On the contrary, criticism in Spanish BRs is roughly one tenth of the presence of praise as evaluative act. What we may infer so far, therefore, is that in general terms, Spanish historians are much more prone to evaluate their colleagues' research in positive terms in BRs than their British peers, and very much avoid criticizing their colleagues' contributions to the (non)advancement of the discipline. When compared to their Spanish peers, British book reviewers feel freer to pour negative opinions over their colleagues' publications if they deem it necessary.

To continue with the present study, it was also my aim to gather observations from the distribution of evaluative acts along the BRs. Previous studies on the distribution of evaluative features along the text have shown the close relation between distribution of evaluation and identification of rhetorical structure (Hyland, 2000; Suárez, 2006). To fulfil my purposes I used Motta-Roth's (1998) four-move schema for BRs, based on the assumption that texts belonging to a certain genre present certain general invariable features of rhetorical organization manifested in a general schematic representation of the genre. Motta-Roth did not include history BRs in her study, but she did choose disciplines that represented the traditional trichotomy of human, social and natural sciences. In addition to her study of linguistics, economics and chemistry, subsequent studies have shown her model to be useful in describing texts in other humanities disciplines (e.g. Suárez, 2005). Therefore, I considered it appropriate to draw on her model as a framework for exploring patterns of evaluation in my corpus of history BRs. Following Motta-Roth's (1998) model, four moves can be identified in terms of the function they play in the genre: Move 1 (Introducing the book), Move 2 (Outlining the book), Move 3 (Highlighting parts of the book) and Move 4 (Providing a closing evaluation of the book).[4] The four moves show a gradual change of focus which reveals a certain text flow. Thus, according to Motta-Roth, BRs present a more global view of the book at the beginning of the text (Move 1) where general information about the book is provided, placing it in the disciplinary context. Then, in Moves 2 and 3 there is a more detailed description of the book, and a focus on more specific aspects. Finally, Move 4 presents again a more general view and the appraisal of the book is given within the disciplinary context.

To explore how evaluation was distributed along the text, I first established the rhetorical structure of each BR in the corpus, following Motta-Roth's model. Once the four moves were identified in each text, a quantitative study was carried out on all the evaluative acts, positive and negative, which appeared in the corpus. A problematic aspect in the identification of evaluation was the case of evaluative acts in which both praise and criticism appeared in the same sequence. The use of praise-criticism pairs is considered as a mitigation strategy (Hyland, 2000) to attenuate the effects of criticism, which in itself is a face-threatening act. Examples (3) and (4) illustrate this case:

Example 3

[1-] *Its style will not excite,* [2+] but *diligent mining of the book will reward the conscientious reader.* (EHR2)

Example 4

[1-] *Y aunque el libro se hace muy corto dada la importancia de los temas y problemas planteados,* [2+] *se convierte también en una referencia clara y sintética de éstos.*

[And although the book seems short due to the relevance of the topics and issues it deals with, it also becomes a clear and synthetic reference for them.] (CHC9)

Sometimes the case was that several evaluative acts were chained in the same sequence:

Example 5

[1+] In a book that avoids patronizing *or moralizing the many disputed accounts presented throughout,* [2+] while *still showing just how constructed local and national histories are,* [3-] *this letter seemed oddly jarring.* (HWJ 5)

Example 6

[1+] *Aunque las páginas dedicadas a la noticia bibliográfica del combativo clérigo son justas,* [2-]quizá *resulten breves y* [3-] *el lector se queda con el deseo de saber más y,* sobre todo, [4-] *echa de menos algunos datos sobre la intimidad de quien se creyó –y esa fama tuvo– tan fervoroso católico.* (PM2)

[Although the pages devoted to the bibliographic note of the fighting clergyman are fair, they may be too few, and readers are left wanting more, and, above all, they feel the need for some information about the intimacy of someone who thought himself to be an ardent Catholic – for such was his reputation.]

In the present study, and for the sake of the quantitative analysis, each act appearing in a sequence or 'cluster' was counted as an instance.

It went beyond the scope of this study to explore the way clusters of evaluation influence readers' interpretation of texts. However, as the phenomenon of mitigation and the interpretation of evaluative acts as more or less critical cannot be ignored, observations were made as to where these mitigated acts tended to concentrate in BRs. Thus, the following data were gathered:

As may be observed, the use of clusters of praise-criticism as a mitigation strategy (Hyland, 2000) occurs in British BRs mainly in Move 3,

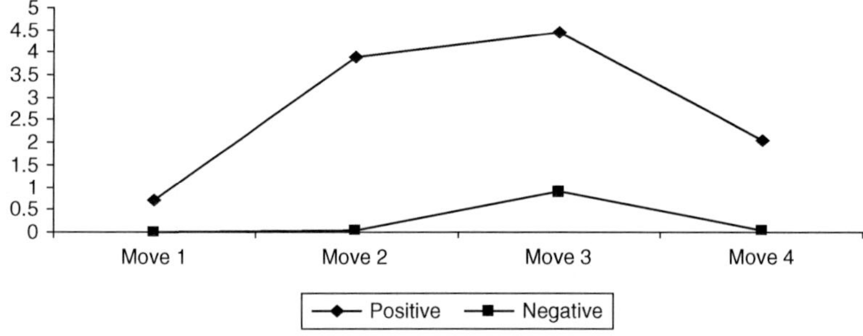

Figure 8.1 Distribution of clusters of evaluation in British and Spanish history BRs

Table 8.2 Clusters of evaluation (two or more evaluative acts in a sequence) in British and Spanish history BRs. Normalized frequencies per 1,000 words and raw numbers in brackets

	Move 1	*Move 2*	*Move 3*	*Move 4*
British BRs	4 (0.08)	3 (0.06)	32 (0.61)	5 (0.09)
Spanish BRs	1 (0.03)	1 (0.03)	5 (0.14)	11 (0.32)

where parts of the book or specific aspects of it are highlighted. As for Spanish BRs it is in Move 4, when a general appraisal of the book is given, that the evaluative acts are redressed. These two moves can in fact be considered as the more face threatening stages of the BR, which explains why it is here where mitigation strategies are found in the form of praise-criticism clusters.

Continuing with the exploration of evaluative acts, the quantitative study yielded the following results:

Table 8.3 Positive and negative evaluative acts in British and Spanish history BRs per move. Normalized frequencies per 1,000 words and raw numbers in brackets

	Move 1		*Move 2*		*Move 3*		*Move 4*	
	Positive	*Negative*	*Positive*	*Negative*	*Positive*	*Negative*	*Positive*	*Negative*
British BRs	0.74 (39)	0.09 (5)	1.85 (97)	0.28 (15)	2.63 (138)	2.42 (127)	0.66 (35)	0.42 (22)
Spanish BRs	0.69 (24)	0	3.91 (136)	0.02 (1)	4.43 (154)	0.89 (31)	2.04 (71)	0.05 (2)

In an attempt to visualize the distribution of evaluative acts in both subcorpora, the previous data were poured onto diagrams which could show us how evaluation flowed along the texts:

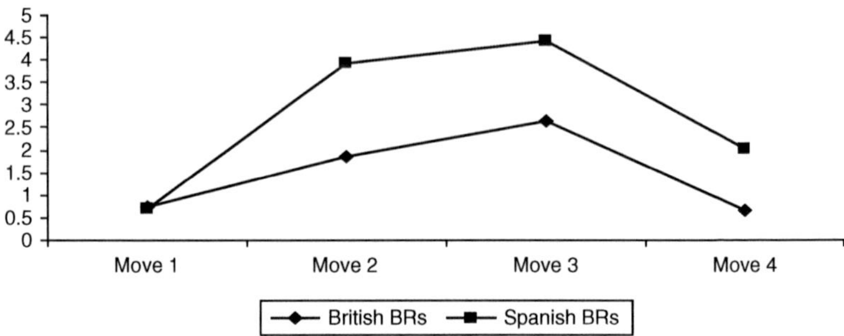

Figure 8.2 Distribution of positive evaluative acts per move in British and Spanish history BRs

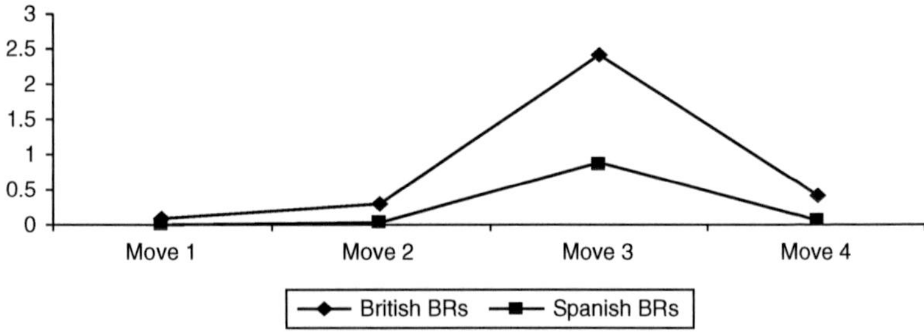

Figure 8.3 Distribution of negative evaluative acts per move in British and Spanish history BRs

When comparing the two graphs we do not observe many differences in the way positive and negative evaluation is distributed along British and Spanish BRs. What we find in both contexts is: (i) a tendency to praise the book in the central moves, both when general aspects of the book (structure and organization) are commented upon (Move 2) and when chapters or detailed aspects are under focus (Move 3); (ii) a tendency to criticize only specific aspects of the book (Move 3). This shows that the flow of evaluation is similar in both cultural contexts, with peaks of praise and criticism in the central parts of the BR. We may, therefore, infer that there are common, conventional generic patterns of evaluation distribution shared by the disciplinary community of historians in both cultures. The difference between both cultures lies, however, in the degree and the intensity with which those patterns are used.

Moreover, further conclusions can be drawn when exploring the way praise and criticism is distributed in each context:

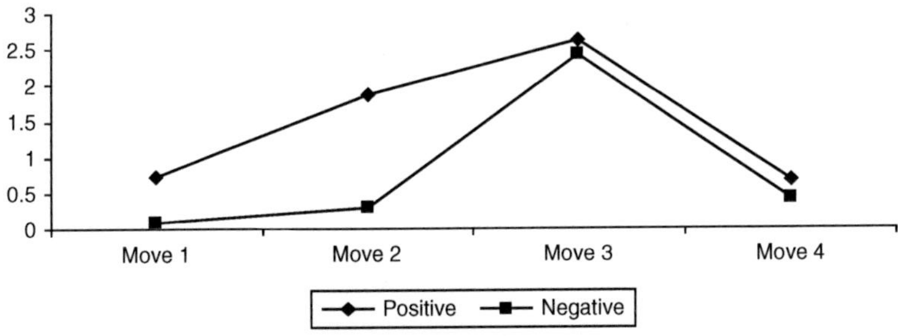

Figure 8.4 Distribution of positive and negative evaluative acts per move in British history BRs

As we observe in this graph, British book reviewers distribute their praise between Move 2 and Move 3 (positive criticism of both general and specific aspects of the book). Their negative evaluation, however, is focused on Move 3, when dealing with more specific aspects of the book, which provides support to Hyland's (2000, p. 48) claim that writers tend to criticize specific issues and praise more global features, which contribute to the dual purpose of book reviews: 'to provide an overview of the text for prospective readers while raising particular problematic issues for the field'. In Move 3, similar degrees of praise and criticism are offered. This is also the case in Move 4 (recommendation of book), where fewer evaluative acts are included but evaluation is both positive and negative. Move 1, in which the book is set in disciplinary context, favours positive evaluation rather than criticism.

Spanish book reviewers also make specific issues the focus of their negative evaluation (Move 3). However, whereas in British BRs positive and negative evaluation showed very similar results at this point, in Spanish BRs criticism makes a very shy appearance when compared to praise. As for Move 4 (recommendation of book), here again the presence of praise is overwhelming if compared to criticism. Move 1, in which the book is set in context, favours positive evaluation rather than criticism, as was the case in British BRs. The absence of criticism both of general

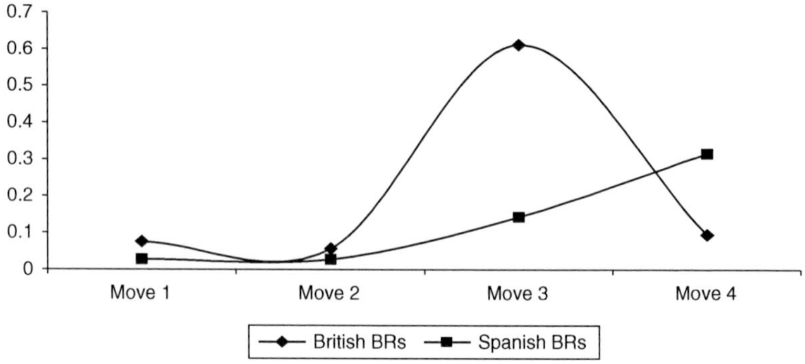

Figure 8.5   Distribution of positive and negative evaluative acts per move in Spanish history BRs

and specific issues in Spanish BRs might indicate, then, that in Spanish BRs issues of the field tend not to be problematized.

Discussion of results: what the professionals have to say

What we gather from the previous results is that Spanish and British book reviewers share conventions as to the degree of 'evaluativeness' and the distribution of evaluation in general. Both disciplinary cultures keep the presence of evaluative acts low in the initial stages and show their view of the book in Move 2, when dealing with general aspects, and in Move 3, when highlighting, for better or for worse, specific aspects of the book. However, they differ in the way that praise and criticism flows along the text: British book reviewers tend to praise general aspects of the book under review; they tend to evaluate specific issues positively or negatively to the same degree and recommend or not the book under review. They tend to use mitigation strategies in the form of praise-criticism clusters in Move 3, when discussing specific aspects of the book, as it is at this point that more negative evaluative acts are used. Spanish book reviewers, on the contrary, tend to praise both general and specific aspects of the book and usually recommend its reading. Criticism is scantly used when highlighting specific points and, in the final stage, when offering general appraisal, and it is precisely at this final stage that mitigation in the form of clusters (praise-criticism) appears.

It is reasonable to cater for these functional and structural divergences between Spanish and English history BRs in terms of a different conceptualization of the genre of the book review in the two cultural milieux as to what its main purpose and function should be. To explore such path, a questionnaire was sent to all the book reviewers and editors of the journals involved in the present study. Although not all of them replied, the answers provided by those who did are enlightening and help to set in frame the results mentioned above and somehow help to see how editors and reviewers corroborate the data drawn from the quantitative study with their views and expectations.

To start with, absence of criticism (although not of evaluation) in Spanish BRs is acknowledged by the book reviewers in answers like this one:[5]

> The purpose of a book review should be to analyze which new elements it contributes to the topic of discussion particularly and more generally to the discipline. It should contain some kind of state of the question, references to who the author is, what the book is about, and what the materials and sources are, and which novelties it contributes with, although sometimes in Spain they become mere summaries of books. (Spanish Informant 3)

In their view, the lack of critical voices in Spanish BRs is related to the issue of trusting or not the information and opinions offered in BRs:

> I have the impression that some reviews just reveal hatred towards the author of the book or a relationship with him/her, who frequently is the person who commissions it. (Spanish Informant 4)

British informants, on the contrary, expressed their trust in the work of review editors as gatekeepers and the prestige of the journal as a guarantee against bias:

> Discounting for known positions, they [book reviews] are no more unreliable/subjective than anything else academic. The incentive structure is generally sufficient to produce reviews that are 'trustworthy', and knowing the review editors their reputation is sufficient as gatekeepers. (British informant 1)

Thus, it seems that even if Spanish and British reviewers and review editors share expectations that this academic genre will be both informative and evaluative, there is a general mistrust in the Spanish academic community of historians with respect to the function of book reviews as an evaluative genre. In fact, as revealed by our quantitative study, critical evaluation is absent from Spanish history BRs.

Then, are book reviews in the Spanish context truly 'the public evaluation of research' (Lindholm-Romantschuk, 1998 in Tse and Hyland, 2006, p. 179)? Whereas no British informant seemed to question their role as disciplinary sites for knowledge construction and discussion, the following are two comments, by a Spanish editor and a Spanish informant, who question the role of BRs as an arena for disciplinary debate:

> Scientific debate is hardly welcomed, and any objection – of approach or method – is interpreted as offensive, if not by the author him/herself, at least by the bulk of the discipline community. (Spanish Editor 3)

> Intellectual dialogue suffers from this lack of public critical debate. The Spanish intellectual production system is funded in such a way that it doesn't need seniors to take part [in book reviewing]. (Spanish Informant 6)

It seems then that participants in Spanish history book reviewing are well aware of the limited role that BRs play as sites for discipline advancement. This fact may be linked to the information gathered regarding the senior or junior status of book reviewers, as this factor was hypothesized to be influential when it came to writing a BR in a more or less critical way. In the British case they seem to be written both by seniors and juniors depending on different factors, such as expertise and the seniority of the book author. With regard to Spanish book reviewers, they mostly agreed that BRs tended to be left in the hands of the junior researchers because of the low rating given to BRs in CVs and professional activity in Spain. The fact, then, that Spanish BRs do not serve as a platform for disciplinary discussion and debate might explain why it is very common for junior researchers to be the ones who usually write them:

> It is usually young researchers who write them, because they are working with bibliography and it's a good way to start publishing and to get to know the authors. Unfortunately, senior researchers do no tend to write book reviews. . . . Seniors make use of more efficient ways to exert power: they control the most important publishing houses, they are part of scientific committees, they evaluate research

programs and assess candidates for tenure or as researchers. (Spanish Informant 6)

Although there is common agreement that BRs fulfill two primary functions, informative and evaluative (Hyland, 2000; Gea-Valor, 2000–01; Salager-Meyer *et al.*, 2005; Suárez, 2006; Moreno and Suárez, 2008a, b; *inter alia*), we can certainly conclude from the present study that the cultural variable influences the degree of 'evaluativeness' history BRs display and thus the primary function they fulfil. This double informative/evaluative role obviously needs to be called into question if one of the functions, that of evaluation, is clearly not performed to the same extent in one of the academic cultural contexts under analysis. This might lead us also to problematize Spanish history BRs as an evaluative academic genre. If purposes differ, or at least if they are not fulfilled to the same extent, are we really dealing with the same academic genre? As far as the present study goes, we are not.

Based on Rothery and Stenglin's (in Martin and Rose, 2008) typology of 'response genres',[6] we could ascribe Spanish and English BRs to two different types of 'text responses': the 'review' and the 'critical response'. We might argue that the 'review' aims at informing the reader about the content of a new publication. The writer of reviews allows a certain degree of evaluation, both of general and specific aspects, but in very positive terms. The absence of a real critical view makes the positive assessment act not as an evaluative parameter but as a strategy of what we might call in-group solidarity, thus strengthening the links between the book reviewer, the author of the book and the reader of both the book and the book review, all of them belonging to the same disciplinary community. On the other hand, writers of 'critical responses' assign a twofold function to their texts: informing the reader about new research and assessing critically both general and specific points of the book under review, thus contributing to the development of the discipline by constructing and discussing new knowledge.

Whereas, in the study presented here, British history BRs seem to follow the pattern of a critical response, Spanish BRs behave clearly as mere rehashes. The reasons for this may be found in the size of the academic community the reviewer belongs to – as Moreno and Suárez (2008b) point to – and the scope of distribution of the journal.[7] However, other factors may also contribute to the explanation for such a divergent profile, which might have to do with socio-cultural beliefs and attitudes ingrained in the corresponding writing cultures. What the present study certainly proves is that further studies across disciplines and across other languages may help support the conclusion that the cultural and linguistic landscape in which a book review is given shape strongly influences the (a) critical voice of their writers.

Notes

*This research has been carried out within the framework of the research project InterLAE, financially supported by the Diputación General de Aragón (245–122) and the Ministerio de Educación y Ciencia (HUM2005–03646). The title of the project is 'El inglés y la ciencia: la voz del autor en la expresión y difusión del conocimiento científico. Análisis contrastivo de los recursos lingüísticos de la valoración en un corpus de textos académicos'. I am also grateful to my colleague, Dr Pilar Mur, for her insightful comments on the contents of this chapter and to both the British and Spanish informants for their generous and valuable answers to the questionnaires.

1. See Suárez (2006) for differences between book note/notice (100–300 words), book reviews (400–3000 words) and book commentaries (more than 5000 words).
2. I would like to thank Dr Ana Moreno for her precious help and time when I was designing the corpus for the present study.
3. Critical acts were tagged with numbers followed by the symbols + or – indicating the polarity of the evaluation provided. As for the identification of sources, abbreviations have been used for all the six journals: EHR (*English Historical Review*), HEI (*History of European Ideas*), HWJ (*History Workshop Journal*), HSP (Hispania), CHC (*Cuadernos de Historia Contemporánea*), PM (*Pasado y Memoria*). Then each of the BRs selected from each journal has been numbered from one to ten.
4. Motta-Roth (1998) provides a much more complex model in which ten different subfunctions are identified in the four moves.
5. All the translations of the Spanish informants' answers are the author's.
6. Rothery and Stenglin (1997) devised a typology of 'text responses' to classify the way students in Australian schools evaluated the stories they read or viewed: 'personal response', 'review', 'interpretation' and 'critical response'.
7. The journals selected in English, published by two main publishing houses (Elsevier and Oxford Journals) have a much wider international distribution than the Spanish journals (published by universities and the Spanish National Research Council).

References

Bloch, J. and Chi, L. (1991) 'A Comparison of the Use of Citations in Chinese and English Academic Discourse' in D. Belcher and G. Braine (eds) *Academic Writing in a Second Language* (New Jersey: Ablex), 231–77.
Bondi, M. and Mauranen, A. (2003) 'Evaluation in Academic Discourse', *Journal of English for Academic Purposes*, II, 4 (Special Issue), 269–71.

Burgess, S. and Fagan, A. (2002) '(Kid) Gloves On or Off? Academic Conflict in Research Articles across the Disciplines', *Revista Canaria de Estudios Ingleses*, XLIV, 79–96.

Connor, U. and Moreno, A. I. (2005) 'Tertium Comparationis: A Vital Component in Contrastive Research Methodology' in P. Bruthiaux, D. Atkinson, W. G. Eggington, W. Grabe, and V. Ramanathan (eds) *Directions in Applied Linguistics: Essays in Honor of Robert B. Kaplan* (Clevedon, England: Multilingual Matters), 153–64.

Fagan, A. and Martín Martín, P. (2002–03) 'Competing for a Research Space: The Criticism of One's Own Scientific Community', *Revista de Lenguas para Fines Específicos*, IX, 10, 139–50.

Gea-Valor, M. L. (2000–01) 'The Pragmatics of Positive Politeness in the Book Reviews', *RESLA*, XIV, 145–59.

Giannoni, D. S. (2006) 'Expressing Praise and Criticism in Economic Discourse: A Comparative Analysis of English and Italian Book Reviews' in G. Del Lungo Camiciotti, M. Dossena and B. Crawford Camiciottoli (eds) *Variation in Business and Economics Discourse. Diachronic and Genre Perspectives* (Rome: Officina Edizioni), 126–38.

Hyland, K. (2000) *Disciplinary Discourses: Social Interaction in Academic Writing* (London: Longman).

Martin, J. and Rose, D. (2008) *Genre Relations: Mapping Culture* (London: Equinox).

Moreno, A. I. (2008) 'The Importance of Comparable Corpora in Cross-Cultural Studies' in U. Connor, E. Nagelhout and W. Rozycki (eds) *Contrastive Rhetoric: Reaching to Intercultural Rhetoric* (Amsterdam: John Benjamins), 25–41.

Moreno, A. I. and Suárez, L. (2008a) 'A Framework for Comparing Evaluation Resources across Academic Texts', *Text & Talk*, XXVIII, 4, 501–21.

Moreno, A. I. and Suárez, L. (2008b) 'A Study of Critical Attitude across English and Spanish Academic Book Reviews', *Journal of English for Academic Purposes*, VII, 1, 15–26.

Motta-Roth, D. (1998) 'Discourse Analysis and Academic Book Reviews: A Study of Text and Disciplinary Cultures' in I. Fortanet, S. Posteguillo, J. C. Palmer and J. F. Coll (eds) *Genre Studies in English for Academic Purposes* (Castelló de la Plana: Publicacions de la Universitat Jaume I), 29–58.

Rothery, J. and Stenglin, M. (1997) 'Entertaining and Instructing: Exploring Experience through Story' in F. Christie and J. R. Martin (eds) *Genre and Institutions: Social Processes in the Workplace and School* (London: Pinter), 231–63.

Salager-Meyer, F. and Alcaraz Ariza, M. A. (2003) 'Academic Criticism in Spanish Medical Discourse: A Cross-Generic Approach', *International Journal of Applied Linguistics*, XIII, 1, 96–114.

Salager-Meyer, F., Alcaraz Ariza, M. A. and Zambrano, N. (2003) 'The Scimitar, the Dagger and the Glove: Intercultural Differences in the Rhetoric of Criticism in Spanish, French and English Medical Discourse (1930–1995)', *English for Specific Purposes*, XXII, 3, 223–47.

Salager-Meyer, F., Alcaraz Ariza, M. A. and Pabón, M. (2005) 'The Prosecutor and the Defendant: Contrasting Critical Voices in French- and English-Written Academic Book Reviews' in K. Fløttum (ed.) *Language and Discipline Perspectives on Academic Discourse* (Newcastle: Cambridge Scholars Publishing), 109–27.

Suárez, L. (2005) 'Is Evaluation Structure-Bound?' in E. Tognini-Bonelli and G. Del Lungo Camiciotti (eds) *Strategies in Academic Discourse* (Amsterdam: John Benjamins), 117–32.

Suárez, L. (2006) *Modes of Evaluation and Rhetorical Patterns: A Contrastive Study of English and Spanish Book Reviews* (Unpublished PhD Thesis, University of Léon, Spain).

Taylor, G. and Chen, T. (1991) 'Linguistic, Cultural and Sub-Cultural Issues in Contrastive Discourse Analysis: Anglo-American and Chinese Scientific Texts', *Applied Linguistics*, XII, 3, 319–36.

Thetela, P. (1997) 'Evaluated Entities and Parameters of Value in Academic Research Articles', *English for Specific Purposes*, XVI, 2, 101–18.

Thompson, G. and Hunston, S. (2000) 'Evaluation: An Introduction' in S. Hunston and G. Thompson (eds) *Evaluation in Text. Authorial Stance and the Construction of Discourse* (Oxford: Oxford University Press), 3–27.

Tse, P. and Hyland, K. (2006) 'Gender and Discipline: Exploring Metadiscourse Variation in Academic Book Reviews' in K. Hyland and M. Bondi (eds) *Academic Discourse across Disciplines* (Bern: Peter Lang), 177–202.

9
Academic Book Reviews in English and Spanish: Critical Comments and Rhetorical Structure

Ana I. Moreno and Lorena Suárez

Introduction

Academic journal book reviews appear at the end of many scientific journals allowing readers 'to keep abreast of new publications they may wish to acquire and provide a forum for the peer review of new theories and ideas' (Spink *et al.*, 1998, p. 364).

Although currently considered as serving two major socially-recognized functions – describing and evaluating a new publication – there has been a continuous tension between these two main purposes since this genre began to incorporate the reviewer's opinion on the book under review at the beginning of the nineteenth century (Hyland, 2000). In fact, recent literature still insists that a good critical book review should not solely inform readers about a particular book, but should also allow them to 'know a book and the judgement of the reviewer of it in relation to other books in the same area and to similar topics treated in them' (Orteza y Miranda, 1996, p. 195). This tension might be easily understood if we consider that reviewers participate in a context of interaction in which 'there is a direct, public, and often critical, encounter with a particular text, and therefore its author' (Hyland, 2000, p. 456). In this context, critical comments on the book can be seen as face-threatening acts that pose great risk of personal conflict. Consider the following two critical comments taken from academic book reviews of literature in English and Spanish respectively:

(1E) His insistence that Shakespeare's disapproval of hunting ... strikes me as questionable.

(1S) Podría decirse que el libro aporta pocas novedades y pocas sorpresas acerca de lo que ya sabíamos ... [It could be said that the book offers little that is new and few surprises in relation to what we already knew . . .] (Our own translation)

Such negative critical comments are likely to create a certain degree of interpersonal friction between the reviewer and the author of the book or its supporters. Therefore, avoiding criticism might be one strategy for minimizing the potential conflict. However, readers expect reviewers to make both negative and positive critical comments since after all they are the key elements that allow readers to judge the quality of a book (Spink *et al.*, 1998). In this situation, a question that is likely to concern many reviewers is how many critical comments and what type they should offer on the book in order to produce an acceptable *critical* book review. This question could be thought ill-considered since the amount and type of critical comments will depend on a number of factors: the quality of each book, its intended purpose, audience and argument, the interest that the reviewer feels, the reviewer's academic background, and so on. However, if we consider results from previous studies that have in one way or another explored critical comments in academic book reviews, we will soon realize that the question is in fact justifiable.

For one thing, it has been shown that providing more or fewer positive vs. negative comments in academic book reviews can be subject to general rhetorical tendencies favoured by broad disciplinary branches. For instance, in his study of praise and criticism in English published book reviews, Hyland (2000) demonstrates that on balance reviewers in the soft knowledge fields tend to be more negatively critical in their evaluations than those in the hard science fields. Also, the frequency and type of criticism is affected by socio-cultural factors across languages. For example, in a study of academic book reviews of literature across English and Spanish, Moreno and Suárez (2008a) reveal that not only do Spanish literary reviewers make far fewer critical comments than their Anglo-American counterparts, but also that their criticisms are almost exclusively positive in contrast to the typically balanced Anglo-American critical approach. Those findings are largely consistent with the observation of Giannoni (2006) for Italian and English reviews.

Thus there seem to be culturally different rhetorical solutions to the ongoing tension between the evaluative demands of this genre and the high interpersonal implications of evaluating a book written by a peer. It might therefore be strategically convenient for novice reviewers to take into account the book reviewing critical practices that are preferred in their own disciplinary contexts. A greater problem, however, may arise when communication is intercultural, such as when scholars from linguistic backgrounds other than English write in English for a wider audience. According to the contrastive rhetoric hypothesis (Kaplan, 2001), writers' first language (L1) rhetorical habits are likely to transfer when they write in a second language (L2). Thus, if Spanish literary scholars wrote an academic book review for an Anglo-American journal of literature without properly adapting their habitual critical approach, then they might have initial difficulties getting their texts accepted. Consider the following observations:

> [The Spanish biased approach would have the effect of] undermining the reliability and credibility of the reviewer and of the book's worth. (Personal e-mail communication with an Anglo-American editor from English studies)

> I ask for changes if the review is too one-sided. (E-mail interview with an Anglo-American editor)

> [Lavish praise could be] unwelcome as superficial and undiscriminating. (Hyland, 2000, p. 45)

Previous genre-based studies of academic book reviews in English have also shown that exemplars of this genre share a rhetorical organization of the text material into four main moves: introducing the book, outlining the book, highlighting parts of the books, and providing a closing evaluation of the book (Motta-Roth, 1998; Gea-Valor, 2000; Burgess and Fagan, 2004). This basic rhetorical structure has been corroborated across various disciplinary and socio-cultural contexts (De Carvalho, 2002; Suárez and Moreno, 2008). In relation to academic book reviews of literature, a question that remains unanswered is that of the relative weight that critical comments have within each move across the Anglo-American and the Castilian Spanish writing cultures. An answer to this question is also interesting because, as will be shown, the relative location of critical comments may have effects on the writer-reader interpersonal relationship that are also worth taking into account.

Thus our major aim in this chapter is to compare how critical comments – both positive and negative – made on the books under review in two comparable samples of academic book reviews of literature (the *LIBRES* corpus) typically distribute across the rhetorical moves that make up the basic book review structure developed by Motta-Roth (1998), thus extending the previously-mentioned research. We will also aim to explain the reasons for the identified distributions across the two *big* writing cultures under comparison in the light of information provided by a sample of the reviewers through e-mail interviews.

The corpus

The *LIBRES* corpus (*Literary Book Reviews in English and Spanish*) contains two samples of comparable (i.e., not translation pairs of) academic literary book reviews written by competent L1 British and North-American and Spanish writers. We chose the field of literary studies on the grounds that scholars from these two discourse communities interact less frequently cross-culturally than in other fields, with the exception of scholars in English departments. This would allow us to study the typical book reviewing behaviours and practices of scholars which are less likely to have been influenced by the globalization process increasingly affecting academic interactions in many fields.

Our corpus design took into account a number of variables that might affect the frequency and type of critical comments, introducing confounding factors. Examples of such factors are time of publication (2000–02), language variety used by the book reviewer (Anglo-American English and Castilian Spanish), place of publication of the book under review (UK, USA and Spain), the size of the audience (half of the Spanish journals also had an international readership), academic discipline and subdiscipline of the reviewed book (novel, drama, poetry, literary theory) and the length of the reviews. The need to control for these factors was suggested by the findings of Hyland (2000), Burgess (2002) and Salager-Meyer (2006). Table 9.1 shows that the two sub-corpora are also comparable in size, each consisting of 20 academic book reviews drawn from four journals well-known in the scholars' disciplinary communities.

Table 9.1   Size of the *LIBRES* corpus

	English	*Spanish*
Number of literary academic book reviews	20	20
Total number of words	21,382	22,084
Average number of words per book review	1,069.1	1,104.2

The rhetorical structure of literary academic book reviews

Method for identifying and quantifying rhetorical moves

The concept of rhetorical structure refers to how textual material is recurrently organized in exemplars of a given genre, when this material is analysed in functional terms (Swales, 1990). In order to analyse the basic rhetorical structure of the reviews in the *LIBRES* corpus, we used the genre-specific moves developed by Motta-Roth (1998) in her study on book reviews. This consisted of looking for text and content clues from which to infer the rhetorical functions of given passages in the reviews. A rhetorical move was defined as a stretch of discourse – irrespective of its linguistic realization – that performs a specific communicative function, representing a stage in the development of the overall structure of information commonly associated with this genre (cf. Swales, 1990; Motta-Roth, 1998) (see Table 9.2).

Table 9.2   Basic rhetorical structure of the reviews in the *LIBRES* corpus

---

Move 1. Introducing the book

(2E) Far more than a handbook to... *The Victorians and the Visual Imagination* is best understood as...

(2E) Los autores de esta obra plantean ya desde el título mismo el criterio que marcará el desarrollo evolutivo de su investigación, es decir, el rescate de...

Move 2. Outlining the book

(3E) Blain organizes the material in chronological order, with four substantive chapters... In the Introduction Blain offers... Chapter one covers... Chapter two examines... Chapter three is devoted to...

(3S) El libro se organiza en cinco partes... En la primera encontramos un capítulo inicial... La segunda parte está dedicada al estudio del... La siguiente sección es... En la cuarta parte, ..., queda patente...

Move 3. Highlighting parts of the book

(4E) If the chapter on... contributes to the latter aim, it does so in a manner that is too understated.

(4S) Se preocupa mucho menos de los aspectos..., y esto, tratándose de una monografía sobre..., resulta poco justificable.

Move 4. Providing closing evaluation of the book

(5E) If there is anything wanting in... it is that...: ... a gifted reader of Bowles' poetry who very certainly achieves her aim in demonstrating..., and that fully warrants a larger hearing.

(5S) En resumen, nos encontramos ante una edición sencilla, pero de calidad, que refleja un claro interés por... consiguiendo de este modo, hacer agradable el libro tanto en su forma, como por su amena lectura.

For instance, when reviewers refer to *this book, volume, monograph, study, collection of essays* in English or *este libro, volume, esta obra, novela edición* in Spanish, or provide its title, and state what it is about and/or what its aims are, they are introducing the book (Move 1 in Table 9.2); when reviewers state how the book is organized, and/or mention its parts and then describe them in objective terms, they are outlining it (Move 2); when reviewers offer their critical observations on that part, then they are highlighting its parts (Move 3); when reviewers attempt to summarize the most relevant achievements of the book and their critical observations, they are closing their review (Move 4).

After describing the texts according to this basic rhetorical schema, we tallied the moves that were present in each review and aggregated the data within each subcorpus. We then asked all the writers in the study which sections they thought a book review should contain and in which order.

Quantitative contrastive analysis of rhetorical moves and authors' own reports

The frequencies of the moves we identified are shown in Table 9.3:

Table 9.3   Basic rhetorical structure of the reviews in the *LIBRES* corpus

	English reviews (20)		*Spanish reviews (20)*	
	N	*%*	*N*	*%*
Move 1. Introducing the book	19	95	20	100
Move 2. Outlining the book	7	35	20	100
Move 3. Highlighting parts of the book	13	65	8	40
Cycling of Moves 2 & 3	3	15	7	35
Move 4. Providing a closing evaluation of the book	18	90	17	85

As can be seen, the introductory and closing moves tend to be obligatory in both subcorpora. Move 1 (introducing the book) occurs in almost all of the reviews and Move 4 (closing evaluation) is also present in the great majority. However, the occurrence of the central moves (Move 2, Move 3 and their recycling) varies substantially across the two subcorpora. While a Move 2 (outlining) is obligatory for the Spanish reviews, it occurs in only 35 per cent of the reviews in English. By contrast, the Anglo-American reviewers clearly prefer to concentrate on Move 3 (highlighting parts). Also, while the Spanish reviewers have a tendency to cycle Moves 2 and 3, this cyclical repetition of functions is rare in the English subcorpus. In book reviews, this 'cyclicity' shows that reviewers tend to highlight parts of the book (Move 3) as they outline them (Move 2), and repeat this cycle at various times along the review.

Results from our e-mail interviews show a correspondence between the rhetorical structure we identified and their understandings about it. While only four Anglo-American reviewers and three Spanish ones replied, their responses echo our findings:

> (6E) I would expect reviews to have the following elements: broad introduction; substantive account of what the book does; critical observations on the field; critical observations on the book's achievements. (Anglo-American)

> (6S) [A review should include an introduction which reveals the contribution made by the book in relation to the field or the author himself, followed by a brief description of the book content, and then a reasoned evaluation, which should be the core of the text, and a final conclusion.] (Translation from Spanish)

As for the order of presentation of the moves, most of our informants considered variability desirable and clearly preferred not to be prescriptive since order tends to depend on the construction of the reviewers' argument, their approach to the audience, or what they liked most about the book (see the following two answers):

> (7E) Reviewing is not a mechanical process. It requires creativity and critical acumen on the part of the reviewer and therefore flexibility to shape the review as s/he sees fit. (Anglo-American)

> (7S) [A review that follows a fixed pattern would not say very much about the book under review. Normally, we end up ordering content attending to which aspect of the book has most attracted our attention.] (Translation from Spanish)

Critical comments in literary academic book reviews

Method for identifying, interpreting, quantifying and locating critical comments

In order to identify critical comments in the two subcorpora, we analysed all the texts manually and searched for text units that contained both an indication of an aspect of the book commented upon and a critical evaluation. Such text units are what we have termed *critical comments on the book under review* (henceforth *critical comments*). Consider the following extracts taken from reviews in the *LIBRES* corpus, where the actual text fragments involved in realizing *critical comments* appear in italics and are preceded by a number in square brackets.

> (8E)[1] *Virginia Blain's Caroline Bowles Southey is an unusual but*[2] *immensely valuable addition to the compendium of resources that seek to restore the works…*
>
> (8S) La historia del teatro y el cine en España enfocada… está aún por escribir…[1] *Comicos ante el espejo llena una laguna bibliográfica…* [The history of theatre and cinema in Spain approached… still remains to be written.…[1] *Comicos ante el espejo fills a bibliographical gap…*]
>
> (9E)…and thus I find that[1] *this volume in 'Perspectives in Romanticism'…* does *not fully deliver what the series promises.*
>
> (9S) Sin duda, el interés por… ha llevado a Francisco Nieva a cerrar esta primera parte con un capítulo dedicado a …[1] *Este capítulo, …, quizá* fuera susceptible de una actualización que incluyera… *algunas de las propuestas más innovadoras…* [Undoubtedly, his interest in… has led Francisco Nieva to close this first part with a chapter devoted to …[1] *This chapter,… might benefit from an update, including… some of the most innovative proposals…*]

As can be observed, critical comments usually contain the following constituent items:

(a) Items that indicate (the aspect of) the book commented upon. The meaning of these items may be added on two different planes of the discourse:

  (1) on the propositional plane (Hyland and Tse, 2004), where because the items refer to the external world for the first time, meaning is presented as new information. This, for instance, occurs when items provide the titles of the book at the beginning of the review, as in examples (8E) and (8S), or state the name or number of chapters at the beginning of Move 2, as in examples (3E) and (3S);

  (2) on the metadiscoursal plane (Hyland and Tse, 2004), where meaning is presented as given information because the items refer to other parts in the text where the external reality commented

upon has been fully determined. This, for instance, occurs with such items as the noun phrase *este capítulo* in (9S), which refers back to the immediately preceding proposition, where we learn what the chapter is about, *un capítulo dedicado a*. Or with the noun phrase *this volume in 'Perspectives in Romanticism'* in (9E), which appears at the end of the review and refers back in an unspecified way to meaning derived from previous parts of the review.

(b) Items that indicate appreciation of a positive or negative quality in (the aspect of) the book commented upon. This kind of evaluation is usually presented as new information on the propositional plane and is realized by means of a text chunk or a single word. For instance, the negative appreciations in (9E) and in (9S) have been textually realized by the phrases *does not deliver what the series promises* and *fuera susceptible de una actualización que incluyera*, respectively. In these examples, the evaluations have been made in relation to the following criteria: *overall value* in (9E) and *how updated content is* in (9S). By contrast, the appreciations made, for instance, in (4E-5E) and (4S-5S) in Table 9.2 have been textually realized by means of single words, such as *understated* and *wanting* in English and *justificable* [justifiable] and *sencilla* [simple] in Spanish. These evaluative phrases or words are text clues that help us to interpret the corresponding comments as either positive or negative. Since evaluation tends to be subjective and is sometimes implicit or ambiguous (Shaw, 2004), we interpreted each case by close reading of the immediate co-text and careful consideration of the larger rhetorical context.

(c) Items that indicate the degree to which the quality appreciated is present in the aspect of the book commented upon. For instance, in (8E) the adverb *immensely* is used to intensify the degree to which the positive quality of being valuable is present in the book. By contrast, in (9E) the evaluative adverb *fully*, in a negative predicate, is used to diminish the degree to which the negative quality of not meeting expectations is present in the volume. The meaning of these items is also added on the propositional plane of discourse.

Critical comments are sometimes accompanied by other items, which add other types of metadiscoursal meanings (Hyland and Tse, 2004) (see non-italicized items in the examples). For example, the hedges *I find that* in (9E) and *quizá [perhaps]* in (9S) or the combined conjuncts *and thus* in (9E) and the main clause *one possible criticism of the book might be that* in (10E). It should be noted that these meanings serve other purposes: to show the reviewers' attitude towards their own critical comments, to signal how critical comments are related to other parts of the text and/or how they should be interpreted. In this sense, these added meanings are part of the same critical acts as the corresponding critical comments, and they are integrated into the meanings encoded or implied by the critical comments (Hyland and Tse, 2004). They are also essential to our interpretation of the text because they allow reviewers to share their critical comments appropriately in a given context and coherently at a given point in the text. However, given that neither of these metadiscoursal items encodes or implies any particular appreciation of the book, they have not been considered as constituent elements of critical comments.

The next stage in the analysis consisted of quantifying critical comments. One problem we encountered was that, sometimes, critical comments do not correspond with full orthographical sentences. For instance, while fragment (10E) consists of five sentences and contains seven critical comments, fragment (10S) consists of two sentences and contains six critical comments. Another difficulty was that sometimes the same sentence includes comments of opposite type, that is, positive and negative, as in fragment (8E). A further problem was that critical comments do not always correspond with full clauses. For instance, in fragment (10S) critical comments *por la gran aportación de material textual y testimonios manejados* and *por la exhaustividad en la anotación filológica* are both realized by means of incomplete clauses, though the elliptical meanings indicating the aspect commented upon can be easily recovered. Therefore, we decided to quantify critical comments on the basis of semantic rather than grammatical criteria (see our definition above), in order to carry out as meaningful a cross-linguistic comparison as possible (Moreno and Suárez 2008b).

(10E) All in all,[1] *Literature, Politics, and the English Avant-Garde makes a respectable contribution to the literature on* ...[2]. *Peppis does not theorize in a historical vacuum but*[3] *admirably achieves his goal of* ..., *paying particular attention to*...One criticism of the book might be that[4] *a certain amount of artificial padding is required* ... *to turn it into a coherent whole.* Also,[5] *Peppis's style is not the most economical and*[6] *he* might have ... Neither criticism, however, seriously detracts from[7] *the book's considerable value.*

(10S)[1] *Nos encontramos, en suma, ante una rigurosísima y completa edición crítica de* ...[2] *Esta carencia ya está subsanada con este volumen,*[3] *muy reseñable*[4] por *su claridad expositiva,*[5] por *la gran aportación de material textual y testimonios manejados que corroboran cada afirmación y*[6] *por* la exhaustividad en la anotación filológica. *[In sum,*[1] *we are faced with a very rigorous and thorough critical edition of...*[2] *This gap has been filled with this volume,*[3] *which is remarkable*[4] *for its clear writing,*[5] *for illustrating each statement with an enormous amount of textual material and testimonies and*[6] *for the exhaustive philological annotation.]*

Finally, we tallied the critical comments occurring in each move of each review and aggregated the data for each move within each subcorpus. This allowed us to compare the general distribution of critical comments throughout the reviews basic rhetorical structure across the two writing cultures.

Contrastive analysis of critical comments in rhetorical structure

Our results show that the move with the lowest frequency of critical comments in both subcorpora is Move 2 (outlining) (see Figure 9.1). Examples are:

(11E) ... although *there is much of value in all the book's chapters* ...

(11S) *la Introducción muestra un panorama bastante completo de la realidad literaria del XVIII.* [*the Introduction shows a rather thorough scene of the literary reality of the 18th century.*]

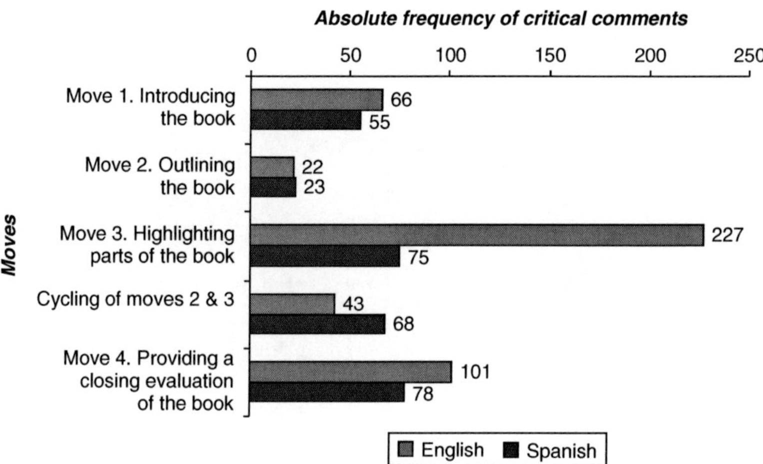

Figure 9.1   Distribution of critical comments throughout the rhetorical structure of the reviews in the *LIBRES* corpus

As expected, critical comments are much more likely to be found in the other moves in both subcorpora, but there is one significant cross-cultural difference: critical comments in Move 3 (highlighting parts) of the reviews in the English subcorpus (227) outnumber by three to one critical comments in the same move of the Spanish reviews (75). This allows us to suggest that the great difference in overall critical attitude across Anglo-American and Castilian Spanish reviewers can be attributed to the significantly lower frequency of critical comments in Move 3 of the Spanish reviews.

Let us now analyse the relative weight of positive and negative critical comments, throughout the texts basic rhetorical structure. This is illustrated in Figure 9.2:

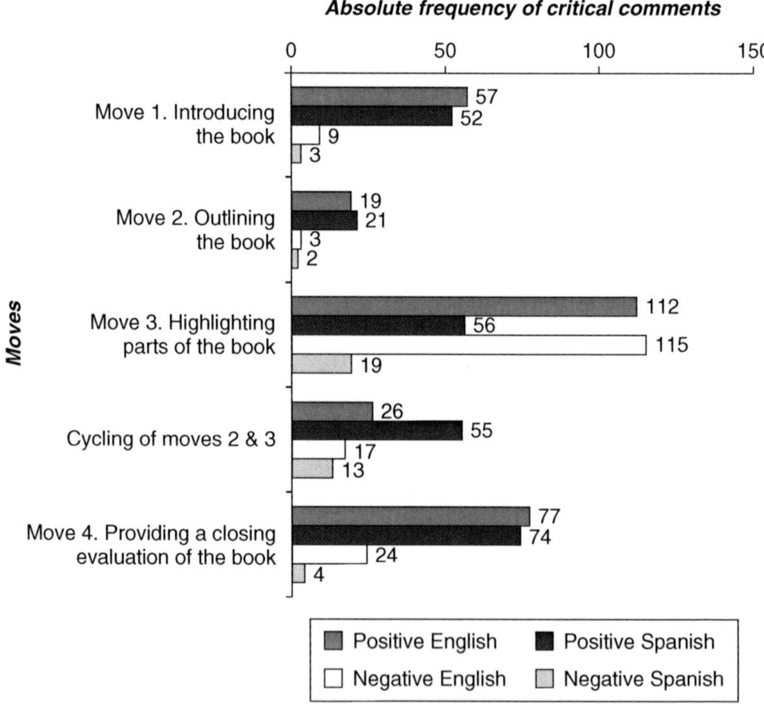

Figure 9.2   Distribution of positive and negative critical comments throughout the rhetorical structure of the reviews in the *LIBRES* corpus

As can be seen, there is a similar tendency for both groups of writers to open the reviews (Move 1) with considerably more positive than negative critical comments. Examples from Move 1 follow:

(12E) *This well-presented...book* is a credit to Professor Berry, his university, and to Cambridge University Press.

(12S) *Libro es éste de larga y rigurosa gestación...* [*Calmly and rigorously conceived, this book...*]

In Move 2 positive comments also predominate in both subcorpora (see fragments (11E) and (11S) above). However, Move 3 and the cycling of Moves 2 and 3 show remarkable differences in critical approach across the two subcorpora. While in Move 3 the Anglo-American reviewers tend to offer a balanced evaluation of the book (112 positive vs. 115 negative critical comments), the Castilian Spanish reviews offer a highly positively biased evaluation of the book (56 positive vs. 19 negative critical comments) when Move 3 is clearly distinguished from Move 2. In the cycling of Moves 2 and 3 the approach tends to be more positive in the English subcorpus, though not as much so as in the Spanish subcorpus, which is even more positively biased than in the isolated Move 3. Examples of critical comments in Move 3 follow:

(13E) *Irwin* therefore *takes great pains to explain such very basic facts as...*

(13S) *la autora salva la dificultad de la desproporción...introduciendo...* [*the author solves the difficulty of disproportion...by introducing...*]

Move 4 also reveals some interesting cross-cultural differences in the frequency and type of critical comments. While Move 4 is the place where Spanish writers make the greatest number of positive critical comments (74), with hardly any negative ones (four) (see fragment (10S) above), the Anglo-American reviewers have a much greater tendency to qualify their positive critical comments (77) with some negative ones (24) (see fragment (10E) above).

Discussion: observations on the data

One striking cross-cultural difference that we observed through our e-mail interviews was that, while our Spanish informants did not seem to see the point in reviewing a book that is very bad, the Anglo-American scholars assumed that very bad books should also be reviewed. In these circumstances, it is understandable that Spanish book reviews would contain fewer negative critical comments. However, given that evaluation is ultimately subjective and that it is always possible to say good or bad things about any given book, irrespective of its overall objective quality, we conjectured that there must have been another underlying assumption or value that might explain this difference better. We then considered our informants' answers to the following question: do you think a book review should necessarily contain a balanced amount of praise and criticism? According to both groups of informants, a balanced approach is always desired. However, as the following extracts illustrate, the *balance* principle seems to be applied more strictly by the Anglo-American scholars than by their Spanish counterparts.

> (14E1) I think the review should be honest. It should look for what is good as well as bad, but if it is honest the review may well at times hugely praise a book as an important work or strongly condemn it. This is not a matter of being kind or unkind, but of professional responsibility.

> (14E2) It is sufficiently balanced for me usually to find good things in bad books, and vice versa, even if I consider MOST of what I read very good or very bad.

> (14S) [If a book is excellent, it [the review] does not need to include negative criticism, though it is normal to include both types, but not *a priori*. One does not need to look for weaknesses where they do not exist simply for the sake of including a criticism, nor does one need to overemphasize a small detail that is not essential for evaluating the book.] (Translation from Spanish)

Given the two different critical approaches adopted by reviewers in the central moves across the English and Spanish subcorpora, one would expect to find in the concluding section (Move 4) an exact reflection of these two critical approaches. However, as Figure 9.2 clearly shows, this is not exactly so. In both subcorpora reviewers show a greater tendency to close their review by reminding the reader of many more positive than negative points. As suggested by Gea-Valor (2000), one possible reason underlying this rhetorical behaviour may be the reviewers' attempt to create an overall good impression that may counterbalance, or redress, the force of the negative critical comments made in preceding moves. In the words of one Anglo-American reviewer, the underlying reason might be a desire to underline what counts more, since 'points made at the end almost always have the feel of greater importance'. Whatever the reason, reviewers in both writing cultures seem to find it more appropriate to finish their reviews in a positive tone. But the question is, why are the concluding moves so positively biased in the Spanish reviews (see Figure 9.2)?

Two considerations about the Castilian Spanish book reviewing writing culture might help to understand this. One is that, since critical comments pose great risk of personal friction between the reviewers and, especially, the authors of the books, an excessive number of them may be interpreted as disrespectful to the author of the book. As one external Spanish informant from the field of English studies remarked on seeing our 2008a results, 'the conclusions...show what most of us already felt: there is more human respect over here' (2008, personal communication). The other consideration is that authors in small academic communities like the Spanish one are more likely to know their book reviewers personally or/and to play a role in their future career. In this circumstance, or the prospect of it, the reviewer's attitude towards the book under review is likely to be affected, however much integrity the reviewer has. Thus, overloading the concluding move with positive critical comments might be a way of managing the potential academic conflict generated by the few negative comments made in the preceding moves. This could be taken to suggest that Castilian Spanish reviewers place much greater importance on establishing a harmonious interpersonal encounter with the author of the book.

By contrast, the Anglo-American informants do not seem to see the personal relationship between the reviewer and the author of the book as a key and central one. As one of them observed, 'this question presupposes that a review is about the interaction of the reviewer and the author. The point of a review is to offer an informed judgment for readers, not to make authors feel good/bad'. Nor do Anglo-American scholars seem to consider that providing criticism on the book may imply lack of respect to the author. As a former reviews editor from English studies remarked via personal e-mail communication, 'I didn't see this as "negative" but as engaging in the discipline and the interests of readers'. This suggests that Anglo-American scholars place greater importance on achieving the key evaluative purpose of the genre. Accordingly, although the Anglo-American reviewers in our corpus tend to finish their reviews with relatively more positive appreciations, probably to comply with the principle of 'being civil' (Tobin, 2003), they also include some negative comments, probably to maintain the consistency of the review.

Conclusions

Our investigation of critical comments across the rhetorical moves of academic book reviews of literature in Castilian Spanish and Anglo-American English has revealed some relevant values, practices and perspectives. Our results have shown that Moves 3 and 4 are the most subject to cross-cultural variation in terms of frequency and type of critical comments. As suggested by the responses to our e-mail questionnaire, these differences may be explained by the greater attention given to *balance* by the Anglo-American scholars than their Spanish counterparts. This seems to reflect different views of what the purpose of the genre is in each writing culture: whether to offer an informed judgement for readers or to establish a harmonious relationship with the author of the book. The result is that, while the academic book review in Anglo-American literary contexts can be considered as a truly evaluative genre, the academic book review in Castilian Spanish contexts can best be taken as a laudatory or/and promotional genre.

We hope that our study will have some practical implications for intercultural communication, especially if the tendencies identified in the Spanish literary writing culture were extensive to fields where Spanish scholars are more likely to have book reviews published in Anglo-American journals. Consider the following remark made by a former reviews editor from English studies via personal e-mail communication:

> When I was reviews editor for…I told reviewers that we would only accept 'balanced' reviews (pointing out flaws and positives). To be honest, I did reject several Spanish reviews because they were insufficiently critical.

Accordingly, Spanish scholars might find it strategically convenient to adopt a more critical approach, particularly in Move 3, whether it is cycled with Move 2 or not, and irrespective of the overall quality of the books. If so, they might also need to write a more balanced conclusion by including some negative comments, although not necessarily in the same proportion as in Move 3.

Finally, on the basis of the present research we would like to propose the hypothesis that Spanish scholars are also less evaluative and negative in other public evaluative academic genres and to suggest that negative criticism on a peers' academic work in Castilian Spanish academic contexts is conveyed more open and freely either in anonymous written interactions or in private spoken communicative events.

Acknowledgements

The present study is part of a research project financed by the Spanish Ministry of Education and Science, Plan Nacional de I + D + i (2005–2008), Ref: HUM2005-01215. We would like to dedicate this chapter to John Swales. We are very grateful to our informants for their generous participation in our study and to Ken Hyland, Giuliana Diani and Mary Ellen Kerans for their useful comments and suggestions on earlier versions.

References

Burgess, S. (2002) 'Packed Houses and Intimate Gatherings: Audience and Rhetorical Structure' in J. Flowerdew and C. N. Candlin (eds) *Academic Discourse* (London: Longman), 197–215.

Burgess, S. and Fagan, A. (2004) 'Genre Analysis and the Novice Researcher: The Book Review and The Poster Presentation' in M. Brito and J. I. Oliva (eds) *Traditions and Innovations: Commemorating Forty Years of English Studies at ULL* (La Laguna: RCEI), 61–77.

De Carvalho, G. (2002) 'Rhetorical Patterns of Academic Book Reviews Written in Portuguese and in English' *Proceedings of the 2nd International Contrastive Linguistics Conference Santiago de Compostela* (Santiago de Compostela: Universidade de Santiago de Compostela), 261–68.

Gea-Valor, M. L. (2000) *A Pragmatic Approach to Politeness and Modality in the Book Review Articles* (València: SELL Monographs. Lengua Inglesa. Universitat de València).

Giannoni, D. S. (2006) 'Expressing Praise and Criticism in Economic Discourse: A Comparative Analysis of English/Italian Book Reviews' in G. Del Lungo Camiciotti, M. Dossena and B. Crawford Camiciottoli (eds) *Variation in Business and Economics Discourse: Diachronic and Genre Perspectives* (Rome: Officina Edizioni), 126–38.

Hyland, K. (2000) 'Praise and Criticism: Interactions in Book Reviews' in K. Hyland (ed.) *Disciplinary Discourses: Social Interactions in Academic Writing* (London: Longman), 41–62.

Hyland, K. and Tse, P. (2004) 'Metadiscourse in Academic Writing: A Reappraisal', *Applied Linguistics*, XXV, 2, 156–77.

Kaplan, R. (2001) 'What in the World Is Contrastive Rhetoric?' in C. G. Panetta (ed.) *Contrastive Rhetoric Revisited and Redefined* (New Jersey: Lawrence Erlbaum), vii–xx.

Moreno, A. I. and Suárez, L. (2008a) 'A Study of Critical Attitude across English and Spanish Academic Book Reviews', *Journal of English for Academic Purposes*, VII, 1, 15–26.

Moreno, A. I. and Suárez, L. (2008b) 'A Framework for Comparing Evaluation Resources across Academic Texts', *Text & Talk*, XXVIII, 6, 501–21.

Motta-Roth, D. (1998) 'Discourse Analysis and Academic Book Reviews: A Study of Text and Disciplinary Cultures' in I. Fortanet, S. Posteguillo, J. C. Palmer and J. F. Coll (eds) *Genre Studies in English for Academic Purposes* (Castelló de la Plana: Publicacions de la Universitat Jaume I), 29–58.

Orteza y Miranda, E. (1996) 'On Book Reviewing', *Journal of Educational Thought*, XXX, 2, 191–202.

Salager-Meyer, F. (2006) 'From "Mr. Guthrie is Profoundly Mistaken…" to "Our Data Do Not Seem to Confirm the Results of a Previous Study on…": A Diachronic Study of Polemicity in Academic Writing (1810–1995)', *Ibérica*, I, 5–28.

Shaw, P. (2004) 'How Do We Recognise Implicit Evaluation in Academic Book Reviews?' in G. Del Lungo Camiciotti and E. Tognini Bonelli (eds) *Academic Discourse – New Insights into Evaluation* (Bern: Peter Lang), 121–40.

Spink, P., Robins, D. and Scamber, L. (1998) 'Use of Scholarly Book Reviews: Implications for Electronic Publishing and Scholarly Communication', *Journal of the American Society for Information Science*, XLIX, 4, 364–74.

Suárez, L. and Moreno, A. I. (2008) 'The Rhetorical Structure of Literary Academic Book Reviews: An English-Spanish Cross-Linguistic Approach' in U. Connor, E. Nagelhout and W. Rozycki (eds) *Contrastive Rhetoric: Reaching to Intercultural Rhetoric* (Amsterdam: John Benjamins), 147–68.

Swales, J. (1990) *Genre Analysis: English in Academic and Research Settings* (Cambridge: Cambridge University Press).

Tobin, R. W. (2003) 'The Commensality of Book Reviewing', *Journal of Scholarly Publishing*, XXXV, 1, 47–51.

10
Historians at Work: Reporting Frameworks in English and Italian Book Review Articles

Marina Bondi

Introduction

Review genres are inherently reflexive and are defined by their need to present critical evaluations of other texts. Their key language features can thus be expected to lie in two interestingly related areas: evaluative language use on the one hand and reporting verbs (or frameworks) on the other.

Evaluation plays a crucial role in the primary function of reviewing – presenting critical views on a text, its academic quality and its value to the field. In its broadest definition, evaluation is understood as 'the expression of the speaker or writer's attitude or stance towards, viewpoint on, or feelings about the entities or propositions that he or she is talking about' (Thompson and Hunston, 2000, p. 5). The growing body of literature on the book review shows increasing emphasis on evaluative language in both praise and criticism (Motta-Roth, 1998; Hyland, 2000; Shaw, 2004; Salager-Meyer *et al.*, 2007; Moreno and Suárez, 2008; Römer, 2008; Tse and Hyland, 2008). The role played by reflexivity in academic discourse has long been the object of great interest (Mauranen, 1993; Hyland, 1998, 2000, 2005; Bondi, 1999). Growing attention has been paid to the argumentative nature of academic writing, as well as to the lexicalization of argumentative processes (Mauranen, 1993, 2003; Bondi, 2001, 2005; Hyland, 2002, 2005; Dahl, 2003).

Studies of academic discourse have also addressed the question of citation extensively, while paying particular attention to disciplinary specificity and variation (Hyland, 1999, 2000; Dahl, 2003; Bondi and Silver, 2004; Thompson, 2005; Bondi, 2007). Academic communities are communities of practice and the representation of research and discourse procedures in text can offer interesting insights into their self-perception.

This chapter combines a focus on the language of 'disciplinary culture' (Hyland, 2000; Hyland and Bondi, 2006) with an interest in contrastive rhetoric (Mauranen, 1993, 2001; Connor 2004), where the emphasis lies on the role of local cultures on rhetorical organization of texts. The aim is to look at the features of a 'cultural identity' in academic prose (Fløttum *et al.*, 2007). The analysis does not look so much at systemic variation across languages, but rather at forms of discourse representation in different languages. The question is not how language resources influence text, but rather how text reflects the values of disciplinary culture, of local academic culture or of transnational academic communities. Reflexive language can be an interesting site of self-representation in communities whose most prominent activity lies in the verbal representation and communication of knowledge.

I focus in particular on verbs of reporting and reporting frameworks, that is, the sequence of elements that signal and qualify the shift between text that is averred and text that is attributed. The distinction originates with Sinclair (1987) who states that responsibility for an averred proposition rests with the writer and an attributed proposition is indicated as deriving from a source. Reporting expressions allow writers to detach themselves from the proposition they introduce by attributing it to others, thus creating a variety of textual voices and the possibility to evaluate reported discourse (Thompson, 1996). The patterns of the reporting verb or noun in question often illuminate discourse features, especially through the representation of consensus and conflict in text (Hunston, 2004).

The study of the connection between reflexive language and cultural or disciplinary identity looks particularly promising in review genres and in the *book review article* in particular. The book review article plays a crucial role in the process of knowledge construction and discussion by providing a forum in which academics can set out their views in the form of arguments.

The genre integrates features of the book review and the position paper: it combines critical evaluation of a book with an extensive discussion of the issues raised with a view to supporting a specific position. Book review articles may be published in the body of the journal or at the beginning of the review section; they may even be isolated as a 'third space', often dividing articles from book reviews. The very existence of the genre reflects disciplinary values, such as the major status attributed to books in the social sciences and the humanities. The structure and features of book review articles have been studied quite extensively by Diani (2004, 2006, 2007), who outlines the functional and formal features of the genre, while also highlighting the key role of the reviewer. The reviewer's argumentative voice is always present: if book reviews typically move from description to evaluation, book review articles also use evaluation to argue a position in the context of academic debate.

The present study focuses on two small corpora of book review articles in history and looks at the lexicalization of discursive procedures in English and in Italian, keeping in mind the tension between narrative and argument that characterizes historical discourse (Bondi and Silver, 2004; Coffin, 2006; Bondi, 2007). Cross-linguistic examination of how argument is represented in both corpora will pay particular attention to the representation of the reviewed author's discourse, while studying the values reflected and implied by the different lexical choices in context. Special attention will be paid to collocation, lexico-grammatical patterns and semantic preference, following a recent upsurge of interest in corpus-based approaches to the phraseological features of academic discourse (Groom, 2005; Charles, 2006; Hyland, 2008). The general questions I address here are: how do historians represent the activity of their community in terms of argument? Is the variety of lexical tools employed in one language peculiarly distinctive? Does it reflect different value systems? After detailing with materials and methods, I focus on reflexive language in frequency data and look at the textual and discourse functions signalled by the lexical units across languages.

Materials and methods

The study is based on the analysis of two comparable corpora of book review articles taken from historical journals published in Italian and English. The English corpus (see Diani, this volume) comprises 42 book review articles published in three American journals over three years (1999–2001): *Journal of Interdisciplinary History, American Historical Review* and *Gender & History.* The Italian corpus includes 41 articles published over six years (1999–2005) in three journals: *Meridiana, Passato e Presente* and *Quaderni Medievali.* Both corpora are between 190,000 and 200,000 words.

No attempt was made to restrict my choice of writers to native speakers, although in both corpora I excluded texts that were explicitly presented as translations. The idea was to look at varieties of Italian and English that get published in authoritative journals. I am aware, however, of the different status of the two languages and of an inherent difference in the scope of the readership, although the difference may be somewhat reduced by the 'local' focus of the discipline.

The analysis combined discourse and corpus perspectives. The initial hypothesis of the centrality of reporting and evaluation was checked against quantitative data by means of the keyword function of Word-Smith Tools 4 (Scott, 2004). The small corpus of book review articles in English was compared to a bigger reference corpus of research articles published in the same journals in the same years (ca. 800,000 words). The data produced – showing words that are statistically more or less frequent in the corpus examined than in the standard set by the reference corpus – confirmed the centrality of both evaluation and reporting.

The tools of attribution were then studied both manually, by identifying reporting frameworks in the corpus of texts, and automatically, by looking at quantitative data through corpus analysis tools. The study looked at the representation of discourse procedures in the lexico-grammar of attribution. Particular attention was paid to the structure of reporting frameworks and to the dialogic sequences they create in the construction of argument, showing for example acceptance or (partial) rejection of a reported claim (cf. 'passive argumentative roles', Stati, 1994, p. 259). Issues of 'voice directionality' (Bondi, 1999, p. 123), that is, patterns of agreement and disagreement, as typically in the reviewers' praise or criticism of the position of the reviewed authors, also took into consideration the variety of textual voices that can be involved in argumentative dialogue with the author – reviewer, reader, discourse community, historical characters and sources (Bondi, 2007).

The analysis then focused on the lexicalization of discursive processes in terms of:

(a) the monologic or dialogic nature of argument;
(b) the patterns of agreement and disagreement shown by the context;
(c) the metaphorical meanings involved in the representation of argument.

The analysis: overview and general issues

The preliminary overview of quantitative data aimed at confirming the centrality of reporting and evaluation in the book review article. Comparison with the research articles produced 393 keywords, most of which could be relatively easily attributed to issues of content identification (e.g. names, places, specific objects of study of the reviewed books). Of the 80 words that remained, another set could be related to the specific book review articles analysed: the fact that they mostly dealt with books written by single male authors, for example, explains the presence of *she* and *their* among negative keywords and the presence of *he* and *his* among the positive.

References to the book itself and its component parts – *book, volume, essays, volumes, essay, chapters, chapter, introduction* – are easily related to the object of the genre in question. Other words relate to the book's pragmatic functions and textual organization. Surfing the concordances of words like *works, literature* and *books* shows that they often contribute to setting the reviewed book in the context of disciplinary debate. Similar functions are revealed by *historians, histories, scholars, authors, study, studies, academic* and *recent.* The word *study* actually includes both perspectives, identifying both the book reviewed and the background literature. Similarly, *history, historiography* and *historical* are often related to content of the reviewed books, to the type of history dealt with and the methodological tools used, while *historian* typically qualifies the identity of the author.

Explicitly evaluative lexis is at first reading rather limited. The presence of *unique, uniqueness* and *intellectual* is mostly linked to specific topics, but a few elements stand out as clearly evaluative: *different, complex, new.* Within the general picture, however, they are much less distinctive than other features that are only shown to be evaluative in context: *is, that, what, it, something,* which are all found in patterns of a local grammar of evaluation (Hunston and Sinclair, 2000). Table 10.1 illustrates the typical functional contexts of the most important keywords, while also showing how easily they combine with evaluative elements and they collocate with each other, thus proving to be useful markers of 'generic language'.

Another interesting set of keywords highlights the role of reporting in the book review article. Reporting can be marked both verbally (*Crosby notes, Landes argues that*) and nominally (*the argument that quantification per se was the key to Western global domination, the question of how historical reality can be established*). Table 10.2 reports the frequencies of potentially reporting word forms, with keyness index, and the number of actual reporting occurrences used in explicit reporting frameworks, that is, forms attributing an explicit reported clause.

Nominal elements like *thesis* are more often used as labelling nouns offering a summary representation of a line of argument (*his famous 'frontier thesis'*), than as linkers introducing the argument itself (*Tom Kemp's thesis that the British model of industrialization is not the only paradigm*). This is true of all of the nominal keywords, even if *question*

Table 10.1 Keywords as 'generic language'

Function	Keyword	Examples
Identifying the object of the review	book – volume – essays – volumes – essay – chapters – chapter – introduction – study	– Despite the **absence of major breakthroughs**, the book is suggestive of some **new** directions taken by Chinese historians. – By highlighting Turner's limitations along with his contributions, **Bogue's scholarly and readable study** sets a **new** standard.
Setting the reviewed book in the context of other disciplinary positions	works – literature – books – study – historians – histories – scholars – authors – study – studies – academic – recent	– In the last ten to fifteen years, citizenship has become a **crucial** term in political and **academic debates.** – In this book, Lu pushes for the adoption of a **new** agenda for **the study of modern Chinese urban life.** – **More recent literature** has begun to **reject** this framing to see a form of female flânerie in women's occupation of the **new** spaces of consumption.
Identifying book content/thesis/ approach/methodology	history – historical – historiography – issues – theses – thesis – claims	– This is an essay in **historiography**, not **history.** – What **historical evidence** does Crosby offer for this thesis? – Let me now attempt to situate the **issues** discussed in a wider context.
Identifying (and qualifying) author	historian	– **An eminent and insightful economic historian of Europe and Egypt,** he has produced a historical tour de force that broaches with wit, intelligence, and more than a hint of impatience topics that in recent years have been highly controversial.

| Expressing opinion | different – complex – new – is – that –what – it – something – but – not | – To defend that thesis would require a far **different** book from the one Landes has written.
– **There is something to these claims**; no two empires are exactly alike.
– His thesis **is** simple, significant, substantial.
– Polo clearly carried European and Christian cultural baggage to the East, but the new baggage that he acquired along the way **is what makes the 'Description' so challenging**. |
| Showing current relevance | has – today | – And it is the kind of knowledge that we must presume **has always been present** but to which historians **have not always lent a ready ear**.
– **Today**, social history, like subaltern history, is seen as **too complex** to be folded into a single rubric. |

Table 10.2   Keywords potentially marking reporting frameworks

N	Keyword	Freq.	%	RC. Freq.	RC. %	Keyness	Reporting
98	argues	83	0.04	118	0.01	56.59	83
121	notes	45	0.02	41		50.06	33
122	thesis	33	0.02	20		49.66	4
123	claims	78	0.04	118	0.01	48.68	17
204	question	110	0.06	243	0.03	33.36	34
225	argument	68	0.03	125	0.01	30.67	26
254	think	54	0.03	92	0.01	27.91	35

and *argument* show greater frequency of use in reporting. Verbal elements also show that specific verbs tend to be associated with specific textual voices – verbs like *argue, note* and *claim* are mostly used in the third person singular (predominantly associated with the reviewed author), whereas *think* is more often attributed to the writer and the reader (25 occurrences out of 35), than to the author, the discourse community or historical characters (10 occurrences out of 35). The trends are confirmed by lemmatizing the three verbs and looking at all of their word-forms. They are also confirmed by looking at an overall proportion of nominal and verbal reporting – the analysis of a random selection of 100 reporting frameworks with *that* shows that verbal reporting accounts for 63 per cent of the occurrences, and nominal reporting for 37 per cent.

The quantitative overview thus confirms that the combination of reporting and evaluative elements is a key feature of the genre. The two elements may be realized as a sequence of acts with different argumentative roles, for example, Reported Claim^Agreement/Disagreement, as shown in example (1) (in this and the following examples, reporting frameworks are italicized, while signals of agreement or disagreement are marked in bold).

(1) The nation-state of the twenty-first century, *he argues*, needs to be less insistent on its own sovereign rights and more accommodating of 'the sub-national and transnational loyalties on which future sites of organizational power may come to rest.' **An obvious point to make, perhaps, but nonetheless vitally important.**

Agreement and disagreement, signalling converging and diverging voices, can also be realized by implication or by qualification of the reporting verb, with different degrees of explicitness. The reviewer's position can be signalled minimally in agreement, by just adding an adverb to the reporting framework: e.g. *Landes argues forcefully, he brilliantly explores* etc. Disagreement, on the other hand, can originate long dialogic sequences, often providing complex counterargument, as in (2):

> (2) *To him*, the British were clearly more humane in their treatment of the indigenous, and this was in keeping with their morally superior nature. Indeed, *Landes argues that*, if confronted with the prospects of torture by either the British or the Spanish, he would have preferred to have been tortured by the British: 'Dead is dead, but that way I might go to my death swiftly and reasonably whole' (p. 77n). This faith in British torture technique **probably would be unappreciated** by the remnants of the Pequot Indian nation attacked by British militiamen and their Indian allies in 1637. During the attack, 'men, women and children burned or were speared to death. Pequot captives were beheaded or sent into slavery,' and the **massacre** decimated this group. **Torture is torture. No one has the moral high ground in such atrocities**, yet Landes has **absolutely no patience** for any historian who questions either the cruelty of the Spanish or the good intentions of the British.

The example draws attention to another interesting feature of reported argument. The reviewer can engage in interaction with other textual voices (Bondi, 2007), such as members of the discourse community or historical characters and sources. In example (2), the reviewer rejects Landes' position by contrasting it first with historical evidence, or (her own) speculation about what the Pequot Indians would think. She then quotes authoritative sources and moves towards positioning through explicitly evaluative lexis (*massacre, torture*). Her disagreement is emphasized by presenting Landes' position as intolerant of other approaches.

Textual voices may be involved in different types of dialogue. In the following example, the reviewer reports current debate on Polo's encounter with Rustichello and, while showing the author's alignment with a generic *current consensus*, attributes the statement to himself (*I think it is fair to say*).

> (3) Larner, *I think it is **fair** to say*, subscribes, for the most part, to the current consensus that Polo related his experiences to Rustichello, a

Pisan writer of romances, while the two shared a cell in a Genoese prison in 1298/99.

Verbs of reporting: cross-cultural comparison

Closer study of reporting verbs in both corpora aimed first at highlighting lexical range and then the peculiarities of the lexical sets that tend to be favoured in the two academic contexts. In both corpora the frequency of the single lexical element is usually low, mostly around 1 per 10,000 words and below, with only few reaching 2 per 10,000 words.

Reporting verbs in English: dialogic argument

The range of verbs referring to the work of historians in the English corpus – *argue, suggest, note, claim, observe, show, believe, conclude, examine, acknowledge, agree, explain, think, reject, say* – reveals much of the attitudes of reviewers towards what is reviewed. Lemmas like *argue* and *claim* are explicitly linked to the argumentative nature of academic discourse, while neutral verbs such as *say* can of course combine with expressions of (lack of) adhesion to the reported statement.

The English corpus is characterized by a significant presence of verbs that represent dialogic roles of agreement or disagreement. The occurrences of these verbs are higher than in the Italian corpus: verbs such as *acknowledge* (50 occurrences), *agree* (49) and *reject* (33) reveal altogether an average presence of 3.1 occurrences per article, whereas the three most frequent verbs in Italian would only account for an average of 1.1.

The representation of argument as dialogic is most explicitly linked to the voice of the reviewed author. Table 10.3 reports the quantitative data of concordance analysis of the most important dialogic verbs. The table shows that the dominant voice is that of the reviewed author, whereas

Table 10.3 Dialogic argument in English

Lemma	Reviewer (+ Reader)	Reviewed author	Discourse community	Historical characters/sources
acknowledge	3/50	21/50	14/50	12/50
agree	9/49	27/49	7/49	6/49
reject	0/33	9/33	12/33	12/33
Total	12/132	57/132	33/132	30/132

the discourse community and historical characters represent a minor, if important, component.

The table also shows that there is great variability across the verbs, themselves representing different types of argumentative dialogue. The partial agreement, typically signalled by *acknowledge,* characterizes rather uniformly reviewer, discourse community and historical characters. Simple agreement (*agree*) is more typically associated with the reviewed author, whereas explicit disagreement (*reject*) shows the opposite profile: its use is null in representing the reviewer's activity and limited when representing the reviewed author, while more consistently attributed to the discourse community and historical characters.

The lemma *reject* has a more limited use of other dialogic verbs, most probably because of its intensely negative value. It is typically accompanied by other signals of strong criticism (*overly sensational, apocalyptic, prudish*), but also by meta-cognitive nouns frequent in the representation of debate (*notion, thesis, framework*). At the level of writer-reader interaction, the verb – with its obvious negative evaluation – implies expected alignment between reader and reviewer and typically leads up to an evaluative statement of the rejected view:

(4) There is one more reason why *diplomatic historians* in particular might *reject Said*: they may be **uncomfortable** with his politics. *Said has always stated* **candidly** *his belief that* intellectuals should have public, political commitments that inform their scholarship.

The verb *agree* can be shown to associate with various forms of 'engagement' (Hyland, 2002) and contribute to involving the reader in an argumentative dialogue with the reviewed text. When looked at in isolation, the lemma suggests strong consensus, but its use in context shows it is quite often part of a concessive sequence: *Perhaps the one argument everyone can agree on is; Few will agree; Culture makes a difference, agreed* etc, even when it does introduce a conclusion to which the reviewer shows unconditional adhesion:

(5) **In conclusion, I believe Vorländer deserves credit** for having ventured onto contested ground, inevitably inviting debate. *I agree with his revision* of Hartz, which makes room for a broader mix of creeds and ideologies in the formation of the American belief system, even if it lacks the clarity and elegance of the Hartzian equation, or the Marxian one, for that matter. History is not mathematics.

Acknowledge typically expresses partial consensus in concessive sequences (*though he acknowledges*), often involving the reviewer (and/or the reader) in the immediate context. Agreement and disagreement combine to produce a complex representation of debate, showing for example agreement between reviewer and author, in conflict with the discourse community. The role of the reviewer is often made explicit, as in the mitigated criticism below:

(6) **My reference** to Popper is **not** intended **to criticize** Scott for revisiting old ground. *Scott himself acknowledges* that his assault on utopian modernism is hardly novel as such.

Reporting verbs in Italian: metaphors of vision

The Italian corpus offers an equally wide range of lexical tools – *parere, sembrare, pensare, sostenere, ipotizzare, notare, osservare, suggerire, rilevare, proporre, sottolineare, credere, dimostrare* – including both neutral expressions like *parere/sembrare* ('seem'), *dire* ('say'), *notare* ('note') and *osservare* ('observe') (*come dice Sabbatini, l'autore nota, osserva Baumann*) and expressions with explicit reference to the argumentative dimension of discourse, such as *sostenere* ('claim'), *dimostrare* ('show') or *ipotizzare* ('hypothesize'). Example (7) provides a sequence where the reviewed author (*Sommariva*) is presented as having claimed (and partly shown) something, which constitutes the basis for further hypotheses; these are in turn contrasted with the views of other members of the community (Scot*t*) and of the reviewer himself, who shows explicit disagreement:

(7) *La studiosa sosteneva (ed in parte dimostrava)* che il poeta mediolatino aveva fatto tesoro…della produzione poetica precedente, classica e tardo-antica (per esempio di alcuni carmi dell'Anthologia Latina). *Partendo da tale assunto, la Sommariva ipotizzava* quindi che la redazione più classicheggiante rappresentasse lo stadio più antico, caratterizzato da una pedissequa imitazione dei modelli. *Con ciò la Sommariva, anche se da un differente punto di vista, confermava* la sequenza cronologica proposta da Scott circa un ventennio prima. **L'elemento, *nel saggio della Sommariva*, che comunque non sono mai riuscito a condividere è il giudizio duro, limitativo e spesso addirittura stroncatorio** che, a più riprese, viene formulato sulle capacità poetiche di Ildeberto, *a dire della studiosa (e cioè partendo da una posizione tipicamente 'classicista')* spesso mediocre e sciatto versificatore.

The representation of dialogic argument in the Italian corpus is thus certainly present. It shows, however, a lesser weight of dialogic verbs of reporting. Verbs like *confermare* ('confirm', 21 occurrences), *ribadire* ('reaffirm', 16), *condividere* ('agree', 'share a view', 9), *riconoscere* ('acknowledge', 9), *ammettere* ('admit', 7), *accettare* ('accept', 7), *concordare* ('agree', 5) and *respingere* ('reject', 6) all have lower frequencies than their English counterparts.

Many of the occurrences also refer to argumentative interaction in the world of reported history, rather than in the world of discourse and disciplinary debates. On the whole then, the dialogue established is varied, but in some cases largely one within the world of history or between the author and the sources: *confermare*, for example, is much more used than English *confirm*, but largely attributed to the reviewed author confirming existing theories (15 occurrences out of 21) or to historical sources confirming the author's thesis (5 occurrences out of 20), thus almost excluding the voice of the reviewer. The emphasis is also quite obviously on convergent voices. The English corpus by comparison is much more explicit in the use of dialogic verbs producing a picture of divergence.

One element that might somehow counterbalance this view is the marked presence of the negative in Italian: *non* is remarkably more frequent than *not*, with its 1596 occurrences (83 per 10,000 words), compared to 1061 in English (54 per 10,000 words). Even adding occurrences of *cannot* (56), *don't* (6), *doesn't* (2) and *needn't* (1), the difference is noticeable. Italian academics seem to identify contrast more often by explicit evaluation or by denying statements rather than by reporting disagreement. Example (8) shows a passage where agreement is signalled verbally and explicitly (*concorda*), but disagreement is shown by denying the interpretation proposed by Fofi and pointing at another question through a series on negatives:

> (8) Fofi parla da tempo di 'due '68': cioè un '68 inizialmente 'buono', ma soffocato prestissimo da un secondo '68, dai gruppi extraparlamentari, dall'ideologia ecc. Resta da capire perché sia stato così facile a questo '68 'cattivo' sopprimere rapidamente quello buono, ma il punto che interessa qui **non** è questo. Chi come me **non** si ritrova in questa lettura, la considera riduttiva, e **concorda però** con Fofi sul pessimismo relativo all'oggi, ha un enorme problema che Goffredo **non** ha.

Another interesting feature of the corpus is the choice of reporting verbs that represent argument through a metaphor of 'vision' rather than 'fight'. These are not 'defended' or 'attacked', but rather 'revealed', 'illuminated', 'highlighted', 'foregrounded'. Arguing means 'seeing', 'showing' and 'letting people see': verbs like *emergere, notare, sottolineare, osservare, evidenziare, mettere in evidenza/luce/rilievo* are very frequent in the corpus. Elements belonging to this metaphoric field are also often presented in clusters, as shown by emphasis in the following extract:

(9) L'oltraggio alla donna da parte dello straniero (o del traditore) è un elemento centrale nell'archeologia del discorso nazionale.... Consente infatti di **mettere in scena** la difesa della donna, della sua purezza, e soprattutto, **sottolinea** Banti, la difesa della purezza della stirpe. Viene così **messo in luce** un aspetto dell'adesione emozionale alla nazione italiana che era stato finora senza dubbio **messo in secondo piano.**

The most obvious example in the field is the verb *sottolineare* ('underline') (88 occurrences, an average of 2 per article by itself). The reviewed author remains the dominant voice as agent of the action (57 occurrences out of 88) (cf. example 9 above), but the reviewer also comes in as the subject of underlining (18 occurrences out of 88), whereas the discourse community and the world of history have a limited role (8 and 5 occurrences respectively). The verb is characterized by an extremely wide extension of meaning. If 'underlining' can be associated to contexts in which it means 'pointing out salient features' of the text reported (as signalled for example by *soprattutto*, 'above all'), it often bears no indication of emphasis, contrast or other form of markedness. It is simply used as a verb of saying and signals 'supporting' a claim or 'inferring' a consequence, as in (10):

(10) La rivoluzione nazionale tedesca avrebbe potuto vincere solo se avesse vinto la rivoluzione nei singoli Stati. Questo dato – **sottolinea** Langewiesche – faceva sì che un avvicinamento delle élite e la concessione della costituzione non fossero sufficienti a condurre a buon fine la rivoluzione.

In similar contexts, English could variously use *mention, note, point out,* etc. If the denotative meaning of these verbs is different, their pragmatic function is similar. Of course English does have a set of verbs based on the same metaphoric field of 'vision', but their use – apart from *point out* (31 occurrences) – is extremely limited in my corpus and mostly directed at introducing elements of emphasis: *underline* is attested only four times and only two of these introduce a reported clause, whereas *highlight* is used ten times, but never in explicit reporting.

It should be noticed then that the frequency of these elements in Italian does not correspond to any significant emphasis. The tension between the frequency of a lexical item and its emphatic function should not go unnoticed: 'markedness' (Merlini Barbaresi, 2003) is reduced by frequency. It is exactly the incidence of the metaphor of vision which makes it metaphorically weaker in Italian and requires use of other emphasizers when actual contrast is needed.

Conclusions

As we have seen, the genre of the book review article finds its specificity – measured against research articles – in a combination of evaluative language and reporting. The reviewer is clearly interested in giving voice to his or her own position in the field. On the level of writer–reader interaction, the dominant voice of the reviewer is manifested through expressions of stance and his or her role as textual interpreter. The multiplicity of textual voices in the book review article also produces a range of textual dialogue. The reader is involved in interaction with the reviewed author and the discourse community through different forms of 'engagement'. The voices of historical characters and sources are also involved, though mostly to confirm or disconfirm the author's claims.

The analysis of lexical elements representing the activity of the various textual voices (the reviewer, the reviewed author, the discourse community or historical characters and sources) revealed different degrees of explicitness in the representation of argument as such, ranging from verbs like *argue, claim* or *reject* to reporting verbs that only take up argumentative meaning in context, such as *believe* or *think* in the English corpus and *notare* or *osservare* in the Italian corpus.

When focusing on the verbal means of representation, the analysis also revealed an interesting difference between the two corpora, that may be related to the ways in which the academic cultures they embody tend to characterize argumentative positions. The English corpus showed preference for lexicalizations that represent argument as dialogic by making explicit reference to the roles of agreement and disagreement. The Italian corpus, on the other hand, showed a preference for monologic representations, where argument is seen as an internal process and the dominant metaphor is one of 'vision', argumentative interaction is represented in terms of giving visual prominence to elements. In both cases, it might be useful to reflect on the degree of markedness of lexical choice and be aware of the fact that lexical items with corresponding denotative meanings might have a different degree of markedness on a pragmatic level.

References

Bondi, M. (1999) *English across Genres: Language Variation in the Discourse of Economics* (Modena: Il Fiorino).
Bondi, M. (2001) 'Small Corpora and Language Variation. Reflexivity across Genres' in M. Ghadessy, A. Henry and R. L. Roseberry (eds) *Small Corpus Studies and ELT* (Amsterdam: John Benjamins), 135–74.
Bondi, M. (2005) 'Metadiscursive Practices in Academic Discourse: Variation across Genres and Disciplines' in J. Bamford and M. Bondi (eds) *Dialogue within Discourse Communities: Metadiscursive Perspectives on Academic Genres* (Tübingen: Niemeyer), 3–29.
Bondi, M. (2007) 'Authority and Expert Voices in the Discourse of History' in K. Fløttum (ed.) *Language and Discipline Perspectives on Academic Discourse* (Newcastle: Cambridge Scholars Publishing), 66–88.
Bondi, M. and Silver, M. (2004) 'Textual Voices: A Cross-Disciplinary Study of Attribution in Academic Discourse' in L. Anderson and J. Bamford (eds) *Evaluation in Oral and Written Academic Discourse* (Rome: Officina Edizioni), 117–36.
Charles, M. (2006) 'Phraseological Patterns in Reporting Clauses Used in Citation: A Corpus-Based Study of Theses in Two Disciplines', *English for Specific Purposes*, XXV, 3, 310–31.
Coffin, C. (2006) *Historical Discourse* (London: Continuum).
Connor, U. (2004) 'Intercultural Rhetoric Research: Beyond Texts', *Journal of English for Academic Purposes*, III, 4 (Special Issue), 291–304.
Dahl, T. (2003) 'Metadiscourse in Research Articles' in K. Fløttum and F. Rastier (eds) *Academic Discourse. Multidisciplinary Approaches* (Oslo: Novus Press), 120–38.
Diani, G. (2004) 'A Genre-Based Approach to Analysing Academic Review Articles' in M. Bondi, L. Gavioli and M. Silver (eds) *Academic Discourse, Genre and Small Corpora* (Rome: Officina Edizioni), 105–26.
Diani, G. (2006) 'Reviewer Stance in Academic Review Articles: A Cross-Disciplinary Comparison' in G. Del Lungo Camiciotti, M. Dossena and B. Crawford Camiciottoli (eds) *Variation in Business and Economics Discourse: Diachronic and Genre Perspectives* (Rome: Officina Edizioni), 139–51.
Diani, G. (2007) 'The Representation of Evaluative and Argumentative Procedures: Examples from the Academic Book Review Article', *Textus*, XX, 1, 37–56.
Fløttum, K., Dahl, T., Kinn, T., Müller Gjesdal, A. and Vold, E. T. (2007) 'Cultural Identities and Academic Voices' in K. Fløttum (ed.) *Language and Discipline Perspectives on Academic Discourse* (Newcastle: Cambridge Scholars Publishing), 14–39.
Groom, N. (2005) 'Pattern and Meaning across Genres and Disciplines', *Journal of English for Academic Purposes*, IV, 3, 257–77.

Hunston, S. (2004) ' "It Has Rightly Been Pointed Out …": Attribution, Consensus and Conflict in Academic Discourse' in M. Bondi, L. Gavioli and M. Silver (eds) *Academic Discourse, Genre and Small Corpora* (Rome: Officina Edizioni), 15–33.

Hunston, S. and Sinclair, J. McH. (2000) 'A Local Grammar of Evaluation', in S. Hunston and G. Thompson (eds) *Evaluation in Text. Authorial Stance and the Construction of Discourse* (Oxford: Oxford University Press), 74–101.

Hyland, K. (1998) 'Persuasion and Context: The Pragmatics of Academic Metadiscourse', *Journal of Pragmatics*, XXX, 4, 437–55.

Hyland, K. (1999) 'Academic Attribution: Citation and the Construction of Disciplinary Knowledge', *Applied Linguistics*, XX, 3, 341–67.

Hyland, K. (2000) *Disciplinary Discourses: Social Interactions in Academic Writing* (London: Longman).

Hyland, K. (2002) 'Directives: Argument and Engagement in Academic Writing', *Applied Linguistics*, XXIII, 2, 215–39.

Hyland, K. (2005) *Metadiscourse. Exploring Interaction in Writing* (London: Continuum).

Hyland, K. (2008) 'Academic Clusters: Text Patterning in Published and Postgraduate Writing', *International Journal of Applied Linguistics*, XVIII, 1, 41–62.

Hyland, K. and Tse, P. (2005) 'Hooking the Reader: A Corpus Study of Evaluative *that* in Abstracts', *English for Specific Purposes*, XXIV, 2, 123–39.

Hyland, K. and Bondi, M. (eds) (2006) *Academic Discourse across Disciplines* (Bern: Peter Lang).

Mauranen, A. (1993) *Cultural Differences in Academic Rhetoric. A Textlinguistic Study* (Frankfurt: Peter Lang).

Mauranen, A. (2001) 'Descriptions or Explanations? Some Methodological Issues in Contrastive Rhetoric' in M. Hewings (ed.) *Academic Writing in Context* (Birmingham: University of Birmingham Press), 43–54.

Mauranen, A. (2003) ' "But There's a Flawed Argument": Socialisation into and through Metadiscourse', *Language and Computers*, XLVI, 1, 19–34.

Merlini Barbaresi, L. (ed.) (2003) *Complexity in Language and Text* (Pisa: Edizioni Plus).

Moreno, A. I. and Suárez, L. (2008) 'A Study of Critical Attitude across English and Spanish Academic Book Reviews', *Journal of English for Academic Purposes*, VII, 1, 15–26.

Motta-Roth, D. (1998) 'Discourse Analysis and Academic Book Reviews: A Study of Text and Disciplinary Cultures' in I. Fortanet, S. Posteguillo, J. C. Palmer and J. F. Coll (eds) *Genre Studies in English for Academic Purposes* (Castelló de la Plana: Publicacions de la Univesitat Jaume I), 29–58.

Römer, U. (2008) 'Identification Impossible? A Corpus Approach to Realisations of Evaluative Meaning in Academic Writing', *Functions of Language*, XV, 1, 115–30.

Salager-Meyer, F., Alcaraz Ariza, M. A. and Pabón Berbesí, M. (2007) 'Collegiality, Critique and the Construction of Scientific Argumentation in Medical Book Reviews: A Diachronic Approach', *Journal of Pragmatics*, XXXIX, 10, 1758–74.

Scott, M. (2004) *WordSmith Tools* (Oxford: Oxford University Press).

Shaw, P. (2004) 'How Do We Recognise Implicit Evaluation in Academic Book Reviews?' in G. Del Lungo Camiciotti and E. Tognini Bonelli (eds) *Academic Discourse – New Insights into Evaluation* (Bern: Peter Lang), 121–40.

Sinclair, J. McH. (1987) 'Mirror for a Text', Manuscript. (Published 1988 *Journal of English and Foreign Languages*, Hyderabad, India), 15–44.

Stati, S. (1994) 'Passive Moves in Argumentation' in S. Čmejrková and F. Stícha (eds) *The Syntax of Sentences and Text* (Amsterdam: John Benjamins), 259–71.

Thompson, G. (1996) 'Voices in the Text: Discourse Perspectives on Language Reports', *Applied Linguistics*, XVII, 4, 501–30.

Thompson, P. (2005) 'Aspects of Identification and Position in Intertextual Reference in PhD Theses' in E. Tognini-Bonelli and G. Del Lungo Camiciotti (eds) *Strategies in Academic Discourse* (Amsterdam: John Benjamins), 31–50.

Thompson, G. and Hunston, S. (2000) 'Evaluation: An Introduction' in S. Hunston and G. Thompson (eds) *Evaluation in Text: Authorial Stance and the Construction of Discourse* (Oxford: Oxford University Press), 3–27.

Tse, P. and Hyland, K. (2008) '*Robot Kung Fu*: Gender and Professional Identity in Biology and Philosophy Review', *Journal of Pragmatics*, XL, 7, 1232–48.

Part IV
Diachronic Variation

11
On the Dynamic Nature of Genre: A Diachronic Study of Blurbs

Maria-Lluïsa Gea-Valor and Marta Inigo Ros

Introduction

There is no doubt that book publishing is a highly competitive industry, especially nowadays. Publishing firms constantly struggle to maintain their space in the market or, in the worst cases, merely to survive. Over the last three decades, international corporations have gradually taken over small and medium-sized companies, so today's independent publishing represents only 1 per cent of the total sales in the industry whereas 90 per cent of the sector is controlled by five major conglomerates, specifically in the United States (Schiffrin, 2001; Mehta, 2006). As Schiffrin indicates, 'In 1999 the top twenty publishers accounted for 93 per cent of the sales, and the ten largest had 75 per cent of revenues' (2001, pp. 2–3). These media multinationals have also come to dominate the UK market. According to the Publishers Association, in all the major publishing sectors 'over half the market by value (and sometimes, as in the case of fiction publishing, 90 per cent) is now controlled by fewer than ten publishing companies' (Richardson and Taylor, 2008, p. 16).

Promotion seems therefore essential for survival and book covers are the most immediate and conspicuous advertising space publishing firms use in order to attract potential customers. It has already been established that book blurbs fulfil a promotional purpose, being widely used by the book industry to promote products and to persuade prospective readers to buy books (Kathpalia, 1997; Bhatia, 2004; Gea-Valor, 2005). But has this communicative intention always been at the core of the blurb genre?

From a critical discourse analysis perspective, Fairclough (1993, 1995) discusses the effects of the generalization of promotion in contemporary culture and argues that 'the genre of consumer advertising has been colonizing professional and public service orders of discourse on a massive scale' (1995, p. 139). This phenomenon, known as marketization of discourse, has given rise to hybrid genres displaying features typically associated with advertising discourse. Bhatia (2004) also addresses this interdiscursivity, contending, in his study of professional and academic discourse, that genre mixing and embedding has become quite common in the last decades, and that promotional strategies are increasingly employed in genres traditionally considered non-promotional in their communicative intention but informative or merely persuasive. Book blurbs belong to this 'colony' of promotional genres, together with advertisements, promotional letters, application letters and reference letters, all of which share a common promotional purpose, although displaying specific realizations.

Also of special interest is Kathpalia's (1997) comparative study of international publishers' book blurbs and those of local Singapore-based publishers, where she underscores the importance of sociocultural factors in the shaping of genres. As this author states, 'genres are socio-culturally dependent communicative events and their success, in part, depends upon their pragmatic value in a specific business/professional environment' (1997, p. 417).

In the light of these insightful works, the purpose of this chapter is to explore the evolution of the blurb genre and to determine the changes it has undergone over the years, especially regarding rhetorical structure and linguistic realizations. It is our contention that blurbs have been greatly influenced by the diversification of the target audience and the dramatic growth experienced by the advertising and marketing industries in the last decades of the twentieth century.

Corpus and method

Our study draws on a corpus of more than 100 blurbs of books published by Penguin, one of the most widely-known and respected publishing companies in the English-speaking world. More specifically, the study focuses on blurbs of fiction books published since the late 1940s in the Penguin Classics series – including Penguin Popular Classics, Penguin Modern Classics, Penguin Twentieth-Century Classics and the most recent Penguin Red Classics. The literature works within these series are clearly of academic interest since they form part of the Western canon, and most of them are required reading in universities and higher-education institutions.

The first step in our study involved the compilation of Penguin titles published since 1946, when the Penguin Classics series was launched. The tracing of older editions proved to be the most difficult part of the collecting process. Some early editions, such as Rieu's translation of *The Odyssey* (1946) or the translation of Perrault's *Fairy Tales* (1957), were excluded from our study since their back covers merely offered a list of translated titles.

At the second stage of our research, we classified the titles gathered into series, a process which was also complex due to the numerous collections created over the years. Nowadays, there are three main classics series: Penguin Classics, Modern Classics and Red Classics.

After scanning and filing all the texts, the third step was to analyse them from a genre-based perspective: at the discursive level – in terms of communicative or rhetorical structure – and at the lexico-grammatical level – most salient linguistic features, especially appraising and persuasive devices.

Communicative intent stands out as the defining factor of genre, which influences rhetorical organization and language use (Swales, 1990; Bhatia, 1993). Regarding blurbs, their main purpose is to promote a book and to persuade potential readers to buy it by providing both description and positive evaluation. This purpose is reflected in the rhetorical structure of the blurb, which consists of five communicative steps or moves, each one 'performing a specific function which contributes to the global function of promoting the book' (Kathpalia, 1997, p. 417):

Move 1 Catchphrase
Move 2 Description
Move 3 Appraisal
    Submove: Endorsement
Move 4 Author's credentials
Move 5 Technical information

Figure 11.1   Rhetorical structure of the blurb (adapted from Kathpalia, 1997; Gea-Valor, 2005)

On the basis of the structural models proposed by Kathpalia (1997) and Gea-Valor (2005), these moves were identified by determining the communicative function fulfilled by the various sections of the text in relation to its overall purpose.

As shown in Figure 11.1, *catchphrases* constitute the opening move of the blurb (Move 1) and, since they are relatively short and visually striking, function as attention-seeking devices, being frequently placed after the heading – which simply includes the firm's name, the title and the author. Example (1) illustrates this move:

(1) James's first really popular fiction work and the first of his great portraits of the American female. (*Daisy Miller. Penguin Classics*)

Catchphrases are followed by *Move 2 description*, which offers a synopsis of the plot and/or a brief description of the characters, and may be considered a central move in the blurb, together with Move 3. The description move is shown in the following example:

(2) It is a poem in which the virtues of a knight, Sir Gawain, triumphant in almost insuperable ordeals, are celebrated to the glory of the House of Arthur. (*Sir Gawain. Penguin Classics*)

Move 3 appraisal focuses on the qualities of the book and, together with laudatory editorial comment, generally displays praising excerpts from renowned journals and magazines, and/or from reputed writers and critics. These quotes, called *endorsements*, function as authoritative, objective voices that recommend the book by praising the author, the book or both; in other words, it is external praise, not one provided by the publisher, and therefore perceived as less biased, more trustworthy. According to Sinclair (1985, p. 159), 'Book advertising for major hardcover fiction and nonfiction is usually filled with quotes. Research shows that serious book buyers want endorsements or recommendations from people they respect – reviewers, commentators, well-known people in various fields'.

In our analysis, endorsements have been considered as a submove within Move 3. An important distinction is thus drawn between appraisal and endorsement: the former encloses not only editorial comment about the qualities of the book and/or the author but also evaluative statements appearing on their own or intertwined with description, whereas the latter refers exclusively to quotes from respected and well-established sources. Examples (3) and (4) illustrate the appraisal move and the endorsement submove respectively:

(3) In *David Copperfield* – the novel he described as his 'favourite child' – Dickens drew revealingly on his own experiences to create one of his most exuberant and enduringly popular works, filled with tragedy and comedy in equal measure. (*David Copperfield. Black Classics*)

(4) The delicate, feline *Washington Square*, perhaps the only novel in which a man has successfully invaded the feminine field and produced work comparable to Jane Austen's – Graham Greene. (*Washington Square. Penguin Modern Classics*)

Move 4 author's credentials, also known as *establishing credentials* (Kathpalia, 1997; Bhatia, 2004), offers the author's professional and personal background, that is, previous publications, current interests, awards won and biographical details:

(5) Winner of the Nobel Prize for Literature. (*East of Eden. Penguin Modern Classics*)

Finally, *Move 5* provides 'technical' information on the special features of the book, such as the source text of the edition, the person in charge of the introduction, the notes and/or the glossary, and details on the cover illustration:

(6) Edited with an Introduction and Notes by Robin Gilmour. (*The Warden. Black Classics*)

It is important to note that move structure is flexible so that moves – and submoves – do not always occur in the same sequence in every instance of the genre. Moves 'can also be discontinuous or embedded one with the other' (Bhatia, 2004, p. 175). More importantly, as we will see in the following section, move frequency may vary significantly according to the characteristics of the blurb – in the case of Penguin, according to the series – so a move considered obligatory or quasi-obligatory in one collection may become peripheral or optional in another. As Bhatia states, variations depend upon 'the nature of the book, the target audience, the publishing house responsible for it and above all the kind of discipline it belongs to' (ibid).

Diachronic change in Penguin blurbs: rhetorical structure and linguistic realizations

This section presents the evolution of Penguin blurbs by focusing firstly on the changes in rhetorical organization, taking as a basis the move-structure shown previously, and secondly the most relevant linguistic realizations, especially those involving the evaluative function.

Rhetorical structure

Regarding rhetorical structure, that is, the communicative organization of the blurb into moves, changes over time seem to have been mainly driven by the need to adapt to an ever-diversifying audience, as evidenced by the percentages of occurrence of each move per series from the 1950s until today, shown in Tables 11.1 to 11.3. Table 11.4 offers the frequency of moves in Penguin Red Classics, a newly-created collection launched in 2006. Although it does not offer any diachronic information, it further illustrates the rhetorical preferences of the modern blurb.

As will be explained in more detail below by focusing on each move, the 1970s seem to be a turning point in the publishing industry and thus

Table 11.1 Evolution of move-structure in Penguin Modern Classics blurbs

	1950–70 (%)	1970–80 (%)	1980–90 (%)	1990–2000 (%)	2000 on (%)
Move 1 Catchphrase	–	50	100	100	100
Move 2 Description	33	33	33	50	25
Move 3 Appraisal	–	33	–	50	15
Submove: Endorsement	33	83	83	67	100
Move 2 & 3 merger	67	50	67	50	75
Move 4 Credentials	100	100	100	100	100
Move 5 Edition	33	–	17	–	90
Move 5 Cover	67	100	100	100	100

Table 11.2 Evolution of move-structure in Penguin Classics blurbs

	1960–70 (%)	1970–2000 (%)	2000 on (%)
Move 1 Catchphrase	–	100	100
Move 2 Description	–	10	9
Move 3 Appraisal	–	45	3
Submove: Endorsement	–	35	97
Move 2 & 3 merger	100	85	84
Move 4 Credentials	100	100	100
Move 5 Edition	–	50	87
Move 5 Cover	100	100	–

Table 11.3   Evolution of move-structure in Penguin Popular Classics blurbs

	Until the 1990s (%)	*From the 1990s on* (%)
Move 1 Catchphrase	100	100
Move 2 Description	28	100
Move 3 Appraisal	–	–
Submove: Endorsement	14	100
Move 2 & 3 merger	72	–
Move 4 Credentials	100	100
Move 5 Edition	–	–
Move 5 Cover	100	–

Table 11.4   Move-structure in Penguin Red Classics

	Penguin Red Classics (%)
Move 1 Catchphrase	100
Move 2 Description	100
Move 3 Appraisal	–
Submove: Endorsement	100
Move 2 & 3 merger	–
Move 4 Credentials	100
Move 5 Edition	–
Move 5 Cover	100

the period where significant changes begin to take place. As Margolis (1985, pp. 167–68) asserts:

> Until the 1970s, publicity was rarely considered very important in most publishing houses.... The 1970s were the decade when the publishing industry went public, in both the financial and the publicity sense.... During the 1970s, more media attention was lavished on books and authors than ever before, not just because there was more to publicise but also because the media had expanded so remarkably.

The new millennium stands out as another crucial time for Penguin, which set out then to redefine its Classics series in an attempt to reassure its share of the market, adapt to the demands of the book-buying public, appeal more effectively to the potential readership and, ultimately, '[survive] in a world of fierce competition' (Baines, 2005, p. 224).

Move 1 catchphrase

The use of catchphrases has increased significantly in the blurb over the years, especially in the 1970s and in the new century, and has spread to all collections. This is particularly evident in the latest Red Classics series where endorsements, used as catchphrases, are used in 100 per cent of the blurbs, not only on the back cover but also on the front cover:

(7) This has everything: murder, passion, injustice, loss, love – Daily Express. (*Tess of the d'Urbervilles. Red Classics*)

(8) A classic tale of the misunderstood outsider made good – Eoin Colfer. (*The Adventures of Huckleberry Finn. Red Classics*)

The only Penguin books which do not offer a catchphrase are the oldest Classics (including Modern Classics) – probably because at that time publicity of the book relied mainly on the author's reputation and the literary interest of the novel – and the new Popular Classics – the main objective of which is to make the classics available at accessible prices; this may explain the simplicity of the design and of the blurbs in particular, which are reduced to the bare minimum.

As evidenced in the Red Classics extracts shown above, catchphrases often resort to quotes from celebrated authors and renowned critics. This rhetorical preference is also present in 67 per cent of the 1990–2000 Penguin Modern Classics blurbs. Nonetheless, it is very common to find praising statements written by the publisher which focus on the impact of the novel or the literary importance of the main character: 72 per cent of the old Popular Classics blurbs and 84 per cent of texts in the old Black Classics series prioritize this alternative, as the following examples show:

(9) *Pamela* created a sensation when it was first published in 1740 – and it has never ceased to be controversial. (*Pamela. Black Classics*)

(10) [It] was sold out in just over two months. (*Far from the Madding Crowd. Penguin Classics*)

(11) Since its publication in 1847 *Jane Eyre* has never ceased to be one of the most widely read English novels. (*Jane Eyre. Penguin Popular Classics*)

In the old Black Classics, complimentary remarks in the catchphrase may be combined with descriptive statements which serve as a quick introduction to the book:

(12) *Barchester Towers* (1857) is Trollope's most popular novel and a great work of English fiction. The second of the *Chronicles of Barsetshire*, it continues the story of Mr Harding and his daughter Eleanor which began in *The Warden*. (*Barchester Towers. Black Classics*)

As for the most recent Modern Classics, endorsements by distinguished writers and renowned newspapers are prevalent in the catchphrase (e.g. in 67 per cent of the 1990–2000 Modern Classics). This is particularly striking in the 2000s Silver classics where quotes, displayed in a larger type on the left side of the cover, are offered in all the blurbs studied:

(13) His final masterpiece... enthralling and indispensable for understanding modern history – Timothy Garton-Ash, New York Review of Books. (*Nineteen Eighty-Four. Modern Classics*)

(14) Lush and evocative... the one Waugh which best expresses at once the profundity of change and the indomitable endurance of the human spirit – The Times. (*Brideshead Revisited. Modern Classics*)

In contrast, the catchphrase in 97 per cent of today's Black Classics blurbs simply consists of a quote from the book, usually by the main character in a key passage, and highlighted in orange lettering:

(15) How am I to dress up in my finery, and go off and away to smart parties, after the sorrow I have seen today? (*North and South. Black Classics*)

(16) Let him feel that he is one of us; once fill his mind with the idea that he has been a thief, and he's ours, – ours for his life! (*Oliver Twist. Black Classics*)

(17) The swift, unseen threshing of the night upon him silenced him and he was overcome. (*The Rainbow. Black Classics*)

Move 2 description

Description, one of the central moves in the blurb, is often combined with praise for the qualities of the book, especially regarding style and literary or social impact. Such merging is present in 85 per cent of the old Black Classics blurbs, 84 per cent in the new series, 50 per cent in the Modern Classics published between 1990 and 2000, and 75 per cent in the Silver Classics. These favourable comments clearly act as appraisal, although their force is somewhat diminished since it is appraisal provided by the publisher selling the book:

(18) After seven years of marriage the beautiful Lady Brenda Last is bored with life at Hetton Abbey, the Gothic mansion that is the pride and joy of her husband, Tony. She drifts into an affair with the shallow socialite John Beaver and forsakes Tony for the Belgravia set. (*A Handful of Dust. Black Classics*)

(19) In the stultified air of the wealthy European holiday resorts, Americans cling to their own ways and traditions. Daisy Miller, with her outspoken honesty and innocence of mind, is anathema to them. (*Daisy Miller. Penguin Popular Classics*)

In general terms, it can be stated that, over the years, description has been gaining relevance in the blurb – although often combined with appraisal – to such an extent that, in the New Popular Classics series, for instance, all blurbs are reduced to a mere summary of the story; here, description is the only move used and no evaluative element is present, as example (20) demonstrates:

(20) When proud and independent Isabel Archer is brought to England from New York by her chaperone, she refuses all suitors, determined to find her own way in life. But unexpectedly left a large fortune by her uncle, Isabel is suddenly vulnerable to charming but worthless men – men like Gilbert Osmond. (*The Portrait of a Lady. New Penguin Popular Classics*)

In this collection, addressed to the general public, costs are reduced to a minimum, as evidenced by their simple format. Apart from description, these blurbs contain a self-promotional statement about the series, which is maintained across titles and reads as follows:

PENGUIN POPULAR CLASSICS are the perfect introduction to the world-famous Penguin Classics series – which encompasses the best books ever written, from Homer's *Odyssey* to Orwell's *1984* and everything in between. For a full list and ideas on what to read next, visit www.penguinclassics.com

This new tendency clearly contrasts with the old Popular Classics series, where pure description is found in only 28 per cent of cases, whereas merging of Moves 2 and 3 prevails in 72 per cent of books.

Move 3 appraisal

The evolution of the blurb's rhetorical structure is especially interesting with regard to this move. Although at first sight this seems to be one of the key communicative sections of the genre, our study reveals a decreasing use of this move on its own. Today's Penguin blurbs generally favour two possible communicative combinations: on the one hand, a merging of description and appraisal and, on the other hand, the display of a catchphrase and/or an endorsement rendering evaluation, always of a positive nature.

As shown in Tables 11.1–11.3, appraisal is present in all earlier blurbs, frequently combined with description. Earlier Modern Classics blurbs tend to discuss a given book at length in the wider context of its author's work and life, whereas more recent blurbs focus on the description of the story and the characters. The most extreme cases of absence of appraisal in the blurb are, firstly, the new Popular Classics, where absolutely no appraisal is present and, secondly, the Red Classics, which displays very few evaluative elements other than endorsements.

A relevant submove that contributes to the appraising function of the blurb is precisely the endorsement, which is often used as a catchphrase and thus placed either at the top or the bottom of the page. In these examples from various collections in several periods, the powerful effect of endorsements, provided by acclaimed authors, is obvious:

(21) There has been nothing as good since – Ernest Hemingway. (*The Adventures of Huckleberry Finn. Penguin Classics*)

(22) This superb romance [stands] at the head of all his works – Virginia Wolf. (*Lord Jim. Black Classics*)

(23) What a jolly thing it is for a man to have written books like these and just filled people's hearts with pity – Robert Louis Stevenson. (*The Christmas Books. Penguin Popular Classics*)

Lately, endorsements have gained importance in the communicative unfolding of the genre, and are pervasively used in the most recent Penguin series (97 per cent of Black Classics blurbs, and 100 per cent in both Red Classics and Modern Classics), to such an extent that blurbs are frequently reduced to the descriptive move and an endorsement (or a string of endorsements), while no other appraisal is offered. In other words, endorsements seem to have fully taken over the appraising function traditionally attributed to Move 3. This responds to an obvious marketing purpose, shown by the fact that in some contemporary series, especially Silver and Modern Classics, the endorsement has been shifted to the left-hand side of the cover, where it acquires special prominence as an eye-catching device:

(24) Graves made Roman history funny and familiar – The Guardian. (*Claudius the God. Modern Classics*)

(25) Everybody knows now that *Ulysses* is the greatest novel of the century – Anthony Burgess, Observer. (*Ulysses. Silver Classics*)

Move 4 author's credentials

It can be observed that, over the years, this move has gradually lost its relevance, as evidenced by the fact that, except for the earliest Classics, information about the author is only offered inside the book. This may be accounted for by the fact that the authors involved are classics or widely-known writers of the time, thus credentials are superfluous. The following extracts belong to editions before 1965, where biographical sketches are offered on the back cover:

(26) Emily Jane Brontë, who was born in 1818, was one of three sisters, who lived in their father's parsonage at Haworth in the Yorkshire moors. Their home's remoteness and the lack of any companionship outside the family forced them, as Charlotte said, to be 'wholly dependent on ourselves and each other, on books and study for the enjoyments and occupations of life.' (*Wuthering Heights. Penguin Books*)

(27) Mr. E. M. Forster is not a prolific writer. He has indeed written only five novels, yet at least two of them – *A Passage to India* and *Howards End* – are widely regarded as masterpieces. (*Howards End. Penguin Modern Classics*)

In later series, this move may occasionally be displayed on the back cover only to offer a brief outline of the writer's career, to refer to the significance of the novel in the author's life or to inform about awards and prizes won. The following examples belong to books published in 1981 and 1999, respectively:

(28) In such terms Nobel Prize winner William Faulkner was described prior to his death in 1962. When he wrote *As I Lay Dying* – in six summer weeks in 1929 during nightshifts at the local power station – Faulkner had already shaken off the influence of Huxley and Joyce. (*As I Lay Dying. Penguin Modern Classics*)

(29) *I, Claudius* received both the James Tait Black Memorial Prize and the Hawthornden Prize. (*I, Claudius. Penguin Twentieth-Century Classics*)

Move 5 technical information: edition and cover illustration

Despite being a secondary move in the rhetorical configuration of blurbs, Move 5 can be considered obligatory in Penguin Classics (87 per cent in modern Black Classics and 90 per cent in modern Silver Classics), where it generally anticipates the information provided in the introduction to the book by making reference to the source text and any possible additional material included in the edition, such as chronologies, notes, lists for further reading, etc. The person in charge of the introduction, the notes and/or the preface, and the editor or translator, are also mentioned here:

(30) Edited by Mark Lilly and introduced by Tony Tanner. (*Villette. Penguin Classics*)

(31) This edition follows the text of Thackeray's revised edition of 1853. John Carey's introduction identifies *Vanity Fair* as a landmark in the development of European Realism, and as a reflection of Thackeray's passionate love for another man's wife. (*Vanity Fair. Black Classics*)

All the Penguin Classics published in the 1970s and 1980s display this move at the top of the back cover following the title and the author, while the Black Classics series, especially since the year 2000, consistently offers it at the bottom. This demonstrates the non-strict nature of move-sequencing in the blurb.

Information about the cover illustration, accompanied in some series by a small-scale reproduction of such illustration, is provided in this move as well and is offered in the totality of blurbs examined:

(32) The cover shows a detail from *The Only Daughter* by Jessica Hayllar by courtesy of Forbes Magazine Collection, New York (photo: Bridgeman Art Library). (*Washington Square. Penguin Popular Classics*)

Linguistic realizations

As mentioned above, catchphrases constitute the move which has more significantly increased over the years. Their function as an attention-seeking element is realized both visually – by being strategically and conspicuously situated, and by displaying attractive colours and varied type fonts – and linguistically – by means of superlatives and boosters that qualify the book in absolute terms, as these examples from the Penguin Classics series illustrate:

(33) *Beowulf* is the most important Old English poem and perhaps the most significant single survival from the Anglo-Saxon period. (*Beowulf. Penguin Classics*)

(34) Elizabeth Gaskell's best work…remarkable, and triumphantly successful, on many levels. (*North and South. Penguin Classics*)

Secondly, even though evaluation of the book is usually associated with Move 3, there is frequent merging of description and evaluation in all series across time. As Kathpalia accurately observes, evaluative language 'permeates throughout the blurb like spreading waves' (1997, p. 425), which certainly contributes to the narrative progression of the text. In examples (35) and (36), appraisal intertwines with description in the form of prepositional phrases filled with positive adjectives (*sensitive, powerful, astonishing*). Also worth noting is the use of syntactic structures reminiscent of advertising discourse (i.e. *one of the most* + string of adjectives), which is common in the modern blurb:

(35) With its sensitive depiction of the wronged Tess and powerful criticism of social convention, *Tess of the d'Urbervilles* is one of the most moving and poetic of Hardy's novels. (*Tess of the d'Urbervilles. Black Classics*)

(36) With their astonishing diversity of tone and subject matter, *The Canterbury Tales* have become one of the touchstones of medieval

literature. The tales are told by a motley crowd of pilgrims as they journey for five days from Southwark to Canterbury. (*The Canterbury Tales. Penguin Classics*)

The analysis also reveals that earlier texts tend to follow conventional clause and syntactic patterns, whereas more recent blurbs employ elliptical structures – which sometimes even flout grammatical rules – in an attempt to sound more colloquial and pique the reader's attention. In the following examples, the ellipsis of the subject (37 and 38) and the use of powerful praising adjectives in minor clauses (39) certainly add to the impact of the catchphrase:

(37) Exquisite . . . captures a twilight world of longing and dreaming – Sunday Times. (*The Great Gatsby. Penguin Classics*)

(38) Impresses me more deeply with every read – Sarah Waters. (*Great Expectations. Red Classics*)

(39) Redeeming, splendid, headlong, endlessly comic and evocative – John Updike. (*Lolita. Red Classics*)

Another strategy that seems to have been gaining relevance in the blurb in the past two decades is the inclusion of 'cliff-hangers' or curiosity arousers at the end of the descriptive move. Experts in the editorial process recommend that description of the book must be done 'in such a way as to entice the potential reader to buy the book' (Rawson and Dolin, 1985, p. 41). As Kathpalia (1997, p. 424) puts it, 'The definition of a good blurb is one that provides only minimal irresistible information without giving away the story and, therefore, compelling the reader to make the purchase'. The clauses in italics at the end of these extracts from the newest Popular Classics collection clearly display this strategy:

(40) An ancient parchment bearing a mysterious cryptogram maps the most hazardous journey of Professor Lidenbrock's career up to the summit of a volcano, down secret passages and across a monster-infested underground sea, *on what may be a voyage of no return.* (*Journey to the Centre of the Earth. New Penguin Popular Classics*)

(41) Glamour, wealth and success mean everything in Regency London. Becky Sharp, quick-witted and alluring, is well suited for the fight, but her sweet and sentimental friend, Amelia, longs only for her

worthless soldier lover. *Who will survive amidst the corruption, betrayals and battles at home and abroad? (Vanity Fair. New Penguin Popular Classics)*

Conclusion

Over the years, the different Penguin imprints and collections have changed considerably in order to reach their intended market more effectively. From the inexpensive paperback publisher aimed at popularizing the classics to the modern publishing monster, Penguin has adapted to the changing times and tastes of readers. This study has focused on the blurbs of the classics collections in order to explore how they have evolved to face the challenges posed by marketing, publicity and competition, while keeping the promise to make the classics available to everyone.

Blurbs clearly reveal the influence of marketing and the need to be competitive in a fast-moving world, without losing sight of audience expectations and the purpose of each collection. Undoubtedly, the diversification of Penguin classics series according to the target audience has had an influence on the rhetorical structure of blurbs and their most salient linguistic realizations.

Penguin Classics and Modern Classics aim at an educated readership whose interests go beyond the mere reading of the book. Readers of these collections look for and appreciate the learned, erudite comments of editors and scholars, so additional material is provided in the form of introductions, notes, glossaries, etc. Accordingly, the blurbs in these series have evolved to include specific information about the edition and the extra material offered. Moreover, these blurbs display the most uniform of designs, with clear guidelines concerning format – colour (i.e. black for Classics, silver for Modern Classics), illustrations, lettering and column layout. This helps distribute information on the cover by giving relevance to the catchiest parts, especially endorsements, which enjoy a prominent place on the left-hand column and, over the years, have taken over the evaluative function typically associated with other moves in the blurb. All in all, the format of these blurbs has been actualized to make them more attractive, both visually and thematically, with a new layout and a special emphasis on the plot and praising quotes.

The new Penguin Red Classics series, in turn, has been launched as a collection of 'classics' best sellers: titles are equated to popular modern texts (e.g. the *Harry Potter* series or the *Da Vinci Code*), emphasizing the fact that they provide the same thrill as a modern best seller with the added value of being classics. Addressed to the general public, Red Classics display blurbs that highlight the value of the book by means of striking catchphrases printed in attractive colours and varied type fonts. Much importance is given to plot description, and endorsements are extensively used both on the front and back covers. Appraisal disappears altogether and so does any technical information about the book: these are not books for scholars or particularly cultivated readers, thus there is no need for any additional material or critical load. The appealing nature of the blurb is reinforced by other features, such as different type fonts, which are somehow related to the plot (e.g. the childlike scribble in *The Adventures of Huckleberry Finn*), and the colourful, suggestive images on the front covers. All these traits aim at popularizing books considered 'absolute' classics.

Finally, the Popular Classics collection appeals to a less specialized or demanding audience, who may just be interested in completing their collection of classics or simply in reading eminent works of literature without the intellectual need to go any further. This is the series which has most radically changed in terms of rhetorical structure: the former Popular Classics generally consisted of a catchphrase, a rather detailed summary of the plot and some editorial comment, whereas the new Popular Classics only includes a brief synopsis and information about the collection, probably leaving to its inexpensive price and easy-to-handle format the role of making them attractive.

In sum, this study has attempted to reveal the ways in which blurbs, considered as a means to publicize and promote books, respond and adapt to the demands of the market. We believe that Penguin is an excellent example to illustrate such evolution, which is inherent to the very notion of genre.

References

Baines, P. (2005) *Penguin by Design: A Cover Story 1935–2005* (London: Allen Lane).

Bhatia, V. K. (1993) *Analysing Genre: Language Use in Professional Settings* (London: Longman).

Bhatia, V. K. (2004) *Worlds of Written Discourse* (London: Continuum).

Fairclough, N. (1993) 'Critical Discourse Analysis and the Marketization of Public Discourse: The Universities', *Discourse and Society*, IV, 2, 133–68.

Fairclough, N. (1995) *Critical Discourse Analysis: The Critical Study of Language* (London: Longman).

Gea-Valor, M. L. (2005) 'Advertising Books: A Linguistic Analysis of Blurbs', *Ibérica*, X, 41–62.

Kathpalia, S. S. (1997) 'Cross-Cultural Variation in Professional Genres: A Comparative Study of Book Blurbs', *World Englishes*, XVI, 3, 417–26.

Margolis, E. (1985) 'Trade-Book Publicity' in A. Dolin, E. A. Geiser and G. S. Topkis (eds) *The Business of Book Publishing: Papers by Practitioners* (London: Westview Press), 166–78.

Mehta, S. (2006) 'The Publishing Industry and Cultural Creation' in A. Soler-Pont, A. Major and V. Miles (eds) *The Futures of the Publishing Industry: Summary and Conclusions of the 2005 Conference* (Barcelona: Ajuntament de Barcelona), 201–16.

Rawson, H. and Dolin, A. (1985) 'The Editorial Process: An Overview' in A. Dolin, E. A. Geiser and G. S. Topkis (eds) *The Business of Book Publishing: Papers by Practitioners* (London: Westview Press), 21–43.

Richardson, P. and Taylor, G. (2008) *A Guide to the UK Publishing Industry* (London: The Publishers Association).

Schiffrin, A. (2001) *The Business of Books* (New York: Verso).

Sinclair, C. (1985) 'Marketing Trade Books' in A. Dolin, E. A. Geiser and G. S. Topkis (eds) *The Business of Book Publishing: Papers by Practitioners* (London: Westview Press), 149–65.

Swales, J. (1990) *Genre Analysis: English in Academic and Research Settings* (Cambridge: Cambridge University Press).

12

The Lexis and Grammar of Explicit Evaluation in Academic Book Reviews, 1913 and 1993

Philip Shaw

Framework and background

Interested and disinterested genres

Evaluative genres can be interested or disinterested. The difference, for example, between blurbs (Cacchiani, 2007; Gesuato, 2007a, b) and reviews (Motta-Roth, 1998; Gea-Valor, 2000; Hyland, 2000; Salager-Meyer *et al.*, 2004, 2007; Römer, 2005, 2008) is that, although both evaluate a book, blurbs adopt an interested stance, clearly intending to promote the book, while reviews adopt a disinterested stance, intending to give the reader an honest, if personal, evaluation. Blurbs are written to maximize sales, whereas the recipients of reviews may justifiably expect them to give impartial advice. Of course an individual review text may have any sort of private purpose (Bhatia, 2004), but in the English-speaking academic world (Moreno and Suárez, 2008) the genre is read as disinterested, and a writer who is somehow involved with the book reviewed is expected to declare an interest.

Blurbs and reviews therefore form a pair of genres dealing with the same sort of content but with different positions on the scale of inter-estedness. This dimension of classification applies to quite a number of genres. Table 12.1 (from Shaw, 2006), in fact, suggests that it is not uncommon to find pairs of disinterested and interested genres dealing with the same referent.

Texts from interested genres normally only give positive evaluation and are characterized by a particular vocabulary, often using extreme, 'intensified' or 'polarized' words like *ideal* (house agent's particulars, Shaw, 2006), *brilliant, fantastic* (blurbs, Cacchiani, 2007). Texts from dis-interested evaluative genres, on the other hand, are expected to give

Table 12.1   Examples of interested and disinterested genres

Referent	Interested (Promotional) genre	Disinterested (Evaluative) genre
Finished book	Blurb	Review
Planned book	Proposal	Referee's report
Journal article	Letter of submission (or one element of actual article)	Referee's report
Company	Company brochure	Stock market analyst's report
Finished product	Sales brochure	Consumer advice review
Job applicant	Application + cv	Consultant's/committee's report
House	Agent's particulars	Surveyor's report
Development project	Tender	Client's internal report

both positive and negative opinions, if they have both reactions, and are typically sparing with intensified words.

Realizing evaluative acts

Thus for the evaluations in disinterested genres to be credible they must have (over a selection of instantiations) evaluations with both positive and negative polarity, and writers have to make it quite clear that a particular utterance is intended as an evaluation and what its polarity is intended to be. They can do this in a number of ways.

Some require no overt marker in the evaluating clause (Thompson and Hunston, 2000), but rely on clause relations (Hoey, 1983; Moreno and Suárez, 2008). However, our understanding of the polarity of these lexically unmarked clauses depends on their being marked clauses in recognizable relations to them, so markers are crucial to identifying evaluation, even where it is locally unmarked. Several writers suggest that contrast relations are particularly common in reviews. Thus, Hyland (2000) and Diani (2007) both draw attention to the mitigation strategy 'praise-criticism pairs'.

Thompson and Hunston (2000) observe that evaluation can also be signalled by syntax (cf. also Römer, 2008). They give lists of constructions and grammatical items that can be used for various evaluative effects. Application of the resulting templates to corpus data produces lists many members of which are evaluations, but looking through a corpus for evaluations does not necessarily produce a large number that have these forms.

However, the most obvious signals of evaluation are lexical items, most often evaluative adjectives (*correct*), nouns (*confusion*) and verbs (*misunderstands*) (examples from Diani, 2007). Evaluative adverbs also occur (*adequately, curiously*).

A terminology for the parts of evaluative acts

The framework developed by Hunston and Sinclair (2000) to map the forms of evaluative constructions on to the elements in an evaluation is very useful. Table 12.2 (adapted from Shaw, 2004) is a set of categories for the components of evaluation in book reviews, based on Hunston and Sinclair's paper, and directly comparable with those discussed in Moreno and Suárez (2008). Two levels of analysis were defined: the evaluative act and the evaluative term. The evaluative act is a text fragment (a sentence or less), which evaluates the book in question and is uniform in polarity – that is, uniformly negative or positive. An act may contain one or more evaluative terms. Thus *the luminous and judicious survey of* X is a single evaluative act with two terms, while the sentence *Apart from all controvertible or controverted matter, too, it is particularly admirable in covering* X was classified as having two evaluative acts and three evaluative terms (*controvertible, controverted, admirable*). The evaluative term is the same as the item defined by Moreno and Suárez (2008), but the acts differ in that critical acts can include both positive

Table 12.2   Invented examples of realizations of the parts of an evaluative act

Term	Examples
Thing evaluated	Smith is right *to draw this conclusion* *This book* might be interesting for some readers
Evaluative word	Negative: This book is *boring*. Smith writes *badly*. The book *fails to* examine
Evaluative item	Positive: Smith is *right* to draw this conclusion … the *sophistication* of this argument
Evaluating response	Your reviewer *was surprised* at the sophistication of this argument
Label (positive or negative)	Item: *In* this book's *favour* one can say that Response: it is *a pity* that
Modification of evaluation	This book is *quite* interesting
Evaluator	*I/Your reviewer* was surprised at the sophistication of this argument
Author (evaluation carrier)	*Smith* is right to draw this conclusion

and negative evaluation if they are within the same clause, while the evaluative act defined here must be of uniform polarity. This allows *This expensive but important book* to be included as an instance of a negative–positive sequence on the same level as a two clause construction with the same content.

The 'thing evaluated' is the part or aspect of the book that is evaluated. Hyland (2000) found that academic book reviews most often evaluated content (60 per cent of positive and 77 per cent of negative evaluations) and then style, readership, the text itself, the author and least frequently physical and commercial aspects of the book. Evaluative expressions may be of positive or negative 'polarity'. It is a fairly robust finding (Hyland, 2000; Giannoni, 2005) that academic reviews overall (not each individual text) contain more praise than blame, that is positive evaluation predominates.[1] Negative evaluation should not be equated with negated clauses or other constructions with grammatically negative markers. These imply contrast and hence evaluation (Thompson and Hunston, 2000), but this does not have to be negative evaluation – one can very well say *This book has no faults.* However, in practice negated structures often carry negative evaluation.

In explicit evaluative acts the evaluation is expressed by an evaluative term, and these can be classified in two ways. First, they can be Items or Responses. The 'evaluative Item' is the expression which actually evaluates the thing being evaluated and puts it into a certain category, good or bad in quality, useful or useless, careful, etc. It thus expresses Martin's JUDGEMENT or APPRECIATION (2000, 2004). Hunston and Sinclair call a corresponding element 'evaluative category', but in this more concrete terminology a word is needed which refers to the expression, not its meaning. The 'evaluating response' is the evaluator's reaction – an alternative or complement to the evaluative Item which expresses Martin's AFFECT. Second, terms are usually 'substantive', saying something about the thing evaluated directly, but they can also be used to 'label' an utterance as an evaluation prospectively or retrospectively (Charles, 2003; Moreno and Suárez, 2008). A label is a term like *merit* or *problem* that gives the polarity of a following or preceding statement without specifying the category. There may be some modification of the evaluation, hedging or boosting. Hedged negative evaluation is typical of academic book reviews (Hyland, 2000) as opposed, for example, to the quite direct negative evaluation in online customers' reviews (Gea-Valor, 2006).

The 'evaluator' is the person who does the evaluation, typically either the reviewer or potential readers (*readers may find that*). Clearly this element is often not realized, except where the evaluation takes the form of Martin's AFFECT (Martin, 2000), that is where an evaluating response rather than an evaluative item is the key evaluator. Hyland (2000) identified realization of the evaluator function (*for this reader, I would have liked*) as a way of making criticism less face-threatening, and several writers (e.g. Salager-Meyer *et al.*, 2004, 2007) have found considerable differences in critic visibility across cultures. In constructions like that illustrated in Table 12.2 (*Smith is right to draw this conclusion*), which are what Hunston and Sinclair call 'third pattern ii',[2] one may also encounter an evaluation carrier; in reviews this is normally the 'author'. In this example *to draw this conclusion* is the thing evaluated and Smith is the carrier. Hyland (2000) includes Author as one of the six dimensions on which books can be evaluated, and it is clear that there are often evaluative acts which evaluate the author as *well-known, thorough, learned*, etc. I suggest Author as a separate category because of examples like *Smith is right to draw this conclusion* which seem to evaluate a specific aspect of content and the author through this.

Aims

It is clear from the above that there has been a good deal of discussion of academic book reviews and related genres at the genre level, but only a rather sporadic amount at the level of linguistic realizations. Most discussion seems to have worked with rather high-inference categories like ways of mitigating a face-threatening act, rather than starting from the linguistic resources and examining how they can be used. The purpose of this chapter is to survey a sample of evaluations from academic book reviews and describe them, bottom-up, somewhat systematically on the basis of the dimensions described above, to establish a baseline for the frequency of various types of realization. Specifically, the aim is to answer, for this limited sample, the following questions:

- At what frequencies are the various elements from Table 12.2 realized in positive and negative evaluations?
- What parts of speech realize these various elements, in particular the evaluating item?
- Does polarity affect the frequency of the various realizations of elements?
- What roles do evaluating items occupy at the clause level? (the question is asked in order to assess to what extent constructions frequently used for evaluation can be identified.)

- At the clause-relation level, what is the balance of blame–praise and praise–blame pairs?

Material and method

The sample is the one whose implicit evaluations are discussed in Shaw (2004). It consists of 11 reviews from the London *Economic Journal* for 1913 and 12 from the *Economic Journal* of 1993 (producing samples of about 25,000 words each).

The analysis was entirely based on paper copies of the reviews; no concordancing was done. The first step in the process of analysis was to read the reviews repeatedly and identify as many instances of evaluation of the book in focus as possible. As a result of this, most of the explicit evaluative acts were identified, and an unknowable proportion of the implicit ones. Most acts were identifiable as realized within individual clauses, or sometimes merely phrases, and within most of these (the explicit ones) one or more evaluative items could be identified.

This resulted in a list of evaluative acts and items. Text extracts were typed into an Excel file, along with an assessment of:

- the polarity of the act (positive or negative);
- the explicitness of the act (explicit or implicit);
- the part of speech of the evaluative item or response(s) in explicit acts;
- any realization of Evaluator or Label;
- any modification of the item that could be regarded as hedging or boosting;
- the item's syntactic role in its phrase (head or modifier);
- the phrase's role in the smallest clause of which it was a constituent or part of a constituent (subject, object, complement, adverbial);
- the subject of verb phrases;
- the clause's relation to the preceding clause or where an act was not clausal, a judgement of the act type (e.g. matching, general–particular, contrast, etc.);
- where appropriate, the relationship of the clause complex to preceding clause complexes was categorized.

Thus the sentence *Apart from all controvertible or controverted matter, too, it is particularly admirable in covering X* was classified as having three evaluative items (*controvertible, controverted, admirable*) and two evaluative acts. The item *admirable* was classified as an adjective boosted by *particularly* and functioning as head in an adjective phrase which itself functioned as complement to a copula clause. This clause was treated as realizing an act in a contrastive (concessive) relation to the previous act, which itself is realized by the phrase headed by *apart from*.

Clearly assessments of grammatical categories are likely to be more reliable than assessments of clause relations and it has to be hoped that the sample is large enough for individual difficult decisions not to bias the results. It will be noted that the recording procedure did not include the realization of Author or Thing Evaluated, and these are not discussed below, though one or the other, at least, is always present.

Results and discussion

Overall figures and polarity

The framework described above was applied to the sample of *Economic Journal* reviews and this produced a total of 419 evaluative acts, all by definition specifying a thing evaluated. Of these, 348 (187 positive and 161 negative) were judged to be explicit because they contained at least one evaluative term. An act may contain more than one evaluative word, and the 348 explicit acts included 394 evaluative Items or Responses, as defined above, 219 of which were positive and 175 negative. Comparison of these figures for acts and Items shows that most acts, both positive and negative, included only one evaluative term, and that positive evaluation was rather more likely to contain two terms than negative. (Do not allow the precision of the numbers to distract from the fuzziness of the categories – but I believe the numbers are of this order.)

There are rather more positive than negative evaluations, as Moreno and Suárez (2008) and Giannoni (2007) also found for their English language samples.

Realization of elements of evaluation

I discuss first the frequencies with which the elements from Table 12.2 are realized in positive and negative evaluations. A total of 137 acts realized some form of modification – boosting or hedging (Table 12.3). About a third of evaluative acts are lexically modified: positive evaluations are much more often boosted than hedged, negative evaluations are rather more often hedged than boosted. Politeness theory explains the broad results here, in that boosting the positive is face-enhancing, while hedging the negative mitigates face-threatening acts. However,

Table 12.3   Acts realizing modification of the claim, by type of realization and polarity

	Positive	Negative	Total	Examples
Mitigation	17	39	56	Dr Scott deals *rather* briefly with … This statement *may* give pause to the reader who recalls that
Boosting	52	24	76	He fails *entirely* to appreciate … But the method itself is *fully* justified
Both	2	2	4	one *may reasonably* wonder whether
Uncertain	1		1	If the implications of … are accepted
Total	72	65	137	

the results show that a substantial number of face-threatening acts are boosted and a number of face-enhancing ones are hedged, so that the writers are trying to do something other than just be polite when they hedge or boost. I would like to argue that they are of course saying what they think, but choose to say these particular things in this way because a disinterested genre requires some demonstration that the writer is not merely being polite but is being balanced and truthful as well.

Table 12.4 shows that only about a tenth of the acts realize an evaluator (*I, readers*). The significant feature is that nearly half of the cases show the writer taking personal responsibility for a negative judgement.

Table 12.4   Acts realizing Evaluator, by type of evaluator and polarity

	Positive	Negative	Total	Actual forms used
Self	4	16	20	I, my (6), we/our (5), one (5), this reviewer (4)
Readers	7	3	10	word readers used 9 (general 8, defined group 1), passive + by (1)
Expert group	4	2	6	economist (3), business man (1), British historical scholarship (1), scholar (1)
Total	15	21	36	

Rather more positive than negative judgements are otherwise ascribed to others. One reason is doubtless, that admitting that an opinion is personal makes it less face-threatening, while ascribing it to third persons may have the opposite effect. Indeed the small number of ascriptions to 'readers' or 'economists' appear predominantly in positive evaluation, where they perhaps strengthen face-enhancing acts. It is, however, a requirement of the disinterested genre that the writer should give an honest opinion, positive or negative. By marking negative judgements as personal writers shows that they stand behind them and are not afraid of damaging the author's face, thus strengthening the disinterestedness of the text.

A separate point is that the norm is for Evaluator not to be realized, so realization of the element is a marked usage. But a higher proportion of negative evaluations than positive ones realize Evaluator, so negative evaluations again appear more marked than positive ones.

Most evaluative words were substantive, rather than retrospective or prospective labels, and in both categories most were Items (*good*) describing the thing evaluated rather than Responses to that thing (*puzzling*). Labels were more often negative than positive. In fact, as Table 12.5 shows, negative evaluation was somewhat predominant in all formal categories except substantive items, much the largest category. In other words positive evaluation was somewhat concentrated in realizations as substantive items, and other realizations like labels and responses were proportionately more likely to be negative. This recalls Giannoni's (2007) comment that negative evaluation is more varied in terms of vocabulary than positive: it also seems to be more varied in terms of the functions that realize it. It suggests that more effort is devoted to negative evaluation. To some extent positive evaluation can just be carried out in the most obvious way, by a substantive evaluative item, while negative evaluation requires more complicated devices.

Table 12.5   All evaluative acts, by type of act and evaluative word

	Substantive			Label		
	Positive	*Negative*	*Total*	*Positive*	*Negative*	*Total*
Item	154	115	269	10	18	28
Response	20	26	46	2	3	5
All	174	141	315	12	21	33

Parts of speech of evaluative words

Table 12.6 and Figure 12.1 show the percentage of all the evaluative terms in the corpus parts in each period which were realized in a particular grammatical form. 'Other' is used when the evaluation seems to be explicit, but does not seem to be localizable to an individual word. In both periods adjectives (and adjectival phrases), verbs (or verb phrases) and nouns (or noun phrases) predominate, with two-thirds of all evaluative items realized by adjectives and verbs.

There are equal numbers of positive and negative explicit evaluations in the 1993 sample but substantially more positive ones in that of 1913, and chi-square shows the difference between the proportions

Table 12.6   Explicit evaluative words, by part of speech, year and polarity

	1913		1993		Total	Examples
	Positive	*Negative*	*Positive*	*Negative*		
Adjective (phrase)	73	18	60	26	177	Distinctly odd; surprising
Verb (phrase)	18	38	7	40	103	[The authors also] exaggerate…Nor did it seem [that many of the participants had fully thought out]
Adverb (phrase)	6	2	9	5	22	[sits] rather oddly [with optimistic statements about]; [the contents relate] only loosely to
Noun (phrase)	24	21	13	17	75	[But there is] some danger of overkill; his almost total neglect of
Other	5	3	4	5	17	may reinforce the gloom of those who feel that a few well-tilled fields are now being subject to open-cast mining…Yet why is this not equally true of a philosophy or an ideology?
Total	126	82	93	93	394	

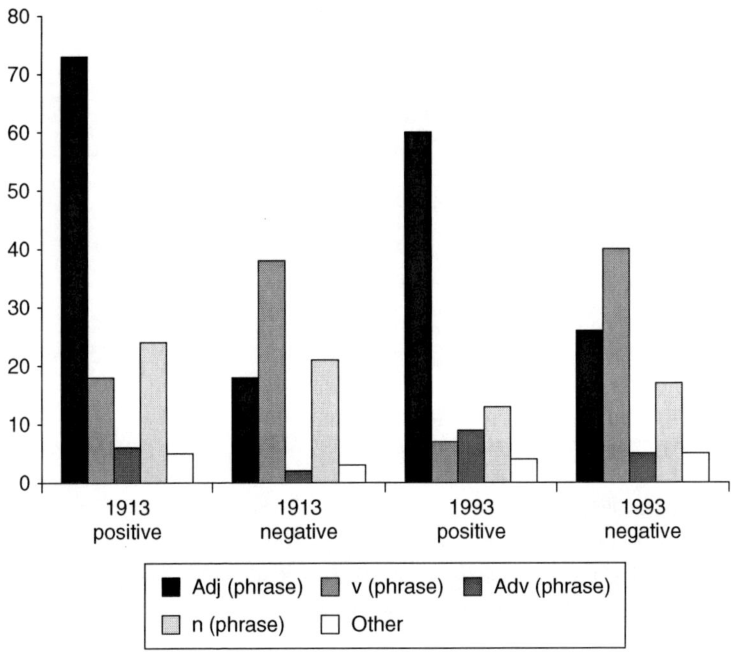

Figure 12.1   Explicit evaluative words, by year and polarity

to be significant at $p=0.035$. Thus the 1993 *Economic Review* texts are more negative than either the English-language or the Spanish-language reviews in Moreno and Suárez (2008), and the 1903 ones are comparable with Moreno and Suárez' English-language texts. One may speculate that positive evaluation was more necessary in the small closed group of 1913 (Shaw, 2004), often reviewing each others' books, than in the more open and competitive environment of 1993.

Otherwise the grammatical proportions for 1913 and 1993 are very similar indeed. Table 12.7 shows the number of occurrences of the evaluative adjectives that were repeated in either 1913 or 1993 and conforms that the vocabulary used is also often rather similar: the familiar standby *interesting* is repeated equally often, for example. One could argue that items like *excellent* and *outstanding* suggest an increased use of intensified adjectives, but at this level of delicacy and with a corpus of this size there has been no significant change over 80 years in the way evaluation is expressed. It may well be that the 1913 texts use a different vocabulary from the 1993 ones – the corpus is too small to say – but in

Table 12.7 Adjectives which occur with a frequency higher than 1 in 1913 or 1993

	1913	1993		1913	1993
acute	3	0	lucid	3	0
amusing	2	0	valuable	2	3
difficult	2	0	outstanding	0	2
excellent	1	8	right	2	1
good	1	2	useful	2	5
important	0	2	unfortunate	0	2
interesting	7	7			

grammatical terms they use a very similar range of forms. This suggests that the register of the (sub)genre 'book review in the *Economic Review*' is mature and stable, or even that evaluations have tended to use the same range of patterns for quite a long time. Given that we do not have much information on the pace of diachronic changes in register within other genres, and for reasons of space and clarity no further investigation is made here on the diachronic dimension.

On the other hand polarity seems to be important: the grammatical-category profile of terms of different polarity tends to be different. Adjectives make up nearly 60 per cent of positive evaluative items but they are only a quarter of the negatives. Verbs and verb phrases (including negated verb phrases) are the most common way of making negative evaluations, but less frequent positive evaluative words.[3] Nouns are at fairly low levels in evaluations of both polarities, as are more complex 'other' realizations of evaluation. If anything can be said of the few adverbs it is that there are more positive than negative evaluations using them. A pattern noted above is repeated here: positive evaluation is more concentrated on a few forms, negative evaluation is more spread across a variety of forms.

Clause-level functions of (phrases containing) evaluative terms

Table 12.8 gives the clause-level functions of phrases containing evaluative adjectives, subclassified by the adjective's phrase-level function. Each cell gives the total number of evaluative adjectives in the category and a breakdown into positive and negative evaluation, marked + and – respectively.

The most common single combination of clause and phrase functions is head of an adjective phrase, which is the complement of a copula, as

Table 12.8 Phrases with evaluative adjectives by clause-level functions of phrase and function of adjective within its phrase (with proportions of positive (+) and negative (–) evaluation)

Function of phrase	Function of evaluative adjective in its phrase			
	Head of AdjP	Head of NP	Modifier in NP	Total
Complement of copula	70 (48+, 22–)	2+	25 (21+, 4–)	97 (71+, 26–)
Subject	–	1+	20 (18+, 2–)	21 (19+, 2–)
Object	–		37 (30+, 7–)	37 (30+, 7–)
Adverbial	–		22 (16+, 6–)	22 (16+, 6–)
Total	70 (48+, 22–)	3+	104 (86+, 18–)	177 (136+, 41–)

in *Finally, C's treatments … are too brief.* Few of these fall into the subsets of copula constructions identified by Hunston and Sinclair (2000) or Römer (2008). The majority of adjectives are actually modifiers in noun phrases, which may be the complement of the copula (as in *there is little discussion of the specialist literature*), the subject (as in *while an excellent and incisive piece by D. occupies only six pages*) the object (as in *These two chapters form a weaker contribution*) or a complement in a prepositional phrase functioning as an adverbial as in *The book ends with a rather speculative (and Niebuhrian) appeal to the reader.* The examples show that most of these grammatical structures result in the evaluative phrase occurring in the rheme. The exception, an evaluative word in the subject and hence regularly the theme, is often a preliminary general evaluation – *another interesting paper, this monumental work* – and often to be classified as a label rather than a substantive evaluation.

It is striking that attributive adjectives are very much more often positive than negative, irrespective of the clause function of their NP. Predicative adjectives are also more often positive than negative, but the difference is not so great. Even though overall numbers of positive and negative evaluations in the corpus are not dissimilar, there are more than four times as many positive as negative attributive adjectives. If this is typical of reviews it means that a negative adjective in this context will stand out as a marked usage, and perhaps have more force.

Table 12.9 shows that noun phrases with evaluative nouns (like *his mastery,* or *real value*) pattern similarly overall to noun phrases with evaluative adjectives, with object roles somewhat more frequent than subject and complement, and occurrence in prepositional phrases functioning as adverbials the least frequent. But the proportions

Table 12.9   Phrases with evaluative nouns, by clause-level function

Function of phrase	Positive	Negative
Complement of copula	10	9
Subject	9	11
Object	10	14
Adverbial	7	5
Total	36	39

of positive and negative evaluation are about equal: the imbalance is not associated with evaluative noun phrases but with evaluative adjectives.

Of the 22 evaluative adverbs and adverb phrases found, most (18) are modifiers in verb phrases and the majority (13) provide positive evaluation in such phrases. There are two negative sentence adverbials (*needless to say* and *curiously*) and one positive (*happily*). Only one adverb provided (positive) evaluation of an (neutral) adjective. (Most evaluative adverbs modifying adjectives functioned as hedges or boosters of evaluative adjectives.) Adverbs are thus like adjectives in being mainly used for positive evaluation.

Verb phrases uniformly play a predicator role at clause level, but verbs are the main category that can be negated. Rather than looking at clause-level function, therefore, we ask what role negation plays, particularly because, unlike the other categories, verbs are predominantly used in negative evaluation. Defining negated phrases as those with *not* (the majority) or a negative indefinite pronoun, Table 12.10 shows that such phrases are indeed predominantly used for negative evaluation (as in *It is not clear why X should be regarded as a failure*), but the converse is not true; the most common form for negative evaluation is in fact a non-negated verb phrase, as in *It is perhaps to be regretted that*. It is clear that negated verb phrases used for positive evaluation, like *never dilates on the*

Table 12.10   Evaluative verb phrases, by polarity and negation

	Negative evaluation	Positive evaluation	Total
Negated verb phrases	28	5	33
Non-negated verb phrases	50	20	70
Total	78	25	103

obvious, and *leaves nothing to be desired* are relatively unusual, and they may be old-fashioned – four out of five are from 1913.

Adjectives and verbs seem to be used to evaluate somewhat different objects. A large majority of evaluative adjectives, positive or negative, modify predicatively or attributively nouns that refer to some aspect of the content of the book, but the most common subject for negatively evaluative verbs is the author (as in *There are some respects in which N. could have improved his presentation* or *he is conflating two issues*). In fact nearly half of the negative evaluations based on verbs (36 out of 78) have the author as subject but only a quarter of the positive ones (7 out of 27) (such as *The problems in economic history … on which Dr Scott throws fresh light*). It almost seems that verbs have been chosen as the vehicle for negative evaluation because they provide a slot for the author to be blamed. This is not easy to explain in politeness terms, since it seems that the finger is pointed at the person responsible more so in face-threatening than in face-enhancing situations. In fact it seems as though this kind of surface-level analysis reveals a genre in which face-threatening acts are valued.

Clause relations

Clause-relations (or evaluative-act relations) are key elements in the structure of reviews but they are not easy to analyse sensibly because of variations in scale and because most clauses are involved in a network of relations that is hard to map. The scale problem may be illustrated through the contrastive or concessive 'praise-blame' or 'blame-praise' relations, which have been much discussed in the literature. Whole reviews can be organized on these principles, paragraphs can be structured on them, sentences (as in *A series such as this has a great deal to recommend it. The particular volumes under review have however encountered four general problems*) and clauses within sentences can stand in these relations, and even evaluative acts within clauses can be contrasted, as in *The author propounds formal theorems with more elaborateness and precision than lucidity* and *These three volumes together make an interesting, if modest contribution*. The network problem arises because a clause usually stands in a hierarchy of clause and sentence relations. It may, for example, be matched with the preceding and following clauses. These three may then represent the particular members of a general-particular pattern. This complex itself might then represent the second member of a contrast relationship and so on. Which of these relations should one count?

I have simplified the task by focusing on contrast sequences in which one member gives a positive evaluation and the other a negative, in any order. I looked for such sequences at any scale within a paragraph and simply asked whether the positive or negative evaluation comes first. This produced a total of 43 sequences of praise followed by blame or vice versa: in 15 of them negative evaluation preceded positive, and in the other 28 positive preceded negative. The rhetorical effect of the pairs was influenced not only by sequence but also by the relative lengths of the members and the strength of the criticism involved. Thus the following example was treated as a praise–blame sequence, but the praise element (*quite properly*) is much shorter than the blame one.

(1) With regard to the more familiar considerations which Professor Pigou from time to time quite properly throws into the balance, we think he might with advantage have more frequently referred to standard versions of similar arguments. (Edgeworth 1913)

Yet this is in a broadly positive review, so that the criticism does not seem harsh.

Thus where evaluative acts are paired in contrastive or concessive relations the sequence positive–negative seems to occur rather more frequently than the reverse. In such sequences one can imagine that each polarity mitigates the force of the other, with the second member receiving more weight because it is more in focus. It is not surprising from a politeness point of view that focused negative evaluation is more often mitigated by preceding positive than the other way around. However, there is a relatively large amount of focused praise mitigated by preceding blame. I interpret this as meaning that in this genre it is almost as important to mitigate face-enhancing acts, so as to publicly preserve one's disinterested status, as it is to mitigate face-threatening acts so as to be interpersonally polite.

Conclusions

At the level of delicacy used here, the formal resources used for evaluation were about the same in 1913 and 1993. There are obviously differences in style, such as the use of authorial *we* in 1913, and in vocabulary, such as, impressionistically, increased use of intensified adjectives, but a larger sample and a different methodology would be needed to specify them. This corresponds to the findings of Salager-Meyer *et al.*

(2004, 2007) that academic reviews in English (in their case medical) did not become less or more aggressive during the last century.

Most evaluative acts in this sample of reviews include an evaluative term of some kind, that is, most are explicit as defined here. This term is most often substantive, not just a positive or negative label for a statement that has just been made or is to come. It is most often an evaluative Item like *excellent* rather than a Response like *surprising*. On this level, as on several others, there is some tendency for positive evaluations to use proportionally more of the least marked realization – a substantive evaluative item – and correspondingly for negative evaluations to be less concentrated on this realization.

Evaluative words are most often adjectives, verbs or nouns, in that order. Positive evaluations are, disproportionately, often represented by adjectives, and negative ones by verbs, even when the artefactual effect of treating negated sentences as having evaluative verbs is discounted. More precisely, positive evaluations use proportionately more of the least marked form – an attributive or predicative adjective – and negative evaluations are less concentrated on this form. This tendency and that for realizations suggest that more rhetorical effort goes into negative than positive evaluation.

A number of findings show that forms of evaluation which might threaten the face of the author of the book under review, such as naming the author, are not as often less frequent for negative than for positive evaluation as one might expect. Some demand other than politeness is being made. The concept of the disinterested genre and the need to distinguish it from a related interested (promotional) one is useful here. Reviews must mitigate praise and balance it with blame just as they must mitigate blame and balance it with praise, not only in order to be polite, but also in order to be judicious, to maintain the essential feature of the disinterested genre. Negative evaluation may require more rhetorical effort and demand various forms of mitigation to maintain politeness. But positive evaluation must also be mitigated and balanced, and some negative evaluation must be boosted, so that the writer maintains credibility as a disinterested judge.

Notes

1. Certainly some journals' review editors discourage wholly negative reviews.
2. That is, link verb + adjective group + *to*-infinitive clause.
3. This result needs to be considered in the light of the decision to treat seven negated copula constructions like *is not always successful in* or *It is not perhaps just what one calls a work of art* as having the negative evaluation in the verb

phrase, while their positive counterparts *is always successful in* and *is a work of art* would be treated as having the positive evaluation in the complement.

References

Bhatia, V. K. (2004) *Worlds of Written Discourse* (London: Continuum).

Cacchiani, S. (2007) 'From Narratives to Intensification and Hyperbole: Promotional Uses of Book Blurbs' in M. Davies, P. Rayson, S. Hunston and P. Danielsson (eds) *Proceedings of the Corpus Linguistics Conference, University of Birmingham, 27–30 July 2007*, http://www.corpus.bham.ac.uk/corplingproceedings07/paper/79_Paper.pdf, date accessed 14 May 2008.

Charles, M. (2003) ' "This Mystery…": A Corpus-Based Study of the Use of Nouns to Construct Stance in Theses from Two Contrasting Disciplines', *Journal of English for Academic Purposes*, II, 4 (Special Issue), 313–26.

Diani, G. (2007) 'The Representation of Evaluative and Argumentative Procedures: Examples from the Academic Book Review Article', *Textus*, XX, 1, 37–56.

Gea-Valor, M. L. (2000) *A Pragmatic Approach to Politeness and Modality in the Book Reviews* (València: Universitat de València).

Gea-Valor, M. L. (2006) 'A Preliminary Approach to the Rhetoric of Online Customers' Reviews: Emotional Involvement and Negative Evaluation', paper presented at the Conference on Academic and Professional Communication in the 21st Century: Genres and Rhetoric in the Construction of Disciplinary Knowledge, Zaragoza, 14–16 September 2006.

Gesuato, S. (2007a) 'Evaluation in Back-Cover Blurbs', *Textus*, XX, 1, 83–102.

Gesuato, S. (2007b) 'Structural and Generic Complexity in Back-Cover Blurbs of Academic books' in L. Jottini, G. Del Lungo and J. Douthwaite (eds) *Proceedings of the 22nd AIA Conference 'Cityscapes – Islands of the Self'*, Vol. 2, *Language Studies Series*, Villasimius, Italy, 15–17 September 2005 (Cagliari: CUEC), 419–32.

Giannoni, D. S. (2006) 'Expressing Praise and Criticism in Economic Discourse: A Comparative Study of English and Italian Book Reviews' in G. Del Lungo Camiciotti, M. Dossena and B. Crawford Camiciottoli (eds) *Variation in Business and Economics Discourse: Diachronic and Genre Perspectives* (Rome: Officina Edizioni), 126–38.

Giannoni, D. S. (2007) 'Metatextual Evaluation in Journal Editorials', *Textus*, XX, 1, 57–82.

Hoey, M. (1983) *On the Surface of Discourse* (London: Allen and Unwin).

Hunston, S. and Sinclair, J. McH. (2000) 'A Local Grammar of Evaluation' in S. Hunston and G. Thompson (eds) *Evaluation in Text: Authorial Stance and the Construction of Discourse* (Oxford: Oxford University Press), 74–101.

Hyland, K. (2000) *Disciplinary Discourses: Social Interactions in Academic Writing* (London: Longman).

Martin, J. R. (2000) 'Beyond Exchange: APPRAISAL Systems in English' in S. Hunston and G. Thompson (eds) *Evaluation in Text: Authorial Stance and the Construction of Discourse* (Oxford: Oxford University Press), 142–75.

Martin, J. R. (2004) 'Mourning: How We Get Aligned', *Discourse and Society*, XV, 2–3, 321–44.

Moreno, A. I. and Suárez, L. (2008) 'A Study of Critical Attitude across English and Spanish Academic Book Reviews', *Journal of English for Academic Purposes*, VII, 1, 15–26.

Motta-Roth, D. (1998) 'Discourse Analysis and Academic Book Reviews: A Study of Text and Disciplinary Cultures' in I. Fortanet, S. Posteguillo, J. C. Palmer and J. F. Coll (eds) *Genre Studies in English for Academic Purposes* (Castelló de la Plana: Publicacions de la Universitat Jaume I), 29–58.

Römer, U. (2005) ' "This Seems Somewhat Counterintuitive, Though..." – Negative Evaluation in Linguistic Book Reviews by Male and Female Authors', in E. Tognini-Bonelli and G. Del Lungo Camiciotti (eds) *Strategies in Academic Discourse* (Amsterdam: John Benjamins), 97–115.

Römer, U. (2008) 'Identification Impossible? A Corpus Approach to Realisations of Evaluative Meaning in Academic Writing', *Functions of Language*, XV, 1, 115–30.

Salager-Meyer, F. and Alcaraz Ariza, M. A. (2004) 'Negative Appraisal in Academic Book Reviews: A Cross-Linguistic Approach' in C. Candlin and M. Gotti (eds) *Intercultural Aspects of Specialized Communication* (Bern: Peter Lang), 150–72.

Salager-Meyer, F., Alcaraz Ariza, M. A. and Pabón Berbesí, M. (2007) 'Collegiality, Critique and the Construction of Scientific Argumentation in Medical Book Reviews: A Diachronic Approach', *Journal of Pragmatics*, XXXIX, 10, 1758–74.

Shaw, P. (2004) 'How Do We Recognise Implicit Evaluation in Academic Book Reviews?' in G. Del Lungo Camiciotti and E. Tognini Bonelli (eds) *Academic Discourse – New Insights into Evaluation* (Bern: Peter Lang), 121–40.

Shaw, P. (2006) 'Evaluative Language in Evaluative and Promotional Genres' in G. Del Lungo Camiciotti, M. Dossena and B. Crawford Camiciottoli (eds) *Variation in Business and Economics Discourse: Diachronic and Genre Perspectives* (Rome: Officina Edizioni), 152–65.

Thompson, G. and Hunston, S. (2000) 'Evaluation: An Introduction' in S. Hunston and G. Thompson (eds) *Evaluation in Text: Authorial Stance and the Construction of Discourse* (Oxford: Oxford University Press), 3–27.

Notes on Contributors

HELEN BASTURKMEN is a Senior Lecturer in the Department of Applied Language Studies and Linguistics at the University of Auckland, New Zealand. She teaches courses in language teacher education, discourse analysis and research methods. Her research interests and publications are in the areas of discourse analysis, pragmatics, English for Specific Purposes and teacher beliefs. She is currently involved in funded research investigating feedback to dissertation writing.

MARINA BONDI is Professor of English and Director of the Department of Studies on Language, Text and Translation at the University of Modena and Reggio Emilia, Italy. She is interested in argumentation, metadiscourse and evaluation in academic texts and her recent published work centres on language variation across genres, disciplines and cultures through the analysis of small specialized corpora.

GIULIANA DIANI is a tenured researcher in English Language and Linguistics at the University of Modena and Reggio Emilia, Italy. She holds an MA in Language Studies from the University of Lancaster, UK and a PhD in English Linguistics from the University of Pisa, Italy. Her research interests are in spoken and written academic discourse from the point of view of genre analysis and evaluation.

MARIA-LLUÏSA GEA-VALOR is a Lecturer in English, Linguistics and ESP at Universitat Jaume I, Castelló, Spain. She is interested in the analysis of evaluative and digital genres. Author of *A Pragmatic Approach to Politeness and Modality in the Book Review* (2000), she has recently co-edited *Language @ Work: Language Learning, Discourse and Translation Studies in Internet* (2005) and *The Texture of Internet: Netlinguistics in Progress* (2007).

DAVIDE SIMONE GIANNONI is a tenured researcher in English Language and Linguistics at the University of Bergamo, Northern Italy and a founding member of the LSP research centre CERLIS (www.unibg.it/cerlis). His research, centred on the textual and sociopragmatic features of academic and professional communication, has been published in various international journals and edited volumes.

NICHOLAS GROOM is a Lecturer in Applied Linguistics, Corpus Linguistics and English Language Teaching at the Centre for English Language Studies, University of Birmingham, UK. He is currently involved in three large-scale research projects that use corpus methodologies to study issues in second language acquisition, EAP and discourse analysis.

KEN HYLAND is Professor of Applied Linguistics in Education and Director of the Centre for Academic and Professional Literacies at the Institute of Education,

University of London. He has published over 130 articles and 14 books on language teaching and academic writing, most recently *Academic Discourse* with Continuum (2009). He is co-editor of *Applied Linguistics* and editor of the *Continuum Discourse Series*.

ANA I. MORENO is a Senior Lecturer in English Philology at the Universidad de León, Spain. She is currently on secondment in the Madrid's Centro de Ciencias Humanas y Sociales (Consejo Superior de Investigaciones Científicas). Her research uses discourse analysis to give an intercultural perspective on scientific communication. She has published in *English for Specific Purposes, The Journal of English for Academic Purposes* and *Text &Talk*.

JUDY NOGUCHI has BA/BS degrees (chemistry) from the University of Hawaii, an MEd (TESL) from Temple University and a PhD (applied linguistics) from the University of Birmingham. She teaches English in Japan to students majoring in science, engineering and medicine. She is interested in examining how language is used in the sciences and in developing materials and methods for these learners.

MARTA INIGO ROS lectures on Methodology of Translation and Linguistics at the École de Traduction et d'Intérpretation, Geneva, Switzerland. Her research concerns are in the areas of sociolinguistics and translation. Her main publications include *Cultural Terms in King Alfred's Translation of the 'Consolatio Philosophiae'* (2004) and *The Stereotyping of Spanish Characters and their Speech Patterns in Anglo-American Films* (*RAEL*, 2007).

ROSA LORÉS SANZ is a Senior Lecturer in the Department of English and German Studies of the University of Zaragoza, Spain. She has co-edited two books and published several articles on pragmatic and systemic-functional aspects of both specialized and academic languages from a contrastive (English-Spanish) point of view. Her latest research focuses on the analysis of rhetorical and metadiscursive aspects of academic texts.

PHILIP SHAW has taught English and Linguistics at universities in Thailand, Germany, England and Denmark, and is currently a professor in the Department of English at Stockholm University. He is co-author (with Gunnel Melchers) of *World Englishes: An Introduction* (Arnold 2003). He is interested in uses of English, mainly in business and academic settings, from both a genre-analytic and reception-process standpoint.

LORENA SUÁREZ received her PhD in English Philology from the Universidad de León, Spain. Her research concerns are contrastive rhetoric, discourse analysis and evaluation in discourse, particularly in book reviews. She has co-authored articles with Ana Moreno in *The Journal of English for Academic Purposes* and *Text &Talk*. She is currently teaching English at the Colegio Jesús Reparador in Burgos, Spain.

PAUL THOMPSON is a Lecturer in Applied Linguistics at the University of Reading, UK. His research interests are: academic literacy, the applications of corpus linguistics (particularly in education) and the uses of computer technologies in language teaching. With Hilary Nesi, he has developed two major corpora of academic English, the British Academic Spoken English (BASE) corpus and the British Academic Written English (BAWE) corpus.

POLLY TSE is an instructor at the Hong Kong University of Science and Technology where she teaches English for Specific and Academic Purposes. She has an MPhil in applied linguistics and is a PhD student at the University of Reading, UK. Her research interests include academic writing, genre analysis and Systemic Functional Linguistics. She has published in various journals including *Applied Linguistics, Journal of Pragmatics, Text & Talk,* and *TESOL Quarterly*.

Name Index

Aalto, M. K., 38, 47
Agar, M., 72, 82
Alcaraz Ariza, M. A., 8, 14, 24, 33,
    143–4, 159, 195, 235
Ames, B., 36, 43, 47, 48
Andersen, J., 29, 31
Anderson, R. G. W., 36, 38,
    47, 194
Arbury, J., 72, 82
Archer, J., 38, 48, 208
Arts, E. J., 48
Atkinson, D., 48, 159

Baines, P., 205, 215
Banerjee, A., 49
Basturkmen, H., 17, 31, 68, 69, 71, 81,
    82, 236
Bazerman, C., 33, 127, 137
Becher, T., 115, 120, 123–6, 131,
    136–7
Bednarek, M., 20, 23, 31
Belcher, D., 106, 120, 158
Bennett, M. K., 36, 48, 127
Benwell, B., 105, 120
Berelson, B., 73, 82
Bhatia, V. K., 19, 31, 68–73, 81, 82,
    199–203, 215, 217, 234
Biber, D., 4, 5, 13, 50, 63, 66, 90, 103,
    129, 137
Blenis, J., 36, 37, 48
Bloch, J., 144, 158
Bloor, T., 114, 120
Blumberg, J., 49
Bondi, M., 7, 13, 67, 98, 103, 104, 138,
    143, 158, 160, 179–82, 187, 194,
    195, 236
Bourdieu, P., 7, 13
Bres, J., 97, 103
Brown, P., 8, 13
Bunton, D., 53, 66
Burgess, S., 143, 159, 163, 164, 177,
    210
Burke, A., 23, 33

Cameron, D., 106, 120
Chafe, W., 4, 13
Chakravarti, D., 38, 48
Charles, M., 138, 181,
    220, 234
Chen, Q., 43, 48
Chen, T., 144, 160
Chi, L., 144, 158, 191
Clarke, M., 46, 47, 48
Clise-Dwyer, K., 48
Coffin, C., 181, 194
Connor, U., 144, 159, 178,
    180, 194
Conrad, S., 4, 5, 13, 66, 103,
    137
Cortes, V., 137
Couzin, J., 46, 48
Crismore, A., 110, 120
Cronin, B., 8, 13, 68, 69, 70, 82

Dahl, T., 103, 179, 194
David, D., 39, 48, 96, 134, 202
De Carvalho, G., 163, 177
Diani, G., 1, 3, 13, 17, 31, 87, 177,
    181, 194, 218–19, 234, 236
Dibble, J., 48
Ditch, S., 49
Dougherty, J. P., 49
Duch, M., 48
Durston, W., 47

Eaton, S., 48
Edersen, F. S., 48

Fagan, A., 143, 159, 163, 177
Fairclough, N., 61, 66, 199, 215
Fan, J., 48
Finegan, E., 4, 13, 66, 103
Fishelov, D., 17, 31
Flick, U., 80, 82
Fløttum, K., 100, 103, 138, 159,
    180, 194
Flowerdew, J., 63, 66, 104, 177

Flynn, E., 106, 120
Francis, G., 32, 50, 66, 106, 110, 112, 120, 121, 126, 138
Frey, O., 106, 120

Gayral, P., 38, 48
Gea-Valor, M. L., 82, 199, 201, 215, 236
Geertz, C., 7, 13
Gerst, J. E., 48
Gesuato, S., 4, 13, 19, 32, 69, 82, 217, 234
Giannoni, D. S., 17, 23, 32, 144, 159, 162, 177, 220, 223, 225, 234, 236
Giora, R., 20, 27, 32
Gledhill, C., 122, 128, 131, 138
Goldman, M. B., 49
Grabczyk, E., 49
Greene, K., 106, 121, 203
Groom, N., 61, 66, 122–31, 136, 138, 181, 194, 236
Grupetta, C., 69, 80, 82

Hagen, T., 43, 47
Hartman, T., 49
Haynes, L., 48
Henry, A., 134, 194
Hicks, G., 49
Hoey, M., 104, 218, 234
Hofstede, G., 82
Holmes, J., 110, 120, 123, 138
Hunston, S., 4, 5, 7, 13–14, 20–1, 30–3, 50, 66, 82, 88, 104, 122, 128–31, 138, 143, 160, 179–80, 183, 195–6, 218–21, 229, 234–5
Huston, G., 48
Hwang, H. I., 46, 48
Hyland, K., 1, 4, 7, 10, 13, 18, 25, 32, 54, 66, 87, 90–3, 96, 98, 103–8, 113, 117, 120, 123, 125–6, 129, 138, 144, 146, 149, 150, 153, 156–64, 168–70, 177–81, 189, 195, 196, 217–18, 220–1, 234, 236

Ivanič, R., 105

Johnson, D. M., 106, 110, 121

Jones, S. C., 41, 42, 48
Jürgens, G., 48

Kaplan, R., 159, 163, 177
Kathpalia, S., 69–70, 80, 82, 199–201, 203, 212–13, 215
Keranen, S., 47
Kirsch, G., 106, 121
Krippendorf, K., 73, 82
Kuhn, T., 26, 32, 34
Kwan, B., 3, 8, 14, 52, 53, 60, 65, 67

La Barre, K., 8, 13, 68–70, 82
Lather, P., 29, 32
Lauber, M. H., 38, 48
Lea, F., 47
Lei, K. Y., 49
Lescot, M., 48
Levinson, S., 8, 13
Lindholm-Romantschuk, Y., 1, 14, 156
Lockhart, B., 48
Lukowitz, W., 48
Lund, A. H., 48

Mailander, P., 48
Manning, E., 138
Margolis, E., 205, 216
Markee, N., 72
Markkanen, R., 120
Martin, J. R., 4, 5, 6, 14, 157, 159, 220, 221, 234
Martín Martín, P., 143, 159
Matsumoto, T., 48
Mauranen, A., 120, 143, 158, 179, 180, 195
Mehta, S., 199, 216
Mikkelsen, J. G., 38, 48
Miller, J. H., 49, 202, 208
Moreno, A., 17, 32, 124, 138, 143–4, 146, 157–63, 170, 177–9, 195, 217–20, 223, 227, 235, 237
Motta-Roth, D., 17, 30, 33, 124, 138, 144, 149, 158–9, 163, 165, 178–9, 195, 217, 235
Myers, G., 17, 33–4

Negroni, M., 48
Noa-Carrazana, J.-C., 48
Noguchi, J., 3, 14, 17, 33–8,
    48, 237
North, S., 123, 138, 164,
    207, 212

Oakey, D., 129, 138
Ochs, E., 4, 14
Orteza y Miranda, E., 2, 14,
    161, 178

Parry, S., 123, 138
Piffanelli, P., 48
Pinney, J. W., 48
Preson, B. D., 49

Rawson, H., 213, 216
Rayson, P., 31, 67, 79, 82, 234
Richards, C., 77, 82
Richardson, P., 199, 216
Robertson, D., 48
Robins, D., 178
Roen, D. H., 106, 110, 121
Römer, U., 17, 21, 33, 179, 195,
    217–18, 229, 235
Ron, Y., 49
Ronne, H., 47
Roper, D., 2, 14
Rose, D., 157, 159
Roseberry, R., 194
Rubin, D., 106, 121
Ruder, E. H., 42, 49
Ryan, G. W., 73, 82

Salager-Meyer, F., 8, 14, 17, 24, 33,
    143–4, 157, 159, 164, 178–9, 195,
    217, 221, 232, 235
Sammarco, M., 41, 49
Scamber, L., 178
Schekman, R., 47, 49
Scheller, R. H., 36, 48
Schiffrin, A., 199, 216
Schmidt, G., 45, 46, 49
Schoene, N. W., 49
Scott, M., 58, 67, 73, 82, 90, 104, 128,
    138, 182, 190, 195, 231
Shaw, P., 17, 20, 33, 169, 178–9, 195,
    217, 219, 222, 227, 235, 237

Shigenaga, M. K., 43, 47
Shih, D. M., 49
Shiu, R., 49
Silver, M., 104, 179, 181, 194–5,
    207–8, 210–11
Simon-Loriere, E., 48
Sinclair, C., 202, 216
Sinclair, J. McH., 61, 87, 104, 122, 138,
    180, 183, 195, 219–21, 229, 234
Spink, P., 161–2, 178
Stati, S., 101, 104, 182, 192, 196
Steffensen, M., 120
Steinmann, T., 48
Stokoe, E., 105, 120
Stubbs, M., 4, 14, 137–8
Sundarababu, S., 48
Swain, S. L., 48
Swales, J., 3, 7, 14, 23, 32–3, 42,
    49–50, 52, 67, 73, 82, 87, 104,
    136, 138, 165, 177–8, 201, 216

Tadros, A., 87, 104
Tannen, D., 106, 108, 121
Taylor, G., 136, 139, 144, 160, 199,
    216
Temin, H., 36, 38, 49
Thetela, P., 147, 160
Thomas, S., 92, 97, 104, 110
Thompson, G., 4–5, 7, 13–14, 20, 33,
    104, 143, 160, 195–6, 218, 220,
    234–5
Thompson, P., 3, 50, 52, 54, 66–7, 87,
    104, 143, 179–80, 237
Thornbury, S., 72, 83
Thue Vold, E., 194
Tobin, R., 175, 178
Todova, E., 72, 83
Tognini-Bonelli, E., 32, 67, 104, 122,
    128, 139, 160, 178, 195–6, 235
Tribble, C., 128, 138
Trowler, P., 115, 120, 123, 137
Tse, P., 4, 13, 105, 108, 120, 144, 156,
    160, 168–70, 177, 179, 195–6, 238

Varela-Echavarri, A., 49

Waizenegger, I., 48
Wallace, D. C., 39, 49
White, P., 4, 5, 14

Wittgenstein, L., 136, 139
Wong, S., 42, 49

Xie, J., 41, 49
Xie, Y., 41, 49

Yang, H., 49
Ye, Y., 7, 14

Zambrano, N., 159
Zhang, J., 38, 49

Subject Index

adjectives, 9, 51, 62, 71, 124, 126, 212, 219, 222–3, 226–30, 233
adverbs, 5, 25, 51, 100, 169, 187, 230
agency, 27, 107, 119
agreement, 88, 100, 101–3, 108, 114, 157, 182, 186–93
argue, 87, 90–103, 186, 188, 193
argument, 3, 8, 11, 27, 29, 42, 56, 88–91, 93, 96, 98, 101–2, 106–8, 111–17, 127, 133, 162, 167, 181–9, 191, 193, 195, 236
attitude markers, 108
attribution, 11, 17, 61, 87, 97, 182
audience, 6, 7, 11, 47, 52, 119, 143–5, 149, 157, 162–4, 174, 181–2, 186, 189–90, 193, 200, 203–5, 213–17, 220–1, 229
averral, 61, 87, 94

blog, 45–9
blurb, 4, 9, 19, 28, 68–71, 77, 79–81, 199–215
book prize, 18–19, 31
book review, 1–6, 8–10, 17–19, 29–30, 51, 87–94, 97–8, 101–2, 107, 119, 122–31, 137, 143–8, 153–67, 173–6, 179–83, 193, 217, 219–21, 228, 237
boosters, 110–13, 212, 230

citation, 6, 26, 29, 35–43, 46–7, 54, 61, 87–8, 94, 102, 155, 179
citation mapping, 35, 37, 39, 47
citation record, 35–6, 46
clause relations, 218, 223
communicative purpose, 19–20, 29, 69, 71, 81
comparative evaluators, 22
concordance, 58, 62, 94, 100, 110, 116, 127–34, 188, 222
corpora, 6, 21, 31, 50–8, 61–6, 73–9, 82–3, 88–91, 94, 97–8, 101, 103, 105, 107–8, 110, 117, 122–30, 133–7, 144–9, 158, 163–5, 168, 175, 181–2, 188–93, 200, 218, 226–7, 229, 234–7
critical voice, 155, 158
criticism, 32–3, 154, 159, 177, 234
cultural difference, 70, 72, 101, 112, 144, 164, 172–6, 180, 188, 199

detractive evaluators, 27, 29
diachronic study, 196, 204, 228
directives, 7
disagreement, 88, 98–103, 182, 186–93
discipline, 13, 33, 66, 104–5, 120, 122, 137–8, 159–60, 194–5, 234
  Agricultural Botany, 50, 54–9, 66
  Agricultural Economics, 50, 54–5, 58, 66
  economics, 3, 88–95, 99–103, 110, 149
  Food Sciences, 54
  History, 3, 25, 35–6, 46, 70, 88–95, 99–100, 102, 111, 119, 122–31, 136–7, 144–9, 154–7, 168, 181, 183, 191–2, 207, 210, 231
  Linguistics, 2–3, 18, 29–30, 70–1, 88–9, 92–5, 99–102, 122, 149, 237–8
  literary criticism, 122, 126–31, 134, 136–7
  Psychology, 50, 54, 58, 60, 66
  sociology, 3, 125
discourse, 2, 5, 7–8, 17, 23, 30–1, 34, 68, 70, 77, 80–1, 87–8, 92–9, 102–3, 105–7, 110–13, 119, 122–4, 128, 130, 132, 137, 147, 164–9, 179–82, 186–93, 199–200, 212, 236–7
discourse analysis, 199, 236, 237

discourse community, 1–12, 34–5, 45, 61, 68, 71–80, 87–8, 91, 94–5, 98, 103, 105, 112, 119, 122, 132, 137, 143–4, 153, 155–7, 164, 175, 179, 180–7, 189, 190, 192–3
dissertations and theses, 50–66, 82, 109

engagement, 1, 7–8, 12, 108, 110–17, 189, 193
English for Academic Purposes (EAP), 31, 66–7
epistemology, 26, 106, 122, 124–5, 136–7
evaluative acts, 17–18, 21, 26, 29–31, 144–5, 218–23, 231–3
evaluative intensity, 5, 25, 29–30, 153
evaluators, 25, 27, 220–1, 224
expert reviews, 18–19, 29, 30

frequency, 25, 30, 50, 58–9, 62–4, 73–5, 88, 90–2, 99, 101, 131, 135, 148, 162, 164, 171–3, 176, 181, 186, 188, 193, 203, 204, 221
functions, 4, 6–7, 10, 29–30, 51, 58, 60–1, 68, 81, 87, 98–101, 108, 125, 127, 146, 149, 155, 157, 165, 179, 182, 192–3, 201–3, 209–12, 214, 221, 228–30

gender, 105–19, 133
genre analysis, 73, 236, 238

hedges, 4–5, 17, 20, 25, 27, 112, 115, 149–54, 218, 220–4, 233
humanities, 2–3, 93, 122, 124, 135–7, 149, 180

identity, 3, 70, 96, 105–10, 119, 180, 183
informants, 36, 155–6, 175
information overload, 45
intercultural, 162, 176, 237
interested genres, 217
interpersonal meaning, 4, 9–12, 19, 29, 31, 63, 110, 162–3, 175
Intertextuality, 66–7, 104, 196
interview data, 111–12, 115, 118, 163

issue review, 35–6
Italian, 144, 162, 179–93, 234

Keywords, 133, 182
Knowledge, 13, 48, 137, 195, 234

language teaching, 24, 26, 71–9
Lemmas
   AGREE, 189
   BE, 51
   DATA, 62
   EFFECT, 58
   EVIDENCE, 59, 61–6
   MODEL, 58, 60, 64–5
   PROBLEM, 62–6
   REJECT, 189
lexicogrammatical patterns, 50–1, 57, 63–5, 146, 201
literature review, 1, 3, 8, 50–66

metadiscourse, 4, 108, 236
move-structure, 9, 36, 42, 53, 70–4, 81, 101, 144, 149, 163–5, 171–2, 175, 181, 201–13

negative evaluation, 5–6, 17, 21–30, 100–2, 127, 133–4, 146–53, 170–6, 189, 220–33
nouns, 50–1, 57–62, 90, 129, 169, 183, 189, 216, 228–30

Penguin Classics, 200–14
phraseology, 122, 125, 128–31, 136, 137
polarity, 18, 20, 23–6, 29, 158, 218–23, 228, 232
praise, 8–12, 17, 22, 25, 27, 30, 31, 68, 80, 81, 88, 110, 114, 144–5, 162–3, 174, 179, 182, 202, 207, 218–22, 231–3
Proceedings of the National Academy of Sciences (PNAS), 35
promotion, 68, 72, 90, 126, 199
pronouns, 90, 94, 103, 108, 110, 128, 230
purpose, 1–2, 4, 8, 10, 17, 19, 50–3, 64–5, 80–1, 153, 155, 162, 175–6, 199–201, 210, 214, 217, 221

Questions, 93, 108–9, 117

reporting verbs, 7, 88, 90–4, 98,
    103–4, 179–93
research article, 1–4, 8–9, 30, 34–5,
    38–9, 42–7, 54, 65, 87–91, 93–4,
    97–8, 101–2, 116–17, 128–9, 136,
    158, 180–3, 188, 192–3, 237
review article, 1–3, 87–103, 179–94
rhetorical effort, 233

scientific fact, 34–5, 126
scientific knowledge, 34, 43, 46
self-mention, 7, 13, 110, 112
semantic sequences, 127–31, 133,
    135–7
Social constructivism, 12, 43, 46–7,
    91, 98, 105, 109, 124, 156, 167,
    180, 182, 220
Spanish, 32, 138, 144–78, 187, 195,
    227, 235, 237
stance, 4–5, 22–3, 62, 108–10, 113–17,
    143, 179, 193, 217

status quo review, 35–6, 47
suggest, 5, 90–103, 186, 188
systemic functional linguistics, 180,
    237

theory review, 35–6

values, 6–7, 12, 17, 21, 31, 68–9, 71–3,
    79–81, 101, 105–6, 114, 122,
    125–6, 131, 135–7, 143, 176,
    180–1
variation, 19, 29, 51, 54, 65–6, 70–1,
    81, 85, 88, 98–9, 115, 123, 125,
    129, 141, 176–80, 196, 236
verbs, 10, 62, 90, 92, 94, 98, 99,
    100–1, 126, 134, 180, 187, 189,
    192, 222, 226, 228, 230, 233
voice, 3, 11, 61, 63–5, 87, 90, 94, 96,
    103, 113, 132, 143–5, 181, 182,
    186, 188–93

Wordsmith Tools, 58, 73, 90, 182